D0896616

Alpine Club Guide Books

PENNINE ALPS CENTRAL

LISKAMM E summit

ALPINE CLUB GUIDE BOOKS

Pennine Alps Central

WEISSHORN – DENT BLANCHE – MONTE ROSA
MATTERHORN CHAINS – ITALIAN VALLEY
RANGES – VALPELLINE SOUTH

companion volumes
Pennine Alps East
Pennine Alps West

compiled and edited by
ROBIN G. COLLOMB

Alpine Club London

PENNINE ALPS CENTRAL
First published in Britain 1975 by
The Alpine Club   London

Copyright © 1975 by West Col Productions

SBN 900523 14 X

Produced from computer information storage and retrieval systems
developed from volumes published under the title
Selected Climbs in the Pennine Alps (Neill) 1962 (one vol.)
Selected Climbs in the Pennine Alps (Collomb) 1968 (2 vols.)

Revised and re-written in three vols. as –
Pennine Alps East
Pennine Alps Central
Pennine Alps West

Designed, produced and sold for the Alpine Club by
West Col Productions
1 Meadow Close   Goring   Reading   Berks. RG8 0AP

Set Olivetti Editor 5C typescript and IBM New Century by
Diana Gould and Rosalind Stayne at West Col Productions

Printed offset in England by Swindon Press Ltd, Swindon, Wilts.

CONTENTS

LIST OF DIAGRAMS AND ILLUSTRATIONS

Codes: PAE, PAC.

New information compiled from:
    Frischer-Roberts Diaries 1967, 1970, 1971, 1974
    A.K. Rawlinson reports 1970, 1971
    West Col Archives, Memoirs 1948, 1956, 1957, 1958, 1961, 1963,
    1964, 1967, 1971, 1974
    Correspondents' reports 1968-1974

Ground survey notes for Valtournanche-Valpelline South chain by:
    P. Charles and K. Rice, August 1974
    P. Charles and R.G. Collomb, August 1974
    R.G. Collomb and E. Roberts, September 1974
    Place Moulin-Prarayer, St. Barthélemy-Pierrey, Torgnon, Buisson,
    Valtournanche, Breuil

Photography and diagrams:
    Frischer-Roberts Archives 1961-1974
    West Col Archives 1946-1974
    Photographic processing: Ray Hebron and Photo Frischer

Text set Olivetti Editor 5C and IBM New Century verified at
West Col Productions by Diana Gould and Rosalind Stayne
Tapes 39A, 42C

Maps and technical publications mentioned in this guidebook are
available from Alpina Technica Productions 1 Meadow Close Goring
Reading Berks. RG8 0AP England

INTERNATIONAL ALPINE DISTRESS SIGNAL

A more elaborate system of signals has been devised in Britain but the International system is basic to the subject of attracting attention in an emergency.

Use a whistle, torch or flashes of the sun on a mirror. Alternatively, shout, or wave bright clothing:

Six regular flashes/notes in a minute, repeated at intervals of a minute.

The reply is three signals per minute.

The previous guidebook to the Pennine Alps (Alpine Club, 1968) attempted to deal with the entire range in two volumes. This proved possible because large areas of ground at the eastern and western ends of the range were omitted or only covered by brief notes. In general throughout the entire length of the range, the Italian side received perfunctory treatment. This was partly due to economics in the amount of information that could be published, lack of first hand accounts and general ignorance of the Valpelline, Valtournanche and other Italian valleys. A lot of this can now be corrected but once again economics are the ruling force and only the most important information in mountaineering terms can be included where previously nothing had been published.

The result is a guidebook for the Pennine Alps in three volumes, of which the second and third are much larger than the first. The divisions of the range are now as follows:

I PENNINE ALPS EAST
Simplonpass to Monte Moropass and the Neues Weisstor
Weissmies, Portjengrat, Mischabel chains.

II PENNINE ALPS CENTRAL
Neues Weisstor to Col des Bouquetins
Monte Rosa, Matterhorn, Dent Blanche, Weisshorn
chains, Italian valley ranges, Valpelline South.

III PENNINE ALPS WEST
Col des Bouquetins to Col Ferret
Bouquetins, Grandes Dents chain, Collon-Pigne-Aiguilles Rouges group, Cheilon-Ruinette group, Otemma-Valpelline North, Grand Combin-Grand St. Bernard group.

To cope with this expansion valuable information has been supplied by over 200 correspondents, most of whom wrote unsolicited letters commenting on the 1968 edition. Letters received containing suggestions for a new edition number over 700. Several correspondents undertook to keep notes of visits to parts of the range unfrequented by British climbers, and the results of their work account for new or completely revised descriptions for 60 routes (Anthony Rawlinson, Eric Roberts, Jeremy Talbot).

An exhaustive edition of this guide to the Pennine Alps will probably never be published in English. But we may reasonably expect in the course of time to see a further improved edition with more complete coverage of the many sub-ranges and divisions of this magnificent part of the Alps.

Robin G. Collomb
Goring on Thames, December 1974

TECHNICAL SOURCE PUBLICATIONS
CONSULTED

The undermentioned publications exclude journals and magazines and concern the complete Pennine Alps from Col Ferret to the Simplonpass. The date of publication/edition is shown in parenthesis.

Anderson, M. Mittel Switzerland. WCP (1974)

Ball, J. Ball's Alpine Guide: The Western Alps (1863, 1870, 1877, revised W. A. B. Coolidge, London, 1898)

Buscaini, G. Guida dei Monti d'Italia. Alpi Pennine. CAI/T CI.
Vol I   Col du Petit Ferret to Col d'Otemma (1971)
Vol II   Col d'Otemma to Colle del Teodulo (1970)

Collomb, R. G. Selected Climbs in the Pennine Alps. AC (1968)
Vol I   Saas Fee, Zermatt and Zinal.
Vol II   Arolla and Western ranges.

- Zermatt and district, including Saas Fee (London, 1969)

Conway, W. M. Climbers' Guide to the Central Pennine Alps (London, 1890)
Climbers' Guide to the Eastern Pennine Alps (London, 1891)

Coolidge, W. A. B. Swiss Travel and Swiss Guide-books (London, 1889)

Dübi, H. Guide des Alpes Valaisannes, CAS (var. vols. 1919, 1922)

Kurz, M. Guide des Alpes Valaisannes, CAS
Vol I   Col Ferret - Col Collon (1937, 1963, revised M. Brandt 1970)

Vol II   Col Collon - Theodulpass (1930, 1947, revised M. Brandt 1970)
Vol III Theodulpass - Simplon (1937)
Vol IIIa Theodulpass - Monte Moro (1952, revised M. Brandt as Vol III, 1970)
Vol IIIb Strahlhorn - Simplon (1952, revised M. Brandt as Vol IV, 1970)
Vol IV   Simplon - Furka (1920)

Lunn, A. A History of Ski-ing (London, 1927)
The Story of Ski-ing (London, 1953)

Pause, W. Im Schweren Fels (Munich, 1960)

Roberts, E. High Level Route, Chamonix-Zermatt-Saas. WCP (1973)

Saglio, S. Guida da rifugio a rifugio. Alpi Pennine. CAI (1951, 1954)

-            I Rifugi del C.A.I. CAI (1957)

- & Boffa, F. Guida dei Monti d'Italia. Monte Rosa. CAI/TCI (1960)

Vanis, E. Im Steilen Eis (Munich, 1964)

Maps

Landeskarte der Schweiz (LK) 1:25,000. Normal grid sheets 1305, 1306, 1307, 1308, 1309, 1324, 1325, 1326, 1327, 1328, 1329, 1344, 1345, 1346, 1347, 1348, 1349, 1365, 1366 (1965-1974)

   1:50,000. Normal grid sheets 273, 274, 282, 283, 284, 285, 292, 293, 294 (1963-1973)

   1:50,000. District sheets 5003 (1968), 5006 (1972)

Istituto Geografico Militare (IGM), Carta d'Italia 1:25,000. Monte Cervino, carta speciale (1960)

   1:25,000. Normal grid sheets old series. Not consulted.

   1:50,000. New series normal grid sheets (series M792) 051, 069, 070, 071. None published at 31 December, 1973.

Carta delle zone turistiche d'Italia, Touring Club Italiano (TCI) 1:50,000 sheet No. 3 Il Cervino e il Monte Rosa (1965). No. 12 Gruppo del Monte Bianco (1968)

Kompass Wanderkarten (KK) 1:50,000. Sheet No. 85 Massiccio del Monte Bianco (1970), No. 87 Breuil-Cervinia-Zermatt (1972). Two unpublished sheets at 31 December 1973 covering the Pennine Alps East area are numbered 88 and 89.

15

SELECTED ENGLISH BIBLIOGRAPHY

A few volumes of general interest content are repeated from
the source publications listed on the previous page.

Ball, J. Peaks, Passes and Glaciers (First Series). 1859

Ball, J. The Alpine Guide: Western Alps. 1898 Coolidge ed.

Clark, R.W. The Early Alpine Guides. 1949

-                 The Victorian Mountaineers. 1953

-                 The Day the Rope Broke, 1965

-                 The Alps. 1973

Collomb, R.G. Alpine Points of View. 1961

-                 Zermatt and district. 1969

Conway, W.M. The Zermatt Pocket Book. 1881

Coolidge, W.A.B. The Alps in Nature and History. 1908

-                 Alpine Studies. 1912

Dent, C.T. Above the Snow Line. 1887

Field & Spencer. Peaks, Passes and Glaciers(Third Series).
                 1932

Finch, G.I. The Making of a Mountaineer. 1924

Gos, C. Alpine Tragedy. 1948

Gos, F. Zermatt and its Valley. 1926

Kennedy, E.S. Peaks, Passes and Glaciers (Second Series).
                 2 vols. 1862

Klucker, C. Adventures of an Alpine Guide. 1932

Lunn, A. Zermatt and the Valais. 1955

-                 A Century of Mountaineering. 1957

Moore, A.W. The Alps in 1864. 2 vols. Blackwell ed. 1939

Mummery, A.F. My Climbs in the Alps and Caucasus, re-
                 published 1974

Norman-Neruda, L. The Climbs of Norman-Neruda. 1899

Pilley, D.E. Climbing Days. 2nd ed. 1965

Ratti, A.A. Climbs on Alpine Peaks. 1928

Rébuffat, G. Starlight and Storm. 1955

-                 Men and the Matterhorn. 1967

Roch, A. Climbs of My Youth. 1949

Rey, G. The Matterhorn. Blackwell ed. 1946

Scott, D. Big Wall Climbing. 1974

Smythe, F.S. Edward Whymper. 1940

Stephen, L. The Playground of Europe. Blackwell ed. 1936

Tyndall, J. Hours of Exercise in the Alps. 1871

Whymper, E. Scrambles Among the Alps in the Years 1860-69. 6th ed. 1936

- Zermatt and the Matterhorn. 1897, republished 1974

Williams, C. Zermatt Saga. 1964

Wills, A. Wandering Among the High Alps. Blackwell ed. 1939

Young, G.W. On High Hills. 5th ed. 1947

- Mountains with a Difference. 1951

ABBREVIATIONS

AACZ	Zürich University Alpine Club
AC	Alpine Club
Aig.	Aiguille
Biv.	Bivouac
c.	approximately
CAAI	Italian Universities Alpine Club
CAI	Italian Alpine Club
CAS	Swiss Alpine Club
Gr.	German
h.	hour(s)
IGM	Italian military map
Ital.	Italian
Kl.	Klein(e)
km.	kilometre(s)
L	left (direction)
LK	Swiss federal map
m.	metre(s)
min.	minute(s)
mtn.	mountain
P, Pta.	Pizzo, Punta
pt.	point (spot height)
Pte.	Pointe (summit)
R	right (direction)
SAC	Swiss Alpine Club
TCI	Italian Touring Club
U.	Unter
WCP	West Col Productions
*	asterisk against an altitude signifies an approximate height, or a height either ascertained from an Italian source or from a foreign publication.
25m.	1:25,000 map (e.g. LK25, LK25m.)
50m.	1:50,000 map (e.g. LK50, LK50m.)

Compass directions are indicated as: N,S,E,W,NE,SW,etc.

Introduction

In the opening remarks to the 1968 edition reference was made to the number of changes which had taken place in the valleys since the 1962 edition had been published; also to the proliferation of mechanical methods of gaining height in the mountains. During the past seven years fewer changes of this nature can be recorded but in some cases they are significant enough to modify the mountaineering aims and instincts of visitors. These changes have been recorded in comments and descriptions embodied in the guide.

Mountaineering is now such an expensive pastime even compared with ten years ago that no purpose is served by giving an indication of costs, or advice on how to travel to the numerous centres in such a diverse area like the Pennine Alps. At the present time all the main centres can be reached by road (except Zermatt village), and where railheads exist these are mentioned in descriptions. Access by helicopters is still a small business (but it would be foolish to predict that it might remain that way), and the irony of many flying journeys is that they are made by climbers to landing pads beside huts above the snowline. For the first time the system of goodwill and reciprocal arrangements over charges made in huts to climbers was put under great strain due to economic factors in 1973. Whereas some order has been restored the future of the system as it has been known for decades between various Alpine countries is likely to remain unsettled, and climbing parties should be prepared to pay more than the rates they believe they are entitled to. In Switzerland the only sure way of securing maximum reductions is to prove membership of the Swiss Alpine Club. In Italy charges are generally higher, certainly more erratic, so that you might stay at one hut for next to nothing and pay exorbitantly at the next; with luck it averages out.

MAPS

The guide is designed for use with the official Swiss map (LK). Wherever possible descriptions are based on consultation with the new grid series on a scale of 1:25,000. The older 1:50,000 map is still being updated by LK, and gradually the variation in heights especially but also other information is being incorporated from the 1:25,000 map. Annoyingly, some information of value to mountaineers appearing on the 1:50,000 map does not appear on the 1:25,000. The Swiss maps extend right across the crest zone of the range into Italy so that in general the official Italian map (IGM, pre-1939 in surveying) has not been consulted. A new IGM map of 1:50,000 is scheduled to be published in a few years (see Technical Source Publications Consulted). The following LK maps refer to the entire Pennine Alps range:

1:25,000 grid series

1287 Sierre	1325 Sembrancher	1347 Matterhorn
1288 Raron	1326 Rosablanche	1348 Zermatt
1289 Brig	1327 Evolène	1349 Monte Moro
1306 Sion	1328 Randa	1365 Gd. St. Bernard
1307 Vissoie	1329 Saas	1366 M. Velan
1308 St. Niklaus	1345 Orsières	1367 Valtournanche
1309 Simplon	1346 Chanrion	1368 Gressoney

A special district map of Saas Fee, consisting of parts of sheets 1328, 1329, 1348, 1349, was issued in 1972 by the Saas Fee Verkehrsverein. Ref: KF 0740. It shows ski routes and emphasises paths, cableways, etc. with additional colours .

1:50,000 grid series

273 Montana	282 Arolla	292 Courmayeur
274 Visp	284 Mischabel	293 Valpelline
282 Martigny	285 Domodossola	294 Gressoney

1:50,000 district series

5003 Mont Blanc - Grand Combin   5006 Zermatt und
                                                     Umgebung

1:100,000 grid series

41   Col du Pillon   46 Val de Bagnes

42   Oberwallis   47 Monte Rosa

Water-resistant syntosil versions of some of the 50m. and 25m. maps are available with ski routes shown; they cost nearly double the price of regular sheets. Warning: prices of maps given in the 1968 edition of the guide have more than doubled in terms of British money.

ALTITUDES AND NOMENCLATURE

All heights are taken from the LK25 map. Where the map does not show an altitude, it has been ascertained from an Italian source, or from a calculation from contour lines on the map. These cases are marked with an asterisk (*). The height given in graded climbing is the vertical distance from the base of a route to its summit (not necessarily the summit of the parent mtn.), and always excludes the height gained in approaching the climb, say from a hut.

Place names are taken generally from the LK25 map. Exceptions are traditional names in popular use which have been changed on the latter map. In these cases the map name appears in parenthesis. Many changes in the spelling of place names on LK25 are due to the adoption of dialectical pronunciation which translates into major variations of spelling. These will confuse climbers for another generation and have already been severely criticised by mountaineering authorities in Switzerland. But the deed has now been done.

French, German and Italian names for climbing routes have been chosen according to popular British usage. These are sometimes an admixture of English and another language. It is appreciated that the choice is arbitrary, and the names believed to be widely understood by British climbers are used. Some have been changed from the 1968 edition of the guide. Thus Younggrat rather than Klein Triftjigrat; Viereselsgrat rather than Arête des Quatre Anes. In this choice German versions predominate, giving way to French as one moves to the W, or to Italian on the frontier ridge.

ORIENTATION

The directions left (L) and right (R) in the sense of direction of movement of the climber - ascent, descent, traverse of slope - have been used consistently throughout. For mountain features such as glaciers, couloirs, rivers, etc. the traditional orographical reference to left and right banks as viewed in the direction of flow, i.e. downward, has been abandoned, due to the number of complaints received over the confusion this system causes. These features are therefore now described in the sense of movement of the climber. For example, you go up the L side of a glacier, which was previously described as ascending the R bank. In some descriptions both ways are given to emphasise orientation. Compass directions are also given to assist route finding.

WINTER AND SKI ASCENTS

Following decades of disagreement on the validity of winter ascents according to dates recorded, a recent UIAA recommendation that the period for counting winter ascents should run from 21 December to 20 March has met with disfavour in some quarters; doubtless general adoption of this period would eliminate many claims to notable first winter ascents made up to 15 April, sometimes later. Without wishing to enter into the argument, in this guide dates from 21 December to 31 March are admitted as winter ascents. The guide also reports important ascents on ski at any time of the year. The contemporary "sport" of "extreme ski", being the descent of snow and ice faces on ski, is recorded for appropriate routes.

CAMPING

There are official campsites with good facilities including shops at the following base centres. Their locations are not always obvious and are generally on the outskirts of villages. If in doubt consult the local tourist bureau, normally found in the centre of a village.

Arolla (poor facilities), Breuil, Gressoney-St. Jean, Les Haudères, Macugnaga, Randa, St. Niklaus, Saas Fee, Saas Grund, Täsch, Zermatt, Zinal.

GRADING OF CLIMBS

In accordance with the UIAA classification system, the grading of rock climbs is numerical from I to VI and A1, A2, A3 and A4 for artificial, with the letter 'e' to denote the use of expansion bolts (e.g. A3e). Grade I is the easiest and VI the hardest. Variations of difficulty are denoted by + and - signs; plus is above the normal rating and minus below (i.e. V-/V/ V+). These variations above Grade IV will matter for the expert climber, and they should be equally helpful in the lower grades for the average performer. It must be stressed that the grade of a climb is determined not only by pure technical difficulty but also by objective danger and length.

Mixed climbs and snow/ice climbs are also graded in six stages. This grading is always more approximate and less precise than the numerical rock grades because of variable conditions in a season and from year to year. Winter climbing will be different again, and apart from severe cold grades could be lower or higher according to the nature of the route. In order of rising difficulty: F (easy), PD (moderately difficult), AD (fairly difficult), D (difficult), TD (very difficult),

ED (extremely difficult). Further refinement is possible by adding plus or minus signs.

The previous guide elaborated on this subject at great length, and went a good deal further by introducing classifications for the sustained nature of routes, and for their relative steepness. While only praise was penned about this treatment, it is felt that climbers must rely on more comprehensive information given in route preambles for these subtleties, and the classifications given for them in the previous guide are now omitted.

MOUNTAINEERING TERMS, LANGUAGE AND GLOSSARY

For the most part terms used in this guide, though not always proper English words, will be known and understood to alpinists. The subject has grown in complexity due to new techniques and slang phrases emerging mainly from the English, French, German and Italian languages. (One ignores just as many coming from modern American mountaineering which no editor would dare apply to descriptions of an Alpine region!). A dictionary of such terms cross referenced in English, Americanese, French, German and Italian is in preparation by Robin Collomb and Eric Roberts for publication in 1975.

Valley bases

ZERMATT VALLEY

One of the best known valleys in the Western Alps. From Visp in the Rhone valley (rail and bus services) you first reach Stalden where the valley divides. The E branch goes to the Saas village resorts (Pennine Alps East), the W to Zermatt. The rack railway follows the valley to Zermatt. Post bus service to St. Niklaus. At this point the motor road can be used by the public up to Täsch, large carpark, the last village below Zermatt. The continuation road is reserved for residents of Zermatt. Trains up and down the valley about 12 times a day.

From Brig:

Visp (663m.). Main line railway and bus services.

Stalden (809m.). Mountain railway and bus services. Junction with Saas valley.

St. Niklaus (1127m.). Mountain railway and bus services.

Randa (1407m.). 34 km. Railway and public road. Shops, hotels, post office, bank, etc. Schools holiday centre. Private camping. Departure point for Dom, Täschhorn, Weisshorn, etc.

Täsch (1438m.). 38 km. Railway and public road terminus. Large carpark, shops, hotels, post office, etc. Campsite. Taxi service to Täschalp. Departure point for Täschhorn - Rimpfischhorn section of Mischabel chain.

Zermatt (1606m.). 44 km. from Brig. Railway terminus. All main services, supermarkets. Main campsite situated

400m. below station on road away from village. There are other private campsites. Youth hostel on the outskirts of the hamlet called Obere Steinmatte (Winkelmatten-Findeln road). English and French widely spoken (native language, German). All inquiries can be dealt with at tourist bureau adjoining the station. Station for rack railway to Gornergrat almost opposite main station. Cableway station terminii are some distance from railway station and a town plan is invaluable for finding the way round this complex resort. In winter one of of the premier ski resorts of the Western Alps.

TURTMANNTAL

This valley runs S from the Rhone valley at Turtmann village. Turtmann-Oberems by cable lift or road. Oberems - Gruben/Meiden (1822m.) by infrequent post bus. Gruben has hotels, shops and a campsite. Car drivers can continue along the small road to the dam wall of the barrage, but not further. Departure point for Turtmann hut.

VAL D'ANNIVIERS

From Sierre in the Rhone valley to Zinal (1675m.), public road and post bus service. The road is motorable for a short distance further up the valley. At Zinal there are hotels in all categories, shops, post office, bank, etc., and a campsite. A cableway project for reaching the Col de Tracuit has so far been resisted. Starting point for the Weisshorn, Zinalrothorn, Ober Gabelhorn, Dent Blanche, etc.

VAL DE MOIRY

From Sierre in the Rhone valley, by Vissoie (junction with Val d'Anniviers) and Grimentz (1570m., village resort facilities) to the Moiry dam wall (2250m., post bus terminus). The road continues along the E bank of the lake to the smaller Moiry

glacier lake (2349m.) near the approach path to the Moiry hut.
Starting point for the Grand Cornier.

VAL D'HÉRENS

From Sion in the Rhone valley via Evolène, Les Haudères
(1452m., junction with Arolla valley, Pennine Alps West) to
La Forclaz (1727m.) and Ferpècle/Salay (1766m., post bus
terminus). The road is motorable a short distance further.
Ferpècle has two or three hotel/inns, a shop and post office.
Departure point for the Dent Blanche, Grand Cornier, etc.

ITALIAN

VALLE ANZASCA - MACUGNAGA

This valley, leading from below Domodossola and Viladoss-
ola, is one of the most important mountaineering centres in
the Alps. Domodossola (270m.), direct rail connections from
Arona, Milan, Turin and Brig (Simplon tunnel). Buses for all
destinations depart from the station forecourt, timetables in
station booking hall and on wall of café across forecourt. About
five buses a day to Macugnaga, journey time, $1\frac{1}{2}$ h. Public
road.

Macugnaga (34 km. from Domodossola) is formed by three
village/hamlets: Borca, Staffa, Pecetto. Staffa (1307m.) is
the largest and the main centre. Hotels, pensions, shops,
garages, tourist office and guides' bureau, camping, cableways, etc. The road continues to Pecetto (1362m.).

VALSESIA - ALAGNA

To Varallo by train, then by bus to Alagna (1190m.). Road in
main valley continues a little beyond the San Antonio chapel
(1391m.). Alagna has numerous hotels, shops, all main

services, camping. Important cableway system to Punta
Indren (3260m.) in three stages, giving easy access to all
approaches on the S side of the Monte Rosa - Liskamm groups.

VALLE DI GRESSONEY (LIS)

From Pont St. Martin (bus and railway from Turin) in the
lower Aosta valley, by road with frequent bus to Gressoney-la
Trinité. An important resort with main services, camping,
and a cableway link towards the Punta Indren system from
Alagna. The road continues up the valley to Staval (1826m.)
where the Carla Rivetti hut/inn is found (24 beds), restaurant
service.

VALLE D'AYAS

From Verres in the Aosta valley by bus to Champoluc and San
Giacomo/St. Jacques (1689m.). Hotels, shops and usual facilities. A small road continues to Alpe Verra (2382m.), parking space, for the Mezzalama and Q. Sella huts. Just above
San Giacomo is the CAI Casale Montferrato hut (1701m.) with
65 beds and restaurant service. There is also a small inn at
Fiery (1878m.).

VALTOURNANCHE - BREUIL

The most notable valley on the Italian side of the Pennine Alps,
road approach with frequent bus service from Châtillon in the
Aosta valley. The main centres and facilities coming up the
valley are: Antey St. André and road junction for Torgnon
(1489m., hotels, shops, etc. and local bus service) above
which is a superb campsite near Septumian, remote however
from main valley. Then Buisson (1115m.) at the Chamois
commune cableway, with an excellent campsite nearby. There
is another campsite, open to end August only, at Moulin below
Maen (1339m.). So to Valtournanche village (1524m.), a main

28

centre with complete services but no campsite. There is a chairlift towards Cheneil and a cableway to the Cime Bianche. At Cheneil there are two inns (for Grand Tournalin). At the head of the valley the road comes to Breuil/Cervinia (2006m.). Bus and public road terminus. Various carparks.

Breuil, modern name, Cervinia, has all classes of hotels, inns, pensions, excellent shopping facilities, tourist office (English spoken), guides' bureau, garage, etc. The campsite has now been overrun by a golf course and is reduced to strips of grass either side of the path approach routes to the Bobba and Balestreri huts. No fresh water or toilet facilities, this site is something of a scandal at present (September, 1974). Breuil is primarily a winter sports resort and facilities for summer visitors leave something to be desired. There is a CAI owned inn in the resort. A private road has been made to the Duca degli Abruzzi (Orionde) hut, jeep service run by the proprietors, and journey possible for private motorists by arrangement. In general English is not spoken in Breuil and French is not widely understood. Cableway system to Plan Maison and from there in separate branches to the Furgggrat and Testa Grigia, the latter called Plateau Rosa by the Italians.

VALLE DI ST. BARTHÉLEMY

From Nus in the Aosta valley by infrequent bus to Lignan (1633m.). Parties going straight up the valley must get off bus at junction with small continuation road up valley to Praz (1737m.). This junction is before Issologne (1515m.) which precedes Lignan on the main road. However, there are no facilities of any kind above the junction. This is the most unspoiled valley of interest in the Italian Pennine Alps. The small continuation road is motorable for some distance. See Route 205 to Nebbia biv. Inns and shop at Lignan.

VALPELLINE

One of the longest and most remote valleys in the Pennine Alps. Bus service from Aosta town up the Gt. St. Bernard road and into the valley to reach Valpelline village (960m.). This infrequent service continues to Oyace (1390m., inns and shop) and Bionaz (1606m., small inn). The road continues for some distance up the valley (no bus) to the dam wall (1950m.) at Place Moulin. The hamlet of La Lechère (1808m., not on road) is now in front of the dam, while just before the road reaches the carpark beside the dam a slip road on R leads down to the Place Moulin inn (c. 1900m.). Detail on all maps is wrong to some degree. There is no unmade (or otherwise) road from the dam along the lake to Prarayer, which is reached in 1 h. by a newly cut and excellent footpath above the lake. A jeep road above the dam is forbidden to motorists. The inn at Place Moulin is a worthwhile and economic base for climbers, albeit distant from real starting points. The owner may agree to a tent being pitched nearby in return for some of your custom.

The only campsite with facilities in this valley is the summer one run by the CAI on the Essert meadow with three pleasant tarns in forest behind. This site is found on S side of road (roadside carpark, and access by driving across a field) at a point midway between LK refs. Chentre (1490m.) and Dzovenno (1575m.). Otherwise not marked on LK, but the location with its lakes is obvious.

Section One

ZERMATT WEST AND ZINAL CHAINS

Huts and other mountain bases

<u>Topali Hut</u> 2674m.

Topalihütte. A small hut situated at the foot of the Distulgrat and below the Barrhorn peaks, above St. Niklaus. Warden sometimes resident, fully equipped, places for 20. Note where water is obtained, some way below the hut and just off the path (red markers), if nothing is coming through the pipe into the hut.

1. From St. Niklaus go up the main road to Zermatt, then fork R along a lane following the railway line, as far as Schwidernu hamlet (1163m.). From the church a path with red waymarks climbs steeply W into the forest. Keep L at all forks, cross a stream, then two rock barriers and reach the Blattbach ravine. Cross the stream and go up (1728m.) into the Blatt forest to the SE, before returning W horizontally to recross the Blatt stream (1978m.). Now climb in zigzags towards Unnerbächji, which is kept on the R. Higher up cross a stream and reach a junction at Scheidchrommo (c. 2400m.). Continue at an easy angle to moraine beside the outfall from the U. Stelli glacier. Leave this and climb S over grassy rocks to the hut (4½ h. from St. Niklaus). Do not attempt to follow more direct paths shown on map.

<u>Turtmann (Tourtemagne) Hut</u> 2519m.

Turtmannhütte or Cabane de Tourtemagne. Situated at the head of the Turtmanntal, just below the true R bank of its glacier and below the Barrhorn peaks. Warden in summer, simple restaurant service, places for 40. At the time of writing (May 1974) LK25 sheet 1307 has not been published and all refs. concern the LK50 map. The latter does not show changes in the Turtmanntal caused by the building of the barrage.

2. From Gruben (bus terminus, 1822m.) the road in the valley continues to Vord-Senntum (1902m.), below the barrage. Continue along the road and descend to cross the stream by the bridge at pt. 2055m. A good path rises along the E side of the barrage, away from the moraine slopes, and passes below the Pipji pastures to reach the hut standing on a promontory (3 h. from Gruben).

Tracuit Hut 3256m.

Cabane de Tracuit. This hut is situated on the Col de Tracuit, to the SE of its lowest point, and directly above Zinal. Warden, simple restaurant service, places for 70.

3. From Zinal take the road to the S to a signpost on the L(E) indicating the way to the hut. Follow the good path, first through forest to Le Chiesso (2061m.) then in broad sweeps across pasture, up into a wide cwm to reach the Combautanna chalets (2578m.). Continue rising up the L-hand side of the cwm to scree, rocks and snow below the pass. Turn R and reach the crest at 3250m. between the lowest point and the hut, which is visible and a few min. away (4 h. from Zinal).

Turtmann - Tracuit huts connection. F+.

4. This connection is used frequently. From the Turtmann hut take the path to the SE, to the foot of a rock barrier split by a conspicuous narrow couloir called Gässi. Climb a scree cone into the couloir which leads to a rounded knoll (2641m.). Continue to the SE and descend moraines to the Turtmann glacier. The exact point at which to cross the glacier depends on the state of crevasses. The usual point is just above the icefall at 2800m. Reach the large rocky rognon called Adlerflüe (2913.4m.) which divides the glacier in two branches. From c. 2780m. there is a path in these rocks which, after crossing a ledge line of white rocks leading R (N), returns L up to pt 2913. 4m. Cross the top of the rognon and descend to the other branch of the glacier to the W. Cross its narrow middle plateau to the L(W) bank at the foot of Les Diablons. Climb beside this bank to the SSW, moraine and snow, traces of a path, to near the Col de Tracuit, then reach the hut a little higher $(3\frac{1}{2}$ h. from Turtmann hut).

Mountet Hut 2886m.

Cabane du Mountet. A fine, large building with a warden, restaurant service and places for 115, situated in the R bank angle formed by the Mountet and Zinal glaciers.

5. From Zinal follow the unmistakable road then path along the Nauisence stream to a triple junction just beyond the Vichiesso chalet (1862m.) (1 h.). Cars can be taken and parked a short distance below the chalet. Take the central path through forest which continues to a moraine and the Petit Mountet inn (2142m.). About 600m. further the path descends from the moraine to the glacier. Ignore this and continue on a path round the flank of a rock bastion above the glacier and rejoin the moraine on the far side. Follow the moraine to a stream coming down from the Pigne de la Lé. Here climb by several zigzags to the lower edge of the Plan des Lettres, cross a slight shoulder near pt. 2464. 9m. and descend to the glacier at c. 2460m., just above the first icefall. Cross the glacier obliquely, going up the medial moraine to the foot of the slope below the hut. Climb this by a steep twisting path (4 h., 5 h. from Zinal).

Tracuit - Mountet huts connection.

6. Much in vogue by parties arrived at the Mountet hut by tra-

34

versing a peak from Zermatt, who then wish to traverse the Weisshorn from the Tracuit hut and return to Zermatt. The connection avoids descending to Zinal.

From the Mountet hut reverse Route 5 to the junction of paths just above the Vichiesso chalet (1862m.). Take the small SE fork which crosses the glacier outfalls (1907m.) and winds up grass and rocks to the Chiesso chalet (2082m.). Continue easily to the N, to a junction. Keep L and mount in the same direction by a good path to the Tsijiere de la Vatse chalet (2388m.). After that cross the shoulder of the Roc de la Vache. Here the path descends into the cwm entered by Route 3, not far from the Combautanna chalets. Follow Route 3 to the Tracuit hut (5½ h. from Mountet hut).

Arpitettaz Hut 2786m.

Cabane d'Ar Pitetta. Property of the Zinal guides, situated remotely below the W flank of the Weisshorn and in the centre of its lower glacier moraines. Door unlocked, places for 30, wood stove and cooking utensils. Normally no warden.

7. From Zinal follow Route 3 to the small fork L from the Mountet path, about 150m. beyond the Vichiesso chalet. Here you join Route 6 which is followed to the junction above the Chiesso chalet. Take the R fork leading SE along a stream then past two small tarns and a cowshed and eventually reach a section rising E in zigzags towards Les Leisses (2567m.). The main path passes below this chalet and continues SE horizontally to the foot of the first moraines below the Weisshorn glacier. Cross two streams before ascending grassy and stony slopes in an open cwm between two moraine crests to reach the hut (4½ h. from Zinal).

A rough but easy route can be made from the Tracuit hut to the Arpitettaz hut across the Col de Milon in about 3 h.

Weisshorn Hut 2932m.

Weisshornhütte. The smallest of the important huts in the Zermatt region, situated on stony slopes below the NE side of the Schali glacier. Warden occasionally resident, places for 22, take your own food (stove installed, wood supplies usually available). Scheduled to be considerably enlarged in 1975.

8. From Randa station walk down the road for 200m. to a path which crosses the railway and river. Climb an old moraine to some chalets, then bear L (signpost) into the rocky forest which is climbed by many zigzags, slanting L, to first one then another open pasture with chalets. Care should be taken to keep L at junctions. Just before Rötiboden (1970m.) fork R and climb in zigzags to the Jatz chalet (2 h.). Now keep R and go up into a large shallow cwm and out again on a traverse line to a shoulder (2472m.). Continue rising to the L (N) till the hut is seen a few min. before it is reached (4½ h. from Randa).

Schalijoch Bivouac c. 3770m.

Biwak Schalijoch. A small aluminium shelter situated about 20m. above the snow saddle of the Schalijoch (3750m.), on the rocks of the Weisshorn. Fully equipped, comfortable, two solid meta fuel cookers (but there may be no fuel in reserve), 8 places.

This is without doubt the most serious hut approach described in the guidebook. The routes are for the col itself - well known to those who have climbed the Schaligrat. The glacier is complex and the middle rock barrier is a distinct obstacle on the Weisshorn hut side. AD. The rock wall and snow/ice slopes on the Zinal side are quite difficult and exposed to stonefall. The latter is unpleasant to descend after the sun has reached it. AD. See also Schalijoch in climbing section.

9. Zermatt side. From the Weisshorn hut a small track leads N to the Schali glacier. Cross an easy snow slope almost horizontally to the L (W), aiming for a little couloir cutting the rock barrier marked by pt. 3145m. Climb the couloir, usually snowy, by rocks on its L, traces of path. Continue across the next level in the glacier to the W, which becomes more problematical due to crevasses and steepness. Aim to reach the big rock barrier separating this part of the glacier from the upper (W) part at precisely 3400m. There are two ways of climbing the barrier. (1) At 3400m. there is a triple couloir forming an X in the rockface. An horizontal ledge line goes R from the centre of the X. Reach the latter by a snow tongue, followed by a rock staircase slanting to the L, to the R-hand end of the ledges. Work along them to the extreme L, descend a few m. and cross a stream. Now climb a rib on the L for about 150m., to where the glacier overlaps the top of the wall. Climb the steep overlap and reach the upper plateau at c. 3600m. (2) On the L of the X couloir system is a prominent pillar. Climb this (III) to the glacier above.

Now make an horizontal traverse across the steep crevassed slopes to the W, and reach the foot of the Schaligrat flank at c. 3620m. Cross the bergschrund and climb straight up for 40m. Then work L across snowy rocks, above a barrier of steeper rocks touching the glacier. On approaching the col further L, climb as directly as possible to the ridge above. Its crest is reached just above the first rocks and a few m. from the hut (4½ h. from Weisshorn hut. 2½ h. in descent).

10. Zinal side. From the Arpitettaz hut climb at an easy angle due E, cross a stream and go up moraine to pass round pt. 2932m. to the R, in order to reach the Weisshorn glacier. Climb the glacier directly towards the foot of the buttress marked pt. 3281m. Climb L(N) round its toe and go up the first couloir on the L, to cross a gap in the buttress and reach the S bay of the glacier above its icefall. Make a rising traverse across the bay to the L, under the W wall of the Weisshorn, to the rocks directly below pt. 4057m. on the ridge above. Cross a bergschrund and climb in a diagonal line to the R, between steeper rocks above and below. The route is now exposed to stonefall. Reach the edge of the crevassed hanging glacier under the Schalijoch, and climb the L-hand side of this, beside rocks, to the lowest rocks on the ridge above the col; this section is steep and delicate (4 h. from Arpitettaz hut).

Rothorn Hut 3198m.

Rothornhütte. Situated at the foot of the Eseltschuggen rocks, on the L bank of the Trift glacier and below the Zinalrothorn. A large building with a warden and restaurant service, places for 104.

11. From Zermatt take one of several possible approach paths (signposts) to the Trift gorge immediately above the resort. These either converge on the R side, which is crossed to the L by a fine bridge, or join the L side above the bridge. A series of zigzags on the L side then lead through the forest and cliffs to the Alterhaupt inn (1961m.). The path continues with a traverse section back to the stream, which is crossed to the R side, followed by a long stretch with zigzags up to the closed Trift hotel (2337m.) (2 h.). Here the hydro electric scheme road can be used for a short way, but one must return to the path in 20 min. It goes along grassy moraines to a stony plateau and streams which are crossed to reach the long lateral moraine on the R side of the glacier. Follow this to where the path leaves the crest and makes big zigzags to the R. Climb up to a final traverse section across snow to the L and a few rocks below the hut ($4\frac{3}{4}$ h. from Zermatt).

Schönbiel Hut 2694m.

Situated on a grassy promontory above the junction of the Zmutt and Schönbiel glaciers. Warden and staff, restaurant service, places for 62.

12. From Zermatt there is practically no advantage in taking the cablelift to Furi. Some time can be gained by taking the lift to Schwarzsee and from there descending via Stafelalp to reach the usual path from Zermatt (plenty of signposts, Schwarzsee to hut, 3 h.).

From Zermatt take the road then path which keeps to the R side of the river and follow it through Zmutt and past wayside teashops to the waterfall section (2311.8m.) above the Zmutt glacier. This is followed by a long moraine section above the glacier to where a zigzag path goes up slopes to the R to reach the hut (4 h. from Zermatt).

Dent Blanche (Rossier) Hut 3507m.

Cabane de la Dent Blanche. Situated on the lowest rocks of a buttress standing below pt. 3717m. on the S ridge of the Dent Blanche. Resident warden, who is sometimes away, places for 30, take your own food. Self cooking is permitted. The warden has limited cooking facilities for which a charge is made.

13. Les Haudères - La Forclaz - Ferpècle (Salay, 1766m., bus, hotel). From Salay a good path behind the church leads above the continuation road to a bridge across a stream at pt. 1984m. On the other side take the L fork to Bricola Alp (2415m.) (1¾ h.). Continue by the same path to the moraine (2640m.) at the foot of the Manzettes glacier. Climb the lateral moraine to where the path descends to the glacier. Go up the middle of the glacier (a few cairns and painted stones) and gradually work to the S side. Reach the ridge on that side at pt. 3105m. (2½ h.). According to conditions on this glacier, it is sometimes better to reach the ridge lower down, then scramble up it. The rocks are marked with paint flashes. From here the direct route to the Col d'Hérens and the Bertol hut branches off to the S. For the Dent Blanche hut climb the ridge called the Roc Noir to the foot of a large glacier hump below the hut.

Go up this following a line of marker poles (crevasses) to the hut (1½ h., 4 h. from Bricola Alp, about 6 h. from Ferpècle. In descent, 3 h. to Ferpècle).

Schönbiel - Dent Blanche huts connection. F+.

14. This is more often used in the reverse direction by parties who have climbed the Dent Blanche and, finding it too late to reach the Schönbiel by nightfall, stop over at the Dent Blanche hut. The obvious connection lies over the Col d'Hérens (3462m.). Clearly it is also possible to reach the Dent Blanche hut by the ordinary route from the Schönbiel hut to the Dent Blanche S ridge; this is more direct but steeper, and parties must suit themselves.

Over the Col d'Hérens (see also entry in climbing section).

From the Schönbiel hut there are two ways to start, because there are lower and upper approaches to the top of the Stockji rognon.

Lower approach: From the hut go down a vague track to the SW, to the edge of the cliff overlooking the glacier junction. There is a complicated route down the cliff, slanting R, short walls, open chimneys; slabs and scree, to reach loose moraine at the bottom. Examine in daylight. Cross the moraine then the dry glacier (open crevasses) to the base of the high lateral moraine (pt. 2624m.) round the foot of the Stockji. Find a small track rising L up to the moraine and follow its crest, then a track over grass to a stone-wall shelter. The track goes up some rocks above pt. 2789m., then below a broken grassy rockface. Climb this in zigzags to the N (the best route is not easy to find in the dark) and reach a stony saddle at the W end of the rognon, pt. 3041m. If the start from the hut is not liked, and the lower route is to be used, you can start as for the upper route described below, then descend the glacier to the foot of the Stockji.

Upper approach: Generally used in descent (glissade carefully!). If climbed in the early hours of morning crampons will be needed to avoid step cutting. From the hut follow the main path to the NW for 10 min., then scramble down moraine to the glacier. Slant across the ice to the N side of the Stockji and climb the large open snow couloir to its top, finishing on a saddle to the L of pt. 3091.8m. A small track leads in a few min. to pt. 3041m. ($1\frac{3}{4}$ h.).

Now climb into the centre of the Stockji glacier, turning several large crevasses (often troublesome), and reach the R side below the Col d'Hérens. The bergschrund is usually large; cross it where the upper rocks are lowest, somewhat L of the col. Climb steep snow then rocks to the top (80m.). A big cornice may be found ($2\frac{1}{4}$ h., $4-4\frac{1}{2}$ h. from Schönbiel hut).

In bad conditions it is much better to go higher up the glacier and climb back to the R across the snowy NE shoulder of the Tête Blanche; then reach the col by a short descent. This variation is called the Col de la Tête Blanche (c. 3580m.) and it is always easy (ski route).

On the other side cross the huge snowfield to the NNE; large crevasses sometimes found lying in the same direction. Keep R, under the Wandflue ridge, and reach the hut by a final short snow slope ($1\frac{3}{4}$ h., $5\frac{1}{2}$ - 6 h. from Schönbiel hut).

Bertol - Dent Blanche huts connection.

15. From the Bertol hut, 3311m. (see Pennine Alps West guidebook) the eastward route across the vast undulating snowfields at the head of the Miné and Ferpècle glaciers, towards the Col d'Hérens, is indicated on LK. In poor visibility the correct direction is easily lost. There are no landmarks and huge crevasses appear in several places. A trade route, however, with a piste in season. Keep somewhat below and to the N of the

Col d'Hérens and join the previous route to the Dent Blanche hut ($2-2\frac{1}{2}$ h. to Col d'Hérens, about $3\frac{1}{2}$ h. to Dent Blanche hut from Bertol hut).

<u>Moiry Hut</u> 2825m.

Cabane de Moiry. An important hut situated on a promontory on the true R bank of the Moiry glacier, at the W foot of the Aigs. de la Lé. Warden, places for 70, simple restaurant service.

16. Postbus from Grimentz to the barrage (2250m.). The road continues along the E side of the lake to a small glacier lake (2349m.) some distance beyond. Cars can be taken to this point, 1 h. on foot. From the roadhead move L(N) to join a path rising to meet the original footpath beyond the point where it has crossed several streams, and continue into a moraine valley (2558m.). From the end of this finish up a steep slope by numerous zigzags to the hut ($1\frac{1}{2}$ h. from roadhead, $2\frac{1}{2}$ h. from barrage).

17. From Zinal the best approach crosses the <u>Col du Gardien</u> (3069m.), also known as the Col de la Cabane, a dip in the ridge of the Aigs. de la Lé. Both sides are easy. Leave Zinal by the main road to the S and reach the triple fork just beyond the Vichiesso chalet on the Mountet hut route (1 h.). Take the R fork in zigzags to the SW, through open forest, to another fork (2142m.) where the L branch leads to a chalet (2184m.). From here climb the L side of the stream above the chalet and at c. 2500m. slant L up scree and snow patches to the SW. Go up a break in a short rock barrier (2600m.) towards the Col du Pigne, then slant R (W) over easy broken rock ledges to the col, above a low relief rock buttress ($2\frac{1}{2}$ h., $3\frac{1}{2}$ h. from Zinal). On the other side slant R down snow and scree to a stream bed which leads to the rocky slope above the hut (15 min, 45 min.

42

in ascent to col, $3\frac{3}{4}$-4 h. from Zinal. In reverse direction, $2\frac{3}{4}$ h.).

18. From La Forclaz (Les Haudères) the usual approach is over the <u>Col de la Couronne</u> (2987m.). From La Forclaz follow the road a short way to a fork on the L, where a path goes to the Saulesses chalets (1951m.) (30 min.). Here take a number of steep zigzags to the NE and so reach the Bréona chalets (2197m.). Follow a water supply channel and contour to the E round the head of a grassy cwm to reach the Remointse chalet (2435m.). Continue to the W by a vague track into the stony cwm below the pass. Climb to the foot of a short rock wall directly below the col. Turn this on the L and return R along a gangway to an earthy couloir which leads to the lowest point in the ridge ($3\frac{1}{2}$ h., 4 h. from La Forclaz). On the other side descend grass slopes to where you bear R under the lower rocks of the P. de Moiry to reach the moraine and true L bank of the Moiry glacier at pt. 2665m. Go straight across the glacier to the opposite side and take a track up rocky slopes to the hut (45 min., 1 h. in ascent. $4\frac{3}{4}$ h. from La Forclaz).

PART I

Weisshorn – Dent Blanche chain

Zermatt West chain to Col de la Dent Blanche

STELLIHÖRNER S. 3409.5m. N. 3405m.

An important outlier of the Barrhörner group, dividing the mtn. scene between the Turtmann (W) and Topali (E) huts. A mtn. of secondary interest with singularly poor rock (limestone), but easily climbed from the W side, and without much difficulty from the Topali side. PD/AD. First ascent of highest pt: W. M. Conway and W. A. B. Coolidge with Chr. Almer jr., 23 August, 1890.

GÄSSIJOCH 3252m.

Between the Stellihörner and the Gässispitz, the easiest passage across the main divide from the Turtmann to the Topali hut. The col is not the lowest pt. in the ridge but a saddle to the NE of the latter (3235m.). PD-. First recorded tourist crossing: Misses Green with guides, 25 August, 1884.

BARRHÖRNER N. 3610m. S. 3583m.

A popular outing from the Turtmann hut, by the W flank on easy scree and snow, and along the main N - S ridges, F. About 3 h. Fine viewpoint. From the Topali hut, by the E ridge of the lower summit then along the main ridge, PD. About 3 h. First ascent of highest pt: Mrs. E. P. Jackson with Aloys Pollinger and M. Truffer, 1 September, 1883.

BRUNEGGHORN 3833m.

A fine secondary mtn. with a huge wall of rotten rocks on the
S side - well seen from Randa, and varied facets and glacier
slopes of snow and ice on the N side, by which it is invariably
climbed. One of the two main excursions from the Turtmann
and Topali huts (with the Bishorn). Recommended to climbers
based in the Zermatt valley and a good reason for visiting the
Topali hut. First ascent: J. and F. Tantignoni with H. Brant-
schen, 1853. First ski ascent: G. Miescher and J. Munck,
10 April, 1913.

<u>West Flank and South-West Ridge (via Bruneggjoch)</u>. The ord-
inary and usual route from the Turtmann hut. More circuitous
but quite convenient from the Topali hut. F. First ascensionists.

19. From the Turtmann hut follow the well marked path SE over
the Gässi rock barrier (couloir, Route 4) and continue in the
same direction L of the moraine crest, which is later reached.
At about 2900m. descend from the crest and cross snow and
rocks near pt. 2941m., below the Chanzilti rocks (3071.9m.),
to reach the Turtmann glacier. This part of glacier is named
Brunegg glacier on LK25 which is not consistent with adjoining
sheets. Climb the glacier hollow SSE under the rocks of the
Schöllihorn, large crevasses, then slant L (E) up to the Bruneggjoch (3365m.) (3 h.). From the col climb on or near the
crest of the NW ridge for a few min., to pt. 3401m., then slant
R and make a slightly curving horizontal traverse across snow
slopes to the S. Cross a bergschrund at c. 3500m. and climb
directly to the SW ridge of the mtn. which is reached either at
a saddle pt. 3649m. or rather higher and better at pt. 3702m.
Now follow the fine narrowing snow ridge to the summit, keeping
L to avoid cornices (2 h., 5 h. from Turtmann hut. 2½ h. in
descent). Clearly it is not necessary to reach the Bruneggjoch, which can be turned on the R by keeping to the main
glacier below some rocks, beyond which the upper cwm leading
to saddle pt. 3649m. is entered. With good conditions on the

glacier this could save 30 min.

20. From the Topali hut a small track descend S and passes under the lower rocks of the Distulgrat before rising slightly to reach stones and snowbeds in the Chella cwm (c. 2700m., cairns). Immediately above is a saddle in the ridge on the S side of the cwm: Satteln (Sattle), 2945m. Climb towards this ridge well to the R of this pt., slanting SW, and reach it near pt. 3020m. where large blocks are perched on the crest (1 h.). From here make a slightly descending traverse SW and S, across the end of the Schölli glacier, and contour moraine slopes and snow round the foot (E side) of a rock spur coming down from pt. 3182m. Another slightly descending traverse now leads SW to the Abberg glacier (30 min.). Climb snow and a few rocks up the R side of the glacier to a short but awkward icefall at c. 3100m. Climb through this (séracs and crevasses very bad late in the season) and continue up the final easy slope under the Schöllihorn to the Bruneggjoch (3365m.) (1¼ h., about 2¾ h. from Topali hut). Here join Route 19 to reach the summit (2 h., 4¾ h. from Topali hut).

21. <u>West Face</u>. This triangular snow facet lies directly L of the upper bergschrund at 3500m. crossed by the ordinary Routes 19, 20. In good conditions it goes easily and quickly in crampons. 300m., 45°, PD+. About 30 min. less than ordinary route, but longer in conditions of ice or poor snow. First ascent: E. R. Blanchet with K. Mooser, 27 July, 1926.

<u>North-West Ridge</u>. On the whole the most direct route from either the Turtmann or Topali huts. The steep part is short with mixed climbing sometimes on ice when it becomes quite delicate. PD/PD+. Descended by F. Gardiner, A. Cust and F. T. Wethered with P. and H. Knubel and L. Proment, 29 July, 1876.

46

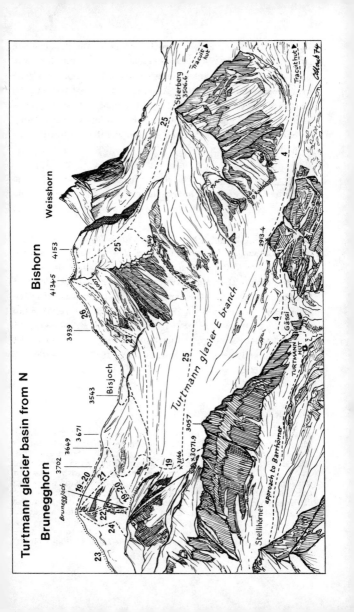

Turtmann glacier basin from N

Brunegghorn   Bishorn   Weisshorn

3702   3649   3671   3543   3939   413+5   4153

Brunegjoch   Bisjoch   Stierberg   3506.6

19-20   3166   x3071.9   3057   2913.4   Tracuit hut

19   25   26   27   25   25

21   22   24   23   Turtmann glacier E branch

Tracuit hut

Gässi

TURTMANN HUT

Stellihörner approach to Barrhörner

22. From the Turtmann or Topali huts reach the Brunegjjoch by Routes 19 or 20 respectively (about 3 h.). Climb the lower easy angled section of ridge on snow and a few rocks to a general steepening at 3500m. A sharp snow crest leads to the first of three rock steps which are ascended in turn keeping R of the crest and returning to the crest at points between them, before reaching a final mixed section and the summit (1½ h., 4½ h. from either hut).

23. <u>North-East Ridge</u>. This is the longest and steepest ridge of the mtn., not easy to approach or climb. Rarely ascended. AD.

24. <u>North-North-East Face</u>. This snow/ice face is about 400m. high and is cut by a diagonal ice ramp from R to L. The main steepness and difficulty occurs above the ramp, which can be reached from either side of the rognon 3419m. in the middle of the Abberg glacier. The face is nearly always a sheet of ice after July. Average 57°, D+/TD, 5 h. from bergschrund to summit. First ascent: E.R. Blanchet with K. Mooser, 14 August, 1925. Ascended from the L(E) side of the rognon by M. Brandt and A. and R. Voillat, 24 July, 1957, and descended by same party.

BISHORN 4153m.

The notable satellite of the Weisshorn, isolated from the greater mtn. by the Weisshornjoch and distantly situated in a magnificent glacier setting from the Brunegghorn by the intervening Bisjoch. The summit is double with rock pt. 4134.5m. to the E. A popular snow climb from the Tracuit hut, with a piste in season almost possible for anyone. A consolation prize for parties unable to climb the Weisshorn. Not infrequently climbed from the Turtmann hut or in a longer day from the Topali hut. In recent years the NE face has become a classic ice climb. First ascent: probably G.S. Barnes and R. Chessyre-Walker with J. Imboden and J.M. Chanton, 18 August, 1884. First winter and ski ascent: the Zinal guides Cotter,

Genoud, Epiney and Theytaz, 22 December, 1912.

<u>North-West Flank</u>.   The usual route from the Tracuit hut,
which is also joined by the usual route from the Turtmann hut.
F.   First ascensionists.

25. From the Tracuit hut traverse E across the   Turtmann
glacier to a snowy saddle (3549m.) to the R (SE) of pt. 3591m.
From here climb snow slopes straight up (SSE) to the saddle
between the two summits, then take a short and sometimes
corniced crest to the highest pt. (2½ h.).

From the Turtmann hut follow Route 19 to pt. 3166m. on the
L(E) side of the Turtmann glacier, directly below the summit
of the Schöllihorn.   Now cross the glacier (crevasses) to the
opposite (W) side, at c. 3200m. where a rock rib descends NE
from saddle pt. 3549m.   Climb this steep rib without special
difficulty past a zone of light-coloured rocks and as directly as
possible to the saddle at the top (1 h. for rib) where the Tracuit
hut approach is joined. PD-.   About 5½ h. from Turtmann hut
to summit.

From the Topali hut, by Route 20 across the Bruneggjoch,
then by a slight descent across the crevassed Turtmann glacier
to the rib at 3200m., join the Turtmann hut route (about 6½ h.
from Topali hut to summit).

<u>East Ridge (via Bisjoch)</u>. A magnificent ridge, one of the finest
of its kind and standard in the region. Not in the same class
as the N ridge of the Weisshorn but finer than its E ridge and
situated in remote surroundings.   You can start either from
the Turtmann (best) or Topali huts: if the latter the Bruneggjoch is traversed. Parties have been known to continue up the
N ridge of the Weisshorn, which makes a very long expedition,
quite possible for a fit party in one day.   Mixed climbing,
mainly narrow and often corniced snow crests. PD+/AD.   First
ascent: Mrs. E. Burnaby with J. Imboden and P. Sarbach,

6 August, 1884.

26. From the Turtmann hut follow Route 19 to below the Bruneggjoch. Continue up the L side of the glacier to c. 3550m., then turn R and cross it SW towards the prominent saddle of the Bisjoch. Cross a bergschrund and go up a short steep ice slope, step cutting often necessary, to the col (3543m.) (3¼ h.). With hard ice on the slope it is better to climb the snow slopes of pt. 3671m. to the E, then descend to the col.

From the Topali hut follow Route 20 across the Bruneggjoch and by traversing below the NW ridge of the Brunegghorn join the Turtmann hut approach on the Turtmann glacier at c. 3400m. This traverse avoids any notable loss of height (about 3½ h. to col).

From the Bisjoch climb the steepening ridge on snow and a few rocks, then more snow to a longer rocky section ending at pt. 3939m. This section is without obstructions but can be icy and delicate. Continue along a fine almost level snow crest rising at the end to the rock pinnacle marking the E forepeak (4134.5m.). Traverse the pinnacle and reach the summit by a nice snow ridge (2½ h., 5¾ h. from Turtmann hut, 6 h. from Topali hut. Because of commonly mediocre conditions, in practice allow at least an additional 1½ h.).

<u>North-East Face.</u> This large symmetrical face of snow and ice is the most conspicuous feature of the Bishorn. It is about 650m. high. A band of séracs runs right across the lower part of the face in the form of a V, the lowest pt. of which is directly below the E forepeak to which the face rises. Ways through the séracs vary from season to season, but generally one is found either a short distance L or R of the V. Most parties have taken the L. Above the séracs the slopes are straightforward but variable conditions ranging from soft snow to ice at an average angle of 48°, rising above 50° in places, makes the climbing delicate. Some danger of falling ice below the

séracs but after a cold night this would appear to be minimal.
TD-. More serious than the Lenzspitze NE face, about equal
to and comparable with the Grand Cornier NE face.

First ascent: E.R. Blanchet with K. Mooser and R. Lochmatter, 21 September, 1924. Second ascent and first descent:
M. Brandt and A. and R. Voillat, 26-27 July, 1957. First
winter ascent: M. Gamma, J. Henkel and G. Leutenegger,
22-23 January, 1969. First British ascent: J.S. Mercer and
A.G.L. Williams, 4 July, 1973.

27. Reach the foot of the face from the Turtmann   or Topali
huts by crossing the Turtmann glacier at c. 3400m. from Routes
19 or 20 (about $3\frac{1}{2}$ h. from either hut). Start in the centre,
cross the bergschrund and climb towards the L side of the lowest part of the V band of séracs. A very steep snow/ice ramp
often slants up from R to L through the séracs. Climb this
with a pitch of at least 60° (Brandt, 67°. British party, 70°
claimed) to a recess under the sérac cornice. Climb the upper
sérac barrier at its weakest pt., where it is usually vertical
and about 6m. high. The British party traversed R at a stated
65° to where the cornice projects only $2\frac{1}{2}$ m., and broke through
at this pt. On reaching the main face above, climb as directly
as possible towards the E forepeak, mostly at an angle of 50°
or less, but rising to 56° at the top (4-6 h. from bergschrund).

WEISSHORN 4505.5m.

One of the most beautiful mtns. in the Alps, and in the Pennine
range only surpassed in height by the Dom and Monte Rosa
group. It is an irregular pyramid of three faces and three
ridges. The faces are practically of no interest, being swept
by stonefall and often of no great technical difficulty. All the
ridges are long and rank as expeditions in the proper sense.
The rock is fairly good but snow/ice difficulties are the main
problem. Combining two ridges for a traverse is highly recommended. Ascents on the W side of the mtn. from Zinal are
still rare and a note about this is included below.

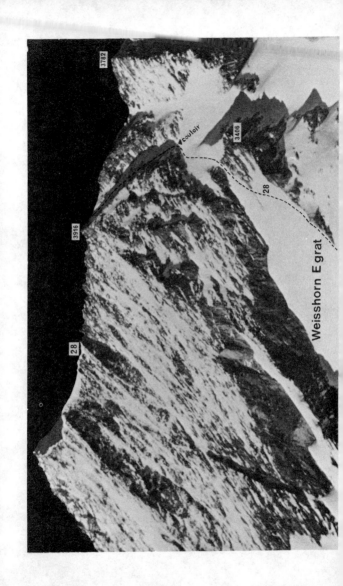

3782

coulair

3406

28

Weisshorn E grat

3916

28

First ascent: John Tyndall with J. J. Bennen and U. Wenger, 19 August, 1861. First winter ascent: L. F. Ryan with A. Pollinger, J. and R. Lochmatter, 10 January, 1902. On ski: Arnold Lunn with Josef Knubel, 27 April, 1920.

<u>East Ridge</u>. The ordinary route and easiest of the ridges. In good conditions there is no difficulty. Some stonefall danger on the face before you reach the ridge. The first part of the crest consists of about two dozen rock thumbs and small gendarmes, the middle part is a short fine snow crest, and the upper section is a long and fairly steep snow/ice slope with a few rocks. PD/PD+. First ascensionists.

28. From the Weisshorn hut take the small track which rises gradually to the glacier (15 min.). Slant L across the snow, horizontally WNW to the rock barrier separating this slope from a higher snow band. The barrier is cut by a small snow couloir just R of pt. 3145m. Climb the couloir by rocks on its L side. At the top move R (N) up rocks at the edge of the snow band, then climb the snow itself to a snow shoulder at c. 3500m. Go up this to where the snow meets a broad buttress coming down more or less from pt. 3916m. on the ridge above. On its R is a large open couloir. The easiest way is to move R along the foot of the buttress wall and climb the L side of the couloir, using a series of rock ribs with alternate snow strips. You emerge on the ridge at the top between pts. 3782m. and 3916m. This route is exposed to stonefall, more often as not from material kicked down by higher parties. Alternatively, climb trending L for a few pitches on good rock, then work up grooves and ribs on the buttress, keeping R near the couloir for the easiest line. Reach the crest a few m. R of pt. 3915m. ($2\frac{3}{4}$ h.).

Follow the crest, climbing over most of the rock teeth. None is higher than 10m. Some are turned more easily on the R, a few on the L. The last big spike is turned on the R (1 h.). Reach the snow ridge, narrow, possibly corniced, and follow its

Weisshorn E grat
from rock teeth
section

28

4178

crest to the broad upper section of the ridge (15 min.). Climb
the almost featureless ridge quite steeply up to an edge of rocks
near the top. A bergschrund may be found halfway up (2 h.,
6 h. from Weisshorn hut, about 4 h. in descent).

<u>North-North-West Ridge (over Bishorn)</u>. Called the N Ridge.
A magnificent climb, snow, ice and rocks up to its Grand Gendarme (4331m.), then a fine snow/ice crest. Comparable with
the Dent Blanche Viereselgrat. The ridge is long and delicate
with a key rock pitch that is often icy. The shortest way of
reaching the ridge is at the lowest pt. between the Weisshorn
and Bishorn, at the col of the Weisshornjoch (4058m.). However, the ice slope below this is generally too serious for climbing at night and it is much simpler and only normally 30 min.
longer to start by traversing the Bishorn. AD with pitches of
III and one of III+. First ascent: H. Biehly with H. Burgener,
21 September, 1898.

29. From the Tracuit hut reach the summit of the Bishorn by
Route 25 (2½ h.). Continue down an easy snow ridge between
ice cliffs and go along the saddle of the Weisshornjoch to the
slight knoll of pt. 4108.9m. (15 min.). Continue along a fine
snow crest, cornices possible, up to pt. 4203m. (15 min.).
This is the first of three flat-topped and square-shaped steps
of serpentine rock. From the top of the first descend the laminated rock crest, nearly vertical (III, or abseil) and go along
a shoulder to the edge of the second. Descend even more
abruptly, in the same manner. The snowy crest now leads to
the third step, from which you descend on the crest more easily.
From a distinct little gap, climb snow or rock slightly L of the
crest to the top of a rock knoll at the foot of the big step rising
to the Grand Gendarme. Climb a few m. direct, then traverse
L on slabs for 6m. to the foot of a vertical chimney. Climb
this (30m., III+) to a shoulder at the top of the step. (In descent,
either climb down the chimney, or abseil down the vertical

WEISSHORN S side

Schalijoch
Gd. Gendarme
Biv.
Schaligrat SW
30
28
4178
4506
E. Grat
3916
3782
3406
28
9
9
3440
R 3492
9
Schali glacier

groove just before it, on the R as you descend, then traverse by ledges to the foot of the step). Continue up the crest on good rock and turn the summit of the Grand Gendarme by easy rocks on the L. Make a slightly descending traverse on this side to reach a snowy shoulder behind the gendarme, and at the start of the upper snow ridge. According to conditions the transition from rock to snow can be tricky ($3\frac{1}{4}$ h.). From the shoulder descend slightly to a saddle and continue along the sharp crest, sometimes corniced and with a few rock outcrops, to the summit, delicate all the way ($1\frac{1}{4}$ h., $7\frac{1}{4}$ h. from Tracuit hut. 4-5 h. in descent).

<u>South-West Ridge (Schaligrat)</u>. In normal conditions this splendid ridge is entirely rock, formed by a series of gendarmes and steps of almost continuous difficulty. There is a sudden dislocation in the line of the ridge near pt. 4350m. at three-quarters height. In the upper part there are linking sections of snow/ice. The ridge is in two main sections, with a vague shoulder at mid-height, just above pt. 4057m. AD+, pitches of III. First ascent: E. Broome with J. M. Biner and A. Imboden, 2 September, 1895.

30. From the Schalijoch bivouac climb on the crest and turn the first series of gendarmes on the R; return to the crest above them at a normally snowy gap behind pt. 4057m. Follow the crest and turn the steepest gendarmes in the next section on the R. Reach the point where the crest peters out at the edge of a large couloir falling down the W face. Cross the head of the couloir, route variable, quite difficult, and join the new ridge rising out of the W face above the couloir. Go up it for a pitch to a large red tower, and climb this direct by its R-hand face. Above, five gendarmes follow, separated by fine snow crests. All this section should be taken more or less direct. A narrow snow ridge leads to the summit ($5\frac{1}{2}$ h. from Schalijoch biv.).

WEISSHORN from E

Schalijoch

Gd. Gendarme
29
N grat
Bishorn
Bisjoch
Brunegghorn

Bis glacier

31. <u>West Face.</u>   The imposing and remote W side of the mtn.
is perhaps the least known versant of any great Pennine summit.   Direct routes on the W face are hard and quite dangerous.
Only the W rib of the N ridge Grand Gendarme has any following, and this is mainly used for descent at present.   This rib
is rightly called the Younggrat.   The main section on rock is
about 550m.   Anyone venturing on it should note that there are
two distinct ways, up and down.   The ascent route keeps on or
near the rib crest and has fixed pegs at tricky points.   III+.
The descent route for this rib keeps to the S of it, in a couloir
line which starts from the snow saddle in the N ridge behind
the Grand Gendarme.   There are good iron stanchions at regular intervals down the upper couloir.   The couloir descent
route joins the rib at a bend (obvious on LK25) where a chimney fault enables one to leave the couloir and reach open rock.
A separate line of abseil pegs on the lower half of the rib does
not correspond to the ascent line and its pegs, but the difference
is slight. It seems probable that the Zinal guides will progressively equip the Younggrat W rib in order to establish a "voie
normale" on this side of the mtn.   G. W. Young with L. and B.
Theytaz, 7 September, 1900.

SCHALIJOCH 3750m.

Between the Schalihorn and Weisshorn. A difficult glacier pass
from Zinal to Randa.   There is a biv. hut just above the col,
on the ridge of the Weisshorn.   See Routes 9 and 10.   First
traverse: J. J. Hornby and T. H. Philpott with Chr. Almer and
C. Lauener, 10 August, 1864.

SCHALIHORN 3974.5m.

A neglected mtn., dominated on either side by the Zinalrothorn
and Weisshorn.   Except for the ordinary route, it is awkward
of access.   Nevertheless a worthwhile day from the Rothorn

WEISSHORN W face

Schalljoch
biv.
30 Schalligrat SW
29
43cz
N grat
Gd. Gendarme
Bishorn
4328t
10
3576
31

hut. Its fine crenellated summit ridge, with a sharp N peak (3955m.), is composed of poor rock. The SE ridge is a good rock climb best reached from the Weisshorn hut by a long tedious traverse on moraine.

First ascent: T. Middlemore with J. Jaun and C. Lauener, 20 July, 1873. First winter and ski ascent: Marcel Kurz with Josef Knubel, 4 February, 1920.

South-South-West Ridge (from Hohlichtpass). The only practical route from the Rothorn hut, a first-rate snow/ice climb, interesting and recommended. Quite popular nowadays, superb scenery. PD. First ascensionists.

32. From the Rothorn hut cross the upper snows of the Rothorn glacier and reach the Unter Äschjoch (3562m.). Now climb the easy snow and rock ridge to the Ober Äschhorn (3669m.) (1¼ h.). Go a few m. further then slant R, down to the upper plateau of the Hohlicht glacier, below the tremendous E face of the Rothorn (30 min.). Cross the plateau N, then climb a steep slope with several large crevasses and possibly ice walls to the foot of the rock spur below the Pte. N de Moming (3863m.). From here an easier slope leads to the Hohlichtpass (3731m.), which cannot be seen till the last moment (1½ h.). Now climb the R-hand side of the broad snow spur forming the SSW ridge, steep and often icy, to finish on a few rocks (1 h., 4¼ h. from Rothorn hut).

33. North Ridge. Though rising little more than 200m. from the Schalijoch, this ridge has been rarely climbed; it appears to have been descended more often. Previous descriptions of the rock made the climb sound most unattractive. The advised time of 3 to 4 h. seemed excessive for such a route. By 1973 several parties had used the ridge in descent by traversing the Schalihorn from the Rothorn hut to reach the Schalijoch bivouac hut. A very detailed description of the ridge descent appears in the December, 1973 monthly bulletin of Die Alpen for the purpose of encouraging this approach to the biv. hut. Sceptics will be pleased to learn that the optimum descent time for the ridge is given as

Col de Moming · P. Nord de Moming · Schalihorn · Schalijoch

S side

Hohlichtpass · 3797 · 32 · Hohlicht glacier · 3418 · 34 · aw. · 9

5 h. (!) - so putting the total approach from the Rothorn hut by ascending the ordinary Schalihorn route first at close to 10 h. The difficulties are described as short pitches of II and III, not technically serious but delicate because of loose rock in places. Descended by E. Davidson with Chr. Klucker and J. Imeich; G. Fitzgerald with U. Almer and F. Boss, 14 August, 1900. First climbed by E. Broome with A. and H. Pollinger, 28 August, 1903.

34. South-East Ridge. This is a worthwhile climb marred by an awkward approach, which consists of a long descending traverse from the Weisshorn hut along the Stockji ledges between rock barriers under the Schali glacier. The ridge is climbed direct, the lower part being loose and unpleasant, the upper sound and interesting. It leads directly to the main summit. AD with pitches of II/II+. About 7 h. from Weisshorn hut. First ascent: J. W. Alexander and H. Whitney, August, 1933.

HOHLICHTPASS 3731m.

Between the Schalihorn and Pte. N de Moming. Not a practical pass but the E side provides normal access to the Schalihorn. See Route 32.

POINTE NORD DE MOMING 3863m.

Rarely climbed for itself, accessible from the Hohlichtpass (Route 32) by the main ridge on loose broken rock with some difficulty in 45 min., or quite easily by the main ridge from the Col de Moming in 30 min. First ascent: H. Pfann and E. Christa, 21 August, 1901.

COL DE MOMING 3777m.

Between the Moming summits, from Zinal to Zermatt. A superb

glacier pass, one of the finest, most interesting and scenic in the Pennine Alps. More varied and less sure than any of the Mischabel chain glacier passes. Much better, surer and safer in the direction Zinal-Zermatt. The Zinal side requires good experience of glacier terrain but is not difficult in favourable conditions. PD+. Unfortunately the great Moming glacier on the Zinal side is riddled with crevasses and is seldom in good condition. The glacier terraces under Besso and the Moming summits used to reach the pass are only relatively undisturbed and may prove troublesome. Consequently very few crossings of the pass are made. The Zermatt side is easier but steep at the top. PD. First traverse: E. Whymper and A. W. Moore with Michel Croz and Chr. Almer, 18 July, 1864.

POINTE SUD DE MOMING 3963m.

Rarely climbed for itself, accessible from the Col de Moming by the main ridge on quite difficult mixed terrain with technical rock pitches, AD, III+. First ascent: H. Seymour King with A. Supersaxo and A. Anthamatten, 6 August, 1886.

ZINALROTHORN 4221.2m.

Probably the most popular rock peak in the Zermatt district, certainly with British climbers, and situated directly above the resort. The ordinary routes deserve a higher grading on technical grounds, but they are too familiar and the difficulties are short and well protected. The rock is an excellent red gneiss, always sound on the ridges. The E face warrants special attention, but otherwise the flanks are loose and very icy. A traverse by the ordinary Zermatt route or the Rothorngrat and the N ridge is one of the finest expeditions of its class in the Alps.

First ascent: Leslie Stephen and F. C. Grove with M. and J. Anderegg, 22 August, 1864. First winter and ski ascent: Marcel Kurz with T. Theytaz, 7 February, 1914.

South-East Ridge (via Gabel Notch). From the Gabel Notch the route finishes up the SW ridge. One of the most frequented climbs on a big mtn. anywhere in the Pennine Alps. Varied and interesting. Contrary to the usual indications there is more work on snow than rock. The Kanzelgrat is the continuation proper of the SE ridge; it ranks as a major variation. The ordinary route

ZINALROTHORN S side

Kanzelgrat

Gabel Notch

Ober Rothornjoch

Schneegrat SE

Rothorn grat SW 37

35

36

35

37

3912

3973

2761

described below is PD/PD+.   The Biner Slab is sometimes a sheet of ice; do not leave crampons at the Gabel notch.   First ascent: C. T. Dent and G. A. Passingham with Alexander Burgener, F. Andermatten and F. Imseng, 5 September, 1872.

35. From the Rothorn hut cross a few rocks to the R(N) and climb NE on the uppermost slopes of the Rothorn glacier, and below a rock wall lying in the same direction. Reach a large snowy break in this wall. Climb sharp L(W) to the foot of a rock promontory, and go up a rock couloir in this, narrowing to a chimney; exit L to the top. Trend L over rocks to a snow band and make a rising traverse L(W) across the snow to a few rocks at the far side; climb these to a broad spur of snowy rocks. Climb R(N) to the highest rocks at the foot of a steep snow slope. Make a rising traverse L(NNW) up this and reach the end of the SE snow ridge, a short distance NW of pt. 3786m. ($1\frac{1}{2}$ h.). Follow the narrow crest of the Schneegrat, sometimes quite delicate, to the first outcrop at the far end (30 min.). Cross this, then a second, after which the ridge steepens. Climb two short steps to below a big vertical step with a horizontal shoulder at its top (15 min.). Now traverse L below the shoulder, rising slightly all the while on to the S face. Go up a short couloir on to the open face. In dry conditions this traverse is mainly on rock; normally the rocks are separated by fairly steep snow beds. Aim for a narrow snow couloir in the upper part of the face, leading to an obvious gap in the SW ridge, L of the summit. Climb rocks and snow to the entrance of the couloir, then take a rock rib on its L side with good flake holds to within a few m. of the Gabel notch. Reach this by a bank of steep snow (45 min.).

From the notch climb the broad ridge direct to a block platform (II+). Move L, pass through a rock window and descend 4m. to a toe traverse. Traverse L, rising slightly, along the crevice line on the Biner Slab to a stance at the foot of the L edge (40m.). Climb L of this edge, usually very steep snow/ice,

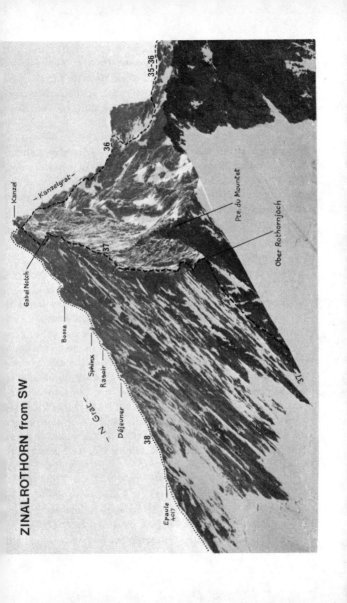

ZINALROTHORN from SW

Kanzel
—Kanzelgrat—
36
35-36
Gabel Notch
37
Pte. du Mountet
Ober Rothornjoch
37
Bosse
Sphinx
Rasoir
Déjeuner
—N Grat—
38
Epaule
4017

to a rib of spiky rocks (30m.). Continue up the rib, or L of it in bad conditions, and regain the crest (15m.). Follow snowy rocks to a platform and gendarme. Turn this on the L by a corner crack, then move R to avoid the top spike of the hooked fore-peak (Kanzel). So reach the summit in a few m. (1 h., 4 h. from Rothorn hut, 3 h. in descent).

Kanzelgrat. South-east ridge direct. A fine piece of rock climb-ing, in good conditions not very serious for skilled performers. D, pitches of IV and IV+. 250m. Several pegs in place. First ascent in three stages spread over five years by E.R. Blanchet with Kaspar Mooser, commencing 31 July 1928.

36. From the point on Route 35 where you go up a short rock couloir on to the S face, instead of working L continue more or less straight up on snow then smooth slabs (III, can be snow covered) until a slanting snow ramp on the R enables the hori-zontal top of the first shoulder step to be joined at the point where the crest steepens again. Climb it briefly to a short step with a chimney on the L. Go up this (III+, 15m.) and continue up the L side of the ridge taking a series of short slabs and walls, gen-erally III+/IV, to a slight angle of grey rock in the L side of the ridge immediately below the break at the foot of the terminal wall. On the R side of the vague angle chimney climb a steep wall (IV+, pegs) then an easier groove trending L to an over-hanging chockstone crack. Go up this (IV+) to ledges under the overhanging forepeak of the Kanzel. Exit L up a slab on nice holds (III) to the main ridge just below the Kanzel where Route 35 is joined about 5 min. from the summit (3 h. from point where Route 35 is left).

South-West Ridge (Rothorngrat). A superb rock climb, very popular. It joins the ordinary SE ridge at the Gabel notch. From either the Rothorn or Mountet huts the ridge can be joined at points as far down as the Trifthorn, but it is normal to join it

68

MOUNTET glacier basin   Zinalrothorn
W side

38

37

45

38

HUT

49

where the real interest begins, at the Ober Rothornjoch (3835m.). This is immediately N of the Pte. du Mountet (3877m.). Fresh snow clears quickly from the rocks. AD with pitches of III, III+. First ascent: C. R. Gross with R. Taugwalder, August, 1901.

37. From the Rothorn hut follow Route 35 to where you reach the broad spur of snowy rocks. Continue traversing L at c. 3560m. over fairly steep snow and rocks and continue across a rock spur from whose crest the traverse descends slightly to reach the glacier flowing down on the S side of the mtn., above its icefall. Cross the glacier NW to the foot of a couloir descending from the Ober Rothornjoch. Climb this direct by snow and rocks to the col ($2\frac{1}{2}$ h.).

From the Mountet hut follow a horizontal track SSE on moraine for a few min. to where the crest levels out. Slant R and reach the Mountet glacier at c. 2950m. Go up diagonally E across the crevassed glacier, over terraces and turning low ice walls, to below the foot of the rock spur under the Pte. du Mountet. On the N side of the rock spur climb crevassed slopes L(NE), then cross two bergschrunds and climb steep, loose but easy rocks to the L(N) of the snow/ice couloir coming down from the Ober Rothornjoch. At the top move R to reach the col (3 h.).

From the col climb the first step direct (III) to a snowy section which can be corniced. After this the first gendarme is easy; continue without incident to the second whose top is turned on the L by a ledge line, followed by a vertical chimney (III+) to regain the crest. Traverse the third gendarme (III) to a snowy gap. Now either traverse the next gendarmes or turn them on the L (III+, or II and III) to the final one with two prongs. Turn this by a block ledge on the R and descend some rocks to the Gabel notch ($2\frac{1}{2}$ h.). Join Route 35 to the summit (1 h., about 6 h. from Rothorn hut, $6\frac{1}{2}$ h. from Mountet hut).

<u>North Ridge.</u> The ordinary route from the Mountet hut, a splendid climb on perfect rock with fine situations. The gendarme pitches are quite difficult when the rock is icy. PD+. First ascensionists.

38. From the Mountet hut follow a good path starting SSE then going NNE along the lateral moraine of the Mountet glacier, up to near the Forcle col (3188m.). Move R on to the glacier and climb its L side round to the E and under the supporting rocks of the Arête du Blanc. Continue in this direction and cross the bergschrund high up, at c. 3740m. So reach the crest of the Arête du Blanc which is followed on snow or ice and rocks to the Épaule (4017m.) (3 h.). Now climb an easy rock ridge to the Gendarme du Déjeuner and turn it on the L. The ridge narrows and rises to an imposing gendarme called the Rasoir. Traverse it by a knife-edge (II+/III, exposed), or turn it more easily, but generally icy, on the R. Continue up the crest to the Sphinx gendarme. Turn this on the R by a ledge line which can be very delicate when icy (II+). At the end of the ledge move L and regain the crest. This is now a knife-edge for 35m. called the Bourrique (II). Arrive at the far end in a gap, at the foot of the Bosse, a tower about 40m. high. Climb it direct (II+/III). This pitch is hard when verglassed; the easiest line is somewhat to the R. From the top of the Bosse climb an easy ridge of rocks and snow to the summit ($1\frac{1}{2}$ h., $4\frac{1}{2}$ h. from Mountet hut).

<u>East Face.</u> There are three routes on this impressive rock wall but only the central and most direct one reaches the summit. The face is raked by stonefall, but the central route is comparatively sheltered. The rock in the lower half is poor; it improves higher up and becomes excellent. A few pegs should be carried. Climbed about 30 times with at least three British ascents to date. D+ with pitches of IV, IV+ and V. 700m. First ascent: André Roch, R. Gréloz and R. Schmid, 6 August, 1945. First British ascent: M. Keen and P.S. Nelson, 10 August, 1956.

ZINALROTHORN E face 39

First winter ascent: P. Etter, A. and E. Scherrer and U. Gant-
enbein, 27-28 December, 1971.

39. From the Rothorn hut follow Route 32 to the upper plateau of
the Hohlicht glacier. Move across this towards the foot of the
face where a deep couloir slants R up to the Sphinx on the N
ridge. Cross the bergschrund (about 2 h. from hut), climb the
L side of the couloir for 50m. (stonefall), then bear L into a
branch couloir. Trend L and climb increasingly steep snowy
rocks towards the base of an enormous triangular wall, dom-
inating the upper part of the face; go up this lower section as
directly as possible, on loose rock and snow/ice plaques, keeping R on more difficult rocks to minimise the stonefall risk (III/
IV). Near the foot of the upper wall is a series of broad gangways
slanting R. Climb the uppermost one to where a sheer buttress
bounds the R-hand side of the wall. Reaching the crest of this
buttress constitutes the crux of the climb, and the buttress gives
the general line of ascent. It has been overcome in at least three
ways, the most usual of which is as follows. Take a chimney/
crack on the edge of the wall itself, about 25m. L of the buttress.
Climb direct on loose rock, nearly vertical, in three pitches of
12m. and another of 40m. (V, fairly sustained, hard, unpro-
tected, peg belays). At the top of this chimney section make a
rising traverse R on to the buttress (IV+/V). The rock improves.
Climb a series of slabs and walls on the broad crest to a large
sloping icy terrace at its top (III/IV). All this section might be
climbed in crampons. Bear L over easy ground towards the
Kanzelgrat, till a steep chimney appears on the R. Climb this
and exit through a hole to finish 5m. L of the summit (7-8 h.
from bergschrund).

METTELHORN 3406m.

Situated on the N side of the Trift glacier basin, and a pendant
for the Untergabelhorn. A traditional training walk. There is
no climbing merit in this, although the panorama is extensive.

Forcle saddle – Besso S side

3217

3595

3667,8

3658

3663

3657
Blanc de Moming

3586
Arête du Blanc

42

43

43,3

82 (sect.)

3188

43

43

38

<u>By Triftchumme</u>. The ordinary route on S side of the mtn., a popular walk for all and sundry. F.

40. From Zermatt follow Route 11 as far as the Trift hotel (2 h.). Further up you reach a road (not shown on map) which can be followed into the Trift cwm. When the road ends join the original footpath working N (signposts) to a boulderfield then snowfields under the Platthorn. Go right up to the saddle/snow spur at the top (3166m.), then bear R(E) up snow and scree to the final rocks (track) and the summit (3 h., 5 h. from Zermatt).

BLANC DE MOMING 3663m.   3657m.

A junction of ridges behind the Mountet hut and on the N side one of the angles containing the great Moming glacier. Usually traversed in combination with the Besso (q.v.).

BESSO 3667.8m.

A good training peak for parties based at the Mountet hut and frequently climbed. First ascent: J.B. Epiney and J. Vianin, about 1862.

<u>South Flank and South-East Ridge</u>. Called the Ladies' Route. The easiest way up, F+, some danger from stonefall caused by other parties on the mtn., especially in descent. First ascensionists.

41. From the Mountet hut follow Route 38 to the Forcla saddle (3188m.). Cross the saddle and descend to a snow slope; descend this NW and go round a moraine and rocks on to the Besso glacier. Cross this due N to the foot of the S flank of the Besso. There is a large couloir in the lower rocks, slanting R. Climb it for about 50m., then exit L along a large horizontal ledge; leave the ledge and rise L to the foot of another large couloir, usually with snow in the bed. Cross it L-wards and climb its L side, parallel

with the SW ridge. This couloir finishes on the SE ridge at a little col. From here follow the rock ridge to the summit, keeping a little R of the crest (about $3\frac{1}{2}$ h. from Mountet hut).

<u>South-West Ridge</u>. The classic route, on perfect red gneiss. PD, pitches of II/III. First ascent: possibly R. L. G. Irving and party, 1906.

42. From the Mountet hut start as for Route 41 and reach the large horizontal ledge in the lower part of the S flank. Cross this to its L(W) end and reach the SW ridge. Climb on the crest to a big step. Either traverse R along its base, descending a little, till a long chimney leads back to the crest above the step. Or climb directly over the step by cracks in a long wall pitch (IV, exposed); finish by moving R along a ledge to enter the ordinary chimney. Keep to the crest, traverse two small gendarmes and reach the summit step. Turn this on the R and reach the top (4 h. from Mountet hut).

Note: A much better climb is made by starting up the ridge from a gap about 150m. R(E) of pt. 3217m. Traverse all the gendarmes (III/IV, sustained, 5-6 h. from hut).

<u>South-East Ridge complete</u>. A pleasant route for making a traverse. To avoid the S flank and stonefall in the afternoon this is the best way to return to the Mountet hut. The route is therefore described in reverse. PD+, bits of III. First ascent: H. Seymour King with A. Supersaxo and A. Anthamatten, 28 July, 1886.

43. From the summit descend a little L of the crest to the gap reached by Route 41. Continue down the ridge to its lowest point (3519m.). Ahead, a number of gendarmes appear; these can be traversed or turned on the L, but the rock is better on the crest; short pitches of III. After this section, reach the fine snow crest which leads to the top of the Blanc de Moming

TRIFTHORN SE side

Col du Mountet

45

44

44

Triftjoch

(3663m.) (2 h.).   Cross the snow dome of pt. 3657m., where the ridge ends. Climb down the easy SW rock ridge towards the Forcla saddle. There is a steep buttress at the foot of this ridge above the saddle. Avoid it by moving R and descending a series of ledges, then traverse back L to the saddle where the path down moraine is taken to the Mountet hut ($1\frac{1}{2}$ h., $3\frac{1}{2}$ h. from summit).

POINTE DU MOUNTET 3877m.

Simple rock pinnacle at the end of the SW ridge of the Zinal-rothorn. See preamble to Route 37.

COL DU MOUNTET 3658m.

In the main ridge NE of the Trifthorn, the easiest crossing in this section from the Rothorn hut to the Mountet hut. Both sides, PD-. Less interesting and used less than the Trifthorn for traversing from one hut to the other.

TRIFTHORN 3728.3m.

A consolation prize when higher peaks are out of condition. A pleasant rock scramble, one of the best of its standard in the Zermatt district, an ideal training peak. The mtn. is often traversed as a convenient and direct way of going from the Rothorn hut to the Mountet hut.   First ascent: Francis Douglas with Peter Taugwalder and P. Inäbnit, 5 July, 1865. First winter and ski ascent: C. Mauler with L. and B. Theytaz, 21 January, 1908.

South Ridge (from Triftjoch).   An exceptionally good scramble on sound rock. The ridge is in two sections with a roof of slabs at mid-height. Many variations possible but obviously keep on or near the crest.   PD with short pitches of II, II+. First ascensionists.

44. From the Rothorn hut follow Route 46 to below the open couloir rising to the Triftjoch.   Cross a bergschrund and climb a

N side

Trifthorn   Wellenkuppe   Ober Gabelhorn

Col du Mountet

Gd Gendarme

45

46

46

50

49

3690

steep snow/ice fan at the bottom of the couloir. Trend L on to steep loose rock and go up this in zigzags till you can work up the earthy/snowy middle and upper bed of the indefinite couloir to the col (1½ h.). Start on the crest and stay there. Fine ridge climbing with plenty of variety, then take a nice chimney on the L to reach the roof. Cross this to the upper ridge and climb walls, cracks and chimneys on or very near the crest; nicely exposed. The summit is at the edge of a small snowfield (1½ h., 3 h. from Rothorn hut. 2¼ h. in descent).

<u>North-East Ridge</u>. This short ridge is merely a snow cap above the depression of the Col du Mountet. A glacier climb throughout, interesting and popular. PD-. First ascent unknown.

45. From the Mountet hut follow a horizontal track SSE on moraine for a few min. to where the crest levels out. Slant R and reach the Mountet glacier at c. 2950m. Go up diagonally E across the crevassed glacier, over terraces and turning low ice walls, to the foot of the slopes leading to the Col du Mountet. Climb snow to a sérac barrier which is turned on the extreme R. Return L to near the col, large cornice, then climb R up the triangular snow cap (one or two crevasses) to the summit (2½ h. from Mountet hut, 1½ h. in descent).

TRIFTJOCH 3527m.

Between the Trifthorn and Wellenkuppe. Formerly a pass equipped with fixed cables on the Mountet side which is very loose and subject to bad stonefall. PD+. Nowadays seldom used to make a crossing between the Mountet and Rothorn huts. The Trift side is climbed frequently to reach the Trifthorn. F. See Route 44. First known tourist traverse: R. Fowler with A. Kehrli and I. Biener, 1 September, 1854.

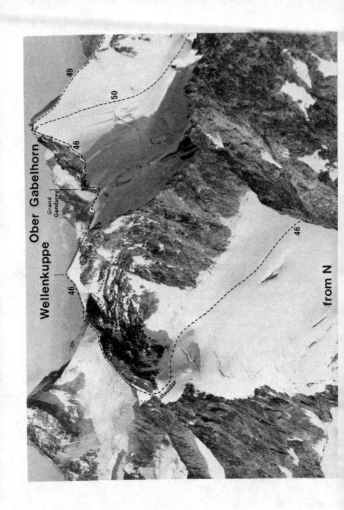

Wellenkuppe Ober Gabelhorn

Grand Gendarme

46

49

50

46

46

Schulter

from N

WELLENKUPPE 3903m.

The prominent satellite of the Ober Gabelhorn, climbed frequently from the Rothorn hut by parties wanting a shorter day than continuing to the parent mtn. A worthwhile short day. PD-. See Route 46. Rarely climbed from the Mountet hut. First ascent: Francis Douglas with Peter Taugwalder and P. Inäbnit, 5 July, 1865.

OBER GABELHORN 4062.9m.

A shapely conical peak of four ridges and four faces, half snow and half rock, with a lot of interesting climbing. All the routes are good and it is customary to traverse the mtn. The summit is a short horizontal snow/rock crest, sometimes corniced. In spite of its comparatively low altitude, the routes are fairly long and serious undertakings. The rocks are generally sound.
First ascent: A. W. Moore and H. Walker with J. Anderegg, 6 July, 1865. First winter and ski ascent: Marcel Kurz with J. Knubel, 3 February, 1920.

East-North-East Ridge (over the Wellenkuppe). See also separate note on Wellenkuppe above. This is easily the most frequented route of ascent, mainly a snow climb with its best moment on rock. Delicate in descent, especially in the afternoon. Between the Wellenkuppe and summit is the Grand Gendarme (3870m.), originally turned on the R by two or three rope lengths on steep snow or ice, now climbed direct with a fixed rope. A splendid outing. PD+. First ascent: L. Norman-Neruda with Chr. Klucker, 1 August, 1890.

46. From the Rothorn hut take a short traverse path over rocks to the upper snowfield of the Trift glacier. Ascend snow slopes in a big curve towards the Trifthorn. Below the Triftjoch bear L (SE) and rise obliquely under the Wellenkuppe to a prominent snow shoulder on its L-hand ridge at c. 3640m. Above, climb a broad snowy rock ridge to a step which is turned on the L, using short slabby walls between the step and a steep snow slope further L. Higher up, cross an open couloir to the L, then climb

83

OBER GABELHORN from NE

Gabel

Gabelhorngrat

47

46

51

Grand Gendarme 3870

directly up pleasant rocks to the crest on your R. Follow this for 100m. to a rock knoll, which is turned on the L by snow; rejoin the crest as soon as possible. Continue up the steep crest to a final riser of 70m. Take this direct and reach an easy snow ridge then a sloping plateau forming the summit of the Wellenkuppe (PD-) (3 h.).

Descend the snow plateau, steepening, into the broad saddle (3827m.) between the Wellenkuppe and Grand Gendarme. Continue along the narrowing ridge, corniced, to slabby ribs below the tower. On the R side, climb the ribs (old cables, stanchions in snow) to the foot of the tower, on the crest. Here is a long vertical cable. Climb it strenuously to the first of two rock knobs (45 min.). You can also climb the fine wall just L of the cable, 25m., IV+. Cross to the second knob, then descend a short wall and snow ridge to the saddle below the summit ridge. Large cornices on L. Climb R of the crest on snow covered rocks which are quite steep near the top. Finish up a short open snow couloir on the crest, just before reaching the summit ($1\frac{1}{2}$ h., $2\frac{1}{4}$ h. from Wellenkuppe, $5\frac{1}{4}$ h. from Rothorn hut; $3\frac{1}{2}$ h. in descent).

South-East Ridge (Gabelhorngrat). The least known ridge of the mtn. and probably the least frequented fine ridge on any major summit within a small circumference of Zermatt. When the Rothorn hut was opened in 1949, both the original ordinary route on the E side of the mtn. and this ridge were abandoned in favour of the ENE ridge. The logical starting point is the now closed Trift inn. Parties must start from the relatively high Rothorn hut and make a descending approach, losing 250m. in height. Nevertheless a fine climb, more serious than the ENE ridge. Conditions on the upper section can vary tremendously. PD+/ AD. First ascent: J. W. Hartley and E. Davidson with P. Rubi and J. Jaun, 3 September, 1877.

47. From the Rothorn hut take a short traverse path over rocks to the upper snowfield of the Trift glacier. Ignore the usual snow

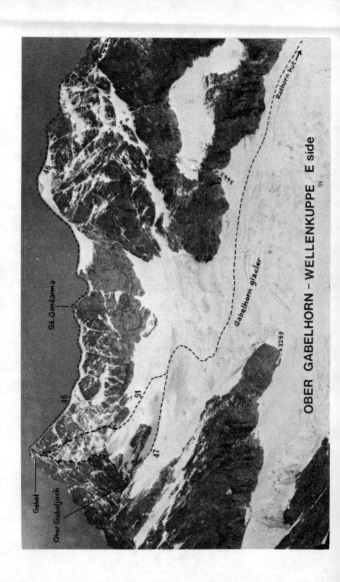

OBER GABELHORN – WELLENKUPPE E side

Gabel
Ober Gabeljoch
Gd. Gendarme
46
46
51
47
×3299
Gabelhorn glacier
3443+
Rothorn hut

trail bearing W and NW.   Cross the glacier plateau SW to the
opposite side, under a supporting triangular lower wall of the
Wellenkuppe. Turn down the R side of the glacier and descend
SE under the rock wall to a moraine junction at pt. 2973m. Turn
the corner and make a rising traverse over moraine to reach
the Gabelhorn glacier. Go up the R side of this, keeping close to
rocks on your R. Several crevasses. When you are opposite an
opening in rocks to the R marked pt. 3443m., move L towards
the middle of the glacier and go up more or less due W between
groups of crevasses to the upper snowfield under the E face of
the Ober Gabelhorn.   Now traverse the small snowfield to the
S and climb a short snow slope to the Ober Gabeljoch (3597m.)
at the foot of the ridge (3 h.).

  At the col a bergschrund must be crossed, sometimes difficult, to reach the first rocks which are climbed trending R till
the top of the first step can be gained on the L.   Climb a rock
ridge to a narrow snow crest and cross this to the foot of a steep
tower. Take this by the crest (III), or more easily but often
delicately by a rising traverse to the R on mixed ground. Continue up a mixed ridge, slightly R of the crest, to a series of
three short steps which lead to a small snow cap and two rock
nicks. Cross these on the crest to a fine and almost level snow
ridge leading delicately to more steep rocks. Work up trending
L to the foot of a large red tower. Traverse R and climb steep
loose rocks and snow in a turning movement to rejoin the ridge
as soon as possible.   This continues as a sharp snow and rock
crest at an exposed angle up to a fine snow tip. From here runs
the narrowest snow crest of all, dipping slightly to cross the
Gabel notch in some 40m., up to a terminal bulge of snowy slabs.
Climb these trending R all the way to reach the summit (4 h.,
about 7 h. from Rothorn hut).

West-South-West Ridge (Arbengrat). Invariably used in descent,
for traversing the mtn. It is a splendid rock ridge; fresh snow

and ice clear quickly. In ascent, AD with pitches of III. In descent, AD-, abseiling over the steepest bits. The rock is excellent and the correct route is scratched. It is vital to leave the ridge at the correct point for descending to Zermatt by the Arben valley. A descent from the Arbenjoch (3570m.) at the bottom of the ridge is steep and unpleasant. This is the fate of those who miss the way, or you can continue over Mt. Durand and descend to the Schönbiel - longer but not difficult. First ascent: H. Seymour Hoare and E. Hulton with J. von Bergen, P. Rubi and J. Moser, 23 August, 1874.

48. From the summit, in a few steps reach the top of a rock wall. Below it the ridge is seen bending L. A few m. R, climb directly down a pleasant chimney system (40m., III) which near the bottom bends L. Reach some slabs. Make a descending traverse L across them to reach the crest which is followed over small rock knobs. Turn minor obstacles easily on the R. Reach a level part of the crest, in front of a short riser marking the top of the Grand Gendarme. From a fixed peg abseil about 30m. to the foot of the gendarme. There is an intermediate peg position, not obvious. Alternatively, and the correct route in ascent, climb down a flat grey rib on the R (NW) side of the ridge, a short distance from the rear side of the gendarme. Nice flaky holds (40m., III, old pegs in place). At the bottom of the rib make a slightly rising traverse over broken snowy rocks below this side of the gendarme, and climb a little on snow to join the crest below the foot of the gendarme.

Continue down the ridge, turning or climbing over obstacles easily, to an indistinct little snow saddle, about 100m. above the upper saddle (3656m.) of the Arbenjoch ($1\frac{1}{2}$ h.). Find a ledge line in the L (S) flank, which resembles a path. Leave the ridge and follow this sharply back to the L for 20m. Enter a snow couloir and descend it, or rocks on its R side, for 100m., to a junction with another couloir coming from the L. Cross this junction and descend in its direction, using a rock rib, till a deep couloir appears on your L. Get into this couloir about 40m. lower down, where it bends R. Follow it to a hanging snowband which runs across the S face. Traverse R along the band and descend towards the first rock knoll, which is turned on the R. Cross a bergschrund and descend snow to a second rock knoll, which forms a buttress dropping into the Arben glacier. Descend its crest and turn the lower step by moving R (W). So reach pt. 3132m. ($1\frac{1}{2}$ h.). Descend the glacier SE, sometimes badly crevassed, to rocks and further L the lateral moraine. There is an old bivouac shelter on the moraine. Follow the moraine crest, called the Arbengandegge, on a poor track, improving lower down, to the Schönbiel footpath at the bottom ($1\frac{1}{4}$ h.) which is taken to Zermatt ($1\frac{1}{2}$ h., about 6 h. from summit).

Note: The Arbengrat provides an interesting and sure way of climbing the Ober Gabelhorn from the Schönbiel hut. This expedition is done more frequently than supposed. The route reaches Col Durand and traverses the easy Mont Durand (q. v.) to cross the head of the Arbenjoch. About $7\frac{1}{2}$ h. from Schönbiel to summit; 5 h. in reverse/descent.

<u>North-North-West Ridge</u>. The usual route from the Mountet hut. The first part is on tedious, quite steep and loose rocks but the ridge itself is a fine piece of climbing on snow or ice. It is generally in poor condition for descent in the afternoon and can be dangerous. The snow tends to avalanche. An alternative approach is used when glacier conditions permit. Inquire at the hut about the best approach route according to prevailing conditions. PD+. First ascent: Francis Douglas with Peter Taugwalder and J. Vianin, 7 July, 1865.

49. From the Mountet hut take a small path to the S which descends scree and moraine to the Durand glacier. Head towards the Ober Gabelhorn, then turn towards Mt. Durand. Later return L towards the rognon called Le Coeur (3089.6m.). The crevasses hereabouts can be bad. Climb round the rognon to the L or R, almost certainly best on the L, to reach a small saddle behind its summit ($1\frac{1}{2}$ h.). It is also possible to climb the rognon direct on sound rocks. Now climb a grey rib to the lower end of a large sloping terrace/ramp rising L. Keep R and climb a rib of yellowish rocks to a large open couloir coming down from the upper rock bastion. So far the rocks are poor but they improve in the couloir. Follow it to the lower end of the snow ridge which is reached at the L end of a large horizontal rock band. Pt. 3690m. (2 h.).

Alternative approach, more satisfactory if the Ober Gabelhorn glacier happens to be in good condition, which is rare. Start as for the approach described above but work SE across the glacier junction to the base of the crumpled opening between two rock outcrops supporting séracs guarding the lower part of the Ober Gabelhorn glacier. Climb through this opening turning crevasses and ice walls according to conditions and reach a narrow plateau under a band of séracs to your R. Climb below these séracs till they relent a little and a way up to the R can be made to a larger glacier terrace lying below the NNW ridge and running up to the N face. Only cross this terrace SW to a bergschrund below a snow and rock prow rising steeply SW to pt. 3690m. at the end of the snow ridge. The bergschrund can sometimes be avoided by starting up to the L. Climb the prow direct in a fine position, 48°. AD ($3\frac{1}{2}$-4 h.).

From pt. 3690m. follow the humpy snow ridge, often corniced, to a bergschrund below the final ridge slope. Cross the bergschrund and climb the steep snow/ice slope to the summit (2 h. on average, about $5\frac{1}{2}$ h. from Mountet).

North Face. A classic snow/ice climb, short, with a complicated approach over a narrow broken glacier and icefall. The face is comparatively easy in conditions of good snow when it can be climbed comfortably in crampons; otherwise hard work on ice.

OBER GABELHORN N face

Comparable with but rather steeper than the Lenzspitze NE face, D/D+, 400m. The angle starts at 47° but soon reaches an average of 55° with a steeper exit, avoidable by moving L. First ascent: H. Kiener and R. Schwarzgruber, 30 July, 1930. First British ascent: D. Baldock and M. F. Baker, 1966. First winter ascent: P. Sala and B. Steulet, 1 March, 1969. Climbed 7 times up to 1960 and many times since then. The face has been climbed in 2 h.

50. From the Mountet hut approach using the alternative way for reaching the NNW ridge described in Route 49, and gain the upper terrace of the Ober Gabelhorn glacier. Go up the terrace crossing a bergschrund to the foot of the face at the top (3½ h.). The face is a plain snow/ice slope with characteristic grooves and ribs in its lower part. Cross the large bergschrund, sometimes very difficult, and climb straight up towards the summit. Near the top move L for an easier finish. Finishing direct, on steep rotten rock, is more serious than the face (4-5 h. in good conditions from bergschrund).

51. East Face. See also remarks in preamble to Route 47 (SE ridge). The route of the first ascensionists and the normal way of climbing the mtn. from Zermatt until in their turn a fixed rope appeared on the NNE ridge and the Rothorn hut was built. The approach is identical to Route 47. Above the highest terrace of the Gabelhorn glacier a rock spur, generally snowy and forming the L part of the face, descends from the fine snow tip marking the Gabel near the top of the SE ridge. Above the bergschrund this spur is reached from its L side and its crest is followed exactly to the Gabel where Route 47 is joined. Probably, AD. About 6 h. in good conditions from Rothorn hut.

South Face. A classic rock climb in the Zermatt district, popular and the scene of many minor "epics" due to unintentional variations being made. In fact this broad rockface has been climbed in various ways, too numerous to record below. The description is confined to the normal and easiest route which finishes near the summit, and a more direct finish to the latter with a note about a similar finish. Routes no harder than the normal one have been made up to the Arbengrat between its Grand Gendarme and the summit. The rock is an excellent gneiss, slabby until the terminal wall sections are reached where it is poor in places but normally protected by pegs in place. Bad stonefall has been experienced by some parties while others have reported none. There is no convenient hut, so it is best to sleep out in the open bivouac shelter at the top of the Arben moraine (Arbengandegge) at pt. 2892m. This is reached by a comfortable walk from Zermatt in 4 h. Normal route: AD with one pitch of IV. Direct finish: IV or harder according to route. First ascent: J.P. Farrer with D. Maquignaz, 28 September, 1892. Original direct finish: E. G. Oliver with A. and A. Aufdenblatten, 29 August, 1923.

52. From the Arben bivouac shelter reverse Route 48 to the hanging snowband which runs across the S face. Go along this upwards to the R to where the band is broken by the rockface, just L of a line directly below the summit. Do not pursue a line up the slabby face towards the summit. A couloir descends to this point from the wall of the Grand Gendarme on the Arbengrat. Climb the rib on the immediate L of this couloir, up to a section of delightful slabs (III) which lead to about 100m. below the Grand Gendarme, where the rocks steepen considerably. Now cross the couloir to the rib on its R side. (This rib is often climbed as an alternative to the L-hand one, by crossing the couloir not not far above its base. It gives more sustained work at the same standard). Now rising above the R-hand rib is a steep buttress. Climb it for a few m. (IV) then trend R up slabs and walls to a terrace at the lower end of the snow/ice couloir descending from the Gabel on the SE ridge. Climb the couloir to the Gabel (stone-

OBER GABELHORN
S face

Arbenjoch 48 (roids)

Arbengrat-

Gd. Gendarme

48

Gabel

52

52

48

48

47

Gabelhorngrat-

Gabelhorngrat-

3465

3492

52

48

Ober Gabeljoch 3597

Ober
scheitel

fall, ice frequent) where Route 47 is joined and the summit reached in another 20 min. (about $6\frac{1}{2}$ h. from Arben biv.).

Direct finishes: From the foot of the Gabel couloir climb rocks at the L side for about 50m. until a higher narrower terrace above the couloir can be reached. This slants upwards below the vertical summit wall. A pillar is formed in this wall directly in the summit line. Pass round its base to the R and enter a chimney. Climb this (15m., III/IV, pegs) and continue by steep slabs to the summit.

The direct finish frequently embarked on by many parties takes a higher line up the buttress starting at the top of the R-hand rib. This buttress gives three fine open pitches of IV (ignore a chimney line on the L) to the narrower slanting terrace rising parallel with and above the Gabel couloir. By following this terrace the usual direct finish is joined further R. A harder finish still consists of climbing the pillar front to the L of the chimney mentioned above in the previous paragraph. The pillar wall is climbed trending L for 4m., then directly for 5m. to a small niche (IV+, exposed). Continue up the wall trending L, over a bulge, to a stance below a dièdre. Continue into the dièdre and by vertical chimney work including an awkward chockstone finish at the summit (20m., strenuous, IV+).

UNTER GABELHORN 3391.7m.

An agreeable little rock peak and a traditional training exercise, taken direct from Zermatt. Critics commenting on the fatigue and dullness of the approach route must be faint hearted and blind to one of the finest views unfolding step by step of the Matterhorn. First ascent: Francis Douglas with P. Taugwalder and P. Inäbnit, July, 1865.

<u>South-East Ridge (from Gabel notch)</u>. The normal route which reaches a gap between the summit and a conspicuous gendarme (3298m.). This gendarme has grown 90m. on LK since the last

guide was published! Standard, F to the gap. The ridge is PD, short pitches of II, but if taken more or less direct, III/III+ according to route. Other variations possible. Good rock. First ascensionists.

53. From Zermatt follow Route 11 to Alterhaupt (1961m.). From here a branch track goes S and SW through forest to the Höhbalmen pastures, to a signpost and cairn where the path climbs R(W) in zigzags near a stream to a higher grassy plateau (2665m.). Continue W along the outer edge of the plateau, poor track, and go round the S corner/foot of pt. 3207m. Cross stony slopes, track gone, to large boulders near the head of an open cwm. Climb R(N) up this into a broad couloir of rocks and snow which leads easily to the Gabel notch (4 h.). Note: on the L-hand is the steep S rockface of the mtn. There are several routes up this, from its foot or from points leading out of the couloir (III to V, 200-300m. of excellent red rock).

From the gap climb on the crest to where it is formed by an angle between reddish slabs on the L and a sub-wall on the R. The crest itself is now very difficult. For the easiest way, move R and work below the sub-wall to a little facet under the summit. Climb this by a choice of short pleasant pitches to the summit. Alternatively, climb exposed slabs L of the crest, with increasing difficulty, to a wall which is taken direct (III+). Easier rocks above lead back to the crest and summit (1 h., 5 h. from Zermatt).

ARBENJOCH 3570m.

Between the Ober Gabelhorn and Mont Durand, a fairly difficult glacier pass from the Mountet hut to Zermatt, rarely crossed, although the top of it is crossed fairly frequently by parties moving between the Ober Gabelhorn and Mont Durand. It has an upper saddle on the Gabelhorn side, pt. 3656m. Traverse proper, AD. First traverse: E. Davidson with L. Lanier, 8 July, 1875.

MONT DURAND 3712.6m.

Also known as Arbenhorn. A secondary summit occasionally climbed for itself as a training exercise from the Schönbiel hut, but overridden in most decisions for this purpose by the Pte. de Zinal. However, traversed often enough from Col Durand to the Arbenjoch in order to reach or leave the Arbengrat. See note at end of Route 48. This traverse is described below. First ascent unknown.

54. From the Schönbiel hut reach Col Durand by Route 55. From the col go up the broad snow ridge to a few rocks culminating in a knoll (3611m.). Above this a steep snow/ice slope leads to a snow/rock crest running L to the summit (1 h., about $3\frac{1}{2}$ h. from hut). In practice Col Durand can be avoided by keeping R on the glacier to reach the rock knoll by a direct ascent.

From the summit descend an easy snow ridge/slope, cornices on R, to a rock pyramid (3678m.). Either traverse this or turn it on the R, according to conditions, and continue down a slightly undulating snow ridge on to the lowest saddle of the Arbenjoch (3570m.) (30 min. from summit, 45 min. in ascent).

COL DURAND 3451m.

Between Mt. Durand and the Pte. de Zinal, a fairly frequented glacier pass from the Schönbiel hut to the Mountet hut. The Schönbiel side is F. The upper slopes of the Zinal/Mountet side are steep, usually ice and cut by large crevasses. PD. First tourist traverse: W. and G. Mathews with J. Vianin, J. B. Croz and M. Charlet, 17 August, 1859.

55. Zermatt side. From the Schönbiel hut a small but well marked track, not shown on map, rises above the main one leading NW, and turns NE into the stony Kumme (cwm). The track is easy to follow right up to the rocky saddle at the top of the cwm (3209m.) ($1\frac{1}{4}$ h.). Traverse horizontally N over scree and large blocks, losing a little height, to a terrace leading out to the Höhwang glacier at 3150m. Climb the glacier plateau keeping L and turn the low icefall ahead by passing close to pt. 3312m., where there are a few large crevasses. Cross another plateau to the col ($1\frac{1}{2}$ h., $2\frac{3}{4}$ h. from Schönbiel hut; $1\frac{1}{2}$ h. in descent).

56. Zinal side. From the Mountet hut a small track makes a slightly descending traverse SSE and crosses moraine to reach the Durand glacier. At first steer SE towards the Ober Gabelhorn, then SSW towards Mt. Durand, finally SW towards the Dent Blanche. This wide circling movement avoids several groups of crevasses. Now climb directly across the glacier to the snow saddle at the S end of the Roc Noir (S of pt. 3150m.). From its crest go along a broad snow ridge between two icefalls to the upper glacier plateau below the Pte. de Zinal. Turn SE to reach the slope below the col, cross the bergschrund (usually wide), and climb as directly as possible. This slope is steep snow or ice, often crevassed, and about 100m. high ($2\frac{1}{2}$ h. from Mountet hut, $1\frac{3}{4}$ h. in descent).

POINTE DE ZINAL 3789m.

One of the best and most popular training peaks in the Zermatt district. In some respects it has a similar profile and configuration to that of the Dent Blanche, with which it is sometimes compared as a poor relation. First ascent: E. Javelle and G. Beraneck, jnr. with J. Martin, 1871.

<u>North-East Ridge (from Col Durand)</u>. The ordinary route, quite direct, interesting. F+. First ascensionists.

57. Reach Col Durand from the Schönbiel hut or Mountet hut by Routes 55 or 56 respectively ($2\frac{3}{4}$ h. or $2\frac{1}{2}$ h.). Climb the snowy ridge, then keep L of the crest when it becomes rocky, and reach the foot of the summit tower. Climb broken snowy rocks to the L and reach the top ($1\frac{1}{2}$ h. from Col Durand).

DENT BLANCHE from NE

Col de la Dent Blanche
Grand Corrier glacier
NNW grat
3124.x
64
68 var.
68
3975
Vlereselsgrat
61
3623.x
62
61
3899
68 VAR.
4350
56
Durand glacier
Col de Zinal
56
56
Pointe de Zinal
57
Col Durand
58
3778.1
3690
49

<u>South Ridge</u>. A good climb, short. If done direct, AD with pitches of III/III+. Many parties turn the initial towers which reduces the difficulty to PD+, pitches of II and III. Good rock. Parties are warned against trying to reach the ridge by a couloir on the W (Schönbiel glacier) side, leading to pt. 3358m. This is steep and very loose. First ascent: L. Norman-Neruda and M. Peyton with Chr. Klucker, 15 August, 1891.

58. From the Schönbiel hut start as for Route 55 and reach the Höhwang glacier at pt. 3150m. Work up snow and rocks at the L side of the glacier till you can climb diagonally R over smooth slabs and snow to a saddle (3358m.) at the foot of the ridge (2 h.). Climb the easy ridge, later broad and snowy, to the foot of a rock tower and forepeak (3778.1m.). Move R and climb a fine chimney (III+) in the E side of the tower and reach the top. Abseil 4m. into a gap and climb on to a second tower. From this abseil about 20m. down the side of a chimney to the continuation ridge. Alternatively, traverse further R along the base of the first tower, climb a short chimney then follow a ledge to the R and finish up a wall giving access to the narrow crenellated ridge behind the two towers. Follow the sharp crest (II) to the foot of the summit tower. Either climb this direct by walls and cracks on splendid rock (III), or turn it on the R (II) and join the ordinary way to the top ($2\frac{1}{4}$ h., $4\frac{1}{4}$ h. from Schönbiel hut).

COL DE ZINAL 3490m.

Between the Pte. de Zinal and Dent Blanche. This difficult pass is rarely used as a passage from the Schönbiel hut to Mountet hut. The former side is used to approach the Dent Blanche Viereselgrat from the Schönbiel hut. First recorded crossing: T. G. Bonney and J. G. Hawkshaw with Michel Croz and J. Kronig, 30 August, 1860.

DENT BLANCHE 4356.6m.

One of the great summits of the Swiss Pennine Alps. A fairly symmetrical mtn. of bold outline, recognisable from afar. It has four ridges, forming a cross. Of the faces between them only the N side merits attention. This N face has received a lot of attention and publicity since the last guide was published. There is more rock climbing on the mtn. than snow/ice work. Some of the rock is poor but most of it is good. In bad conditions the ascent by the usual S ridge route can be quite trying. This ridge is climbed much more frequently than any other route.

First ascent: T. S. Kennedy and W. Wigram with J. B. Croz and J. Kronig, 18 July, 1862. First winter and ski ascent: F. F. Roget and M. Kurz with J. and M. Crettex, L. Murisier and L. Theytaz, 13 January, 1911 (as a variation to the High Level Route!). During the centenary year, 1962, all four ridges were climbed within a week of each other.

South Ridge (Wandflue Route). The easiest and usual route. Starting from the Dent Blanche hut the ridge is reached at the foot of a rocky staircase rising to the summit. This avoids the Wandflue approach. The latter is used to reach the ridge from the Schönbiel hut, i. e. direct from Zermatt. Once attained, the ridge is much longer than it appears from below. In normal conditions it gives pleasant scrambling on sound rock over several gendarmes. When ice glazed (not infrequent) the route is delicate and even dangerous for inexperienced alpinists. PD+. pitches of II. First ascensionists.

59. From the Schönbiel hut follow the main track W over grass, then descend slightly, close to moraine. Cross a stream, confusing cairns, and work across to the lateral moraine of the Schönbiel glacier. Follow a clearly marked track NW along this, then up its steep head slope by zigzags to the R, and reach a dome of large boulders at the edge of the upper glacier plateau (3042.1m.) (1¼ h.). Cross the glacier plateau in a slight curve NE, N and NW, up to c. 3180m. Now work L and cross it with crevasses in the same direction due W towards the Wandflue cliffs. At the R-hand (N) end of the cliffs is a square-shaped snow bay. A broad rock buttress descends from below pt. 3882m. and this marks the R-hand edge. Its base is defended by

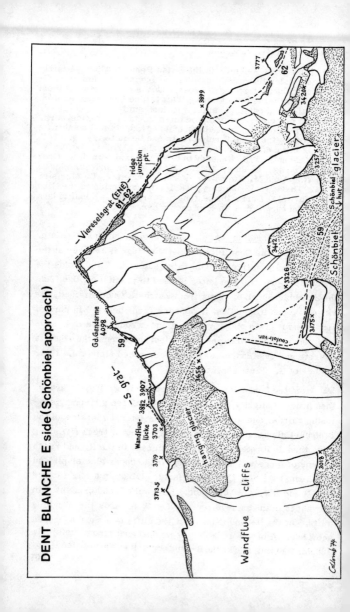

DENT BLANCHE E side (Schönbiel approach)

Viereselsgrat (ENE) 61–62
ridge junction pt.
× 3899
3777
62
34 20×
3257 ×
Schönbiel glacier
hut
59
3442
3326 ×
couloir var.
3175 ×
S grat
Gd.Gendarme 4098
59
Wandflue-lücke 3703
3882 3907
3719
3713.5 ×
3656 ×
hanging glacier
Wandflue cliffs
3018 ×

Coleman 74

a vertical rock wall. Climb across the bay from R to L (crevasses) to near the upper L-hand corner, and under the side of the buttress. This side is cut by two vague gangways, slanting steeply from R to L (45 min.). Step off the slope awkwardly and climb either of these gangways, normally the upper one, on loose rock to the front of the buttress. Arrive on a large terrace cutting the lower part of the Wandflue cliffs at this point. Either climb the large rounded buttress tediously, keeping to the approx. crest or R of it, with snow patches and shallow couloirs in the top part. Or, traverse L(S) along the terrace and near its end climb into a hidden couloir slanting up to the R, which marks the L-hand side of the buttress. When full of snow this couloir gives a rapid way up most of the rockface, but otherwise it is detestable scree. The final rocks of the buttress are steep and firm and lead suddenly to the edge of a small snow plateau extending like a balcony from the low-relief S ridge behind it. Cross the snow and reach the ridge at the small saddle of the Wandfluelücke (3703m.) (2 h.).

Climb the rocky ridge over pt. 3882m., keeping a little R of the crest, and descend snow keeping L of the crest, to where the ridge narrows, cornices possible. Alternate snow and rock sections now lead to the foot of the Grand Gendarme (4098m.) (45 min.). In good conditions you can climb the gendarme direct, by the R-hand wall, then the crest (IV, III, IV). Normally it is turned on the L. For this make a horizontal traverse over broken ledges and ribs to a short rock/snow couloir, leading to a saddle which is marked on the L (above) by a pinnacle. Climb the R side of the couloir and continue up a short snow crest, trending R to steep rocks. Climb these direct on good holds (II) to the ridge immediately behind the Grand Gendarme (30 min.). Follow the crest to the next step, which is climbed so that its top can be turned on the R, using a horizontal ledge line formed by large blocks (overhang above). Regain the crest by a short couloir and continue along it to a short steep step.

Turn this on the L, crossing steep slabby rocks with a slight descent under a vertical wall (10m. of II+, delicate when icy, crux), then traverse horizontally for 40m. to a large platform corner below the rear end of the step. Climb the corner by a crack (10m., II-). On the crest, turn a rotten-looking thumb on the R and descend a few m. to an open saddle. The ridge is now broad, half snow, half rock, and easy. Climb it keeping to the crest or slightly L of it and reach the fine snow crest forming the summit. Cornices possible (2 h., 7½ h. from Schönbiel hut).

60. Starting from the Dent Blanche hut, climb the broad and fairly easy rock rib behind the hut to the short steep snow/ice spur leading to a small snow plateau below pt. 3882m. Bear L and join the previous route at the Wandfluelücke (1 h. to pt. 3882m., about 4 h. to summit).

East-North-East Ridge (Viereselsgrat). Properly called on LK: Arête des Quatre Anes. The classic route, a notoriously variable climb. Sometimes the upper snow ridge is so thin, after cornices have fallen off, that it is pierced by holes. In these conditions the ridge is very dangerous. At c. 4030m. the ridge divides into two branches. The Viereselsgrat proper drops NE to the Grand Cornier glacier (pt. 3000m.). The other branch descends SE to the Col de Zinal (3490m.); the latter is used by parties starting from the Schönbiel hut. Either way, a serious route, long, delicate, exposed, interesting, with a variety of obstacles. Popular, and the easiest route from the Mountet hut. AD/AD+. First ascent: J. Stafford Anderson and G. P. Baker with U. Almer and A. Pollinger, 11 August, 1882. Ulrich Almer remarked on reaching the summit: "We are nothing less than four asses - vier esel - to have climbed up this way". It was also from the summit of the Dent Blanche that Melchoir Anderegg uttered his famous remark about the Zmutt ridge opposite: "It goes, but I'm not going."

DENT BLANCHE
W side

S. grat.

Gd Gendarme

Col de la
Dent Blanche

3719
3703
60
3907 3982
59
63
63
63vk
63vk

Dent Blanche 14-15 hut

61. From the Mountet hut follow Route 56 as for the Col Durand, as far as the small glacier plateau at the NE foot of the Col de Zinal. Work R and reach the side of the ridge at c. 3250m. (2 h.). This point is to the L of a R-angle snow bay, at the foot of a couloir/ramp slanting R up to the crest. Cross a berg-schrund and climb the snow/scree couloir and a few rocks at the top to the crest, just L of a gendarme. The couloir/ramp is well drawn on LK25. Climb the easy rock crest to the foot of a large yellow tower with icy walls on either side. Follow the crest as near as possible, moving R at awkward bits (III), tricky and dangerous when verglassed. Arrive just below its summit and move R to a small col between the tower and a red-dish knoll. Climb over this and continue to the main junction of ridges (4 h.). Climb over a rocky point to the foot of a large gendarme and climb it by an obvious chimney on the crest (III). From the top, drop down to the snowy upper section of the ridge. This is at a reasonable angle but there are sometimes huge cornices, separated by outcrops. Proceed delicately to the summit (3 h. , 9 h. from Mountet hut).

62. Starting from the Schönbiel hut, follow Route 59 to the upper plateau of the Schönbiel glacier which is climbed near its R side to below the Col de Zinal (2 h.). Cross a bergschrund and climb steep snow/ice to the R of a rock band. Immediately above it, move L into the centre of the broken wall defending the col (stonefall). Make a rising traverse L on steep snow/ ice and rock, aiming for a small snow shoulder above the col. Reach this as quickly as possible (30 min.). Climb the loose ridge for a short while, then work L across the Schönbiel flank, below a serrated, horizontal section of the crest (3777m.). Reach a saddle at the foot of a large red buttress (3899m.). Turn this by a ledge line rising L, which leads to a saddle behind the buttress; before reaching this saddle, trend L up steep and fairly easy rock and arrive at the junction of ridges where the

Viereselsgrat proper is joined (2 h.). Then as for Route 61 (2-3 h., $6\frac{1}{2}$ - $7\frac{1}{2}$ h. from Schönbiel hut).

West (Ferpècle) Ridge. A long straight ridge which in good conditions is entirely rock. It finishes somewhat N of the summit. The rock is fairly good. AD+, pitches of III and IV, not sustained, 850m. The ridge has only recently become popular, especially with British parties. O. G. Jones was killed on it in the dramatic accident of 1899. First ascent: W. Gröbli with Aloys Pollinger, 29 July, 1889.

63. From the Dent Blanche hut make a slightly descending traverse N, then rise a little and cross the rock spur coming down from pt. 3882m. Pass just above pt. 3613. 6m. (cairn on knoll) and reach the glacier branch situated between this spur and the wall of the Dent Blanche. Make a descending traverse across this branch, going down its R side and passing pt. 3548m. at the foot of the mtn. At 3500m. you reach the foot of the large WSW couloir rising directly to the summit. L of this is a broad ledge of scree, leading horizontally L to the W ridge at a point where it steepens noticeably. It is usual to cross the bergschrund near the start of the ledge, and from there climb directly up a steep snow slope, then scree and rocks to another ledge line which slants steeply L to the ridge above the first buttress/ step at c. 3700m. ($2\frac{1}{4}$ h.). Climb the crest with continuous interest and some difficulty (slabs, III), turning small gendarmes on the L or R. Half-way up reach an obvious ledge which cuts the face to the L. Above is the grand gendarme. Turn this on the R (III) and regain the ridge by pleasant walls and slabs (III/IV). Continue up the crest, getting easier, to the summit ($4\frac{1}{2}$ h., 7 h. from Dent Blanche hut).

North-North-West Ridge (from Col de la Dent Blanche). Much the shortest but most difficult of the ridges. A famous climb of uneven difficulty. The crux passage is excessive for the ridge

DENT BLANCHE NW face

Gd. Gendarme

Col de la
Dent Blanche

Dent Blanche glacier

59

63

64

63

65

64

67

3549

63

63 var

as a whole, and for this reason it has not been climbed often. A number of attempts were made before it was finally climbed, when it was regarded as "one of the last great problems". It therefore has a certain glamour - enhanced in British mountaineering literature by Dorothy Pilley Richards' account in "Climbing Days". The ridge is seldom in good condition. Some parties have bivouacked on the col; the approaches are otherwise quite long. A bivouac hut is scheduled to be built in the future, and this has been a subject of some debate since the last guide was issued. D+, with pitches of IV, IV+ and two bits of V. First ascent D. Pilley Richards and I. A. Richards with Joseph Georges and A. Georges, 20 July, 1928. Second ascent: A. Roch, G. de Rham, A. Tissières and G. Chevalley, 2 August, 1943. First winter ascent: P. Crettaz and J. Gaudin, 1-2 March, 1963. Climbed about 45 times to date. A major variation on the crux section was made by B. Devaux with C. Bournissen, 23 October, 1968, harder and unlikely to be adopted.

The whole of the lower part of the ridge, the slabs traverse and the pitches leading to immediately below the crux section of the ridge were avoided by climbing steep ice and a big rib at the L side of the NW face (i. e. to R of the ridge) by G. Perrenoud and H. Weber, 23 September, 1961, pitches of IV and V.

In an early attempt to make the second ascent of the ridge, Miss M. Cairney with T. and H. Theytaz, on 11 August, 1928, left the ridge low down and made a rising traverse L on to the NNE face, which was climbed on bad rock, steep snow and ice to a point where the modern Bournissen route (see NNE face) follows the upper rocks towards the summit, after which the 1928 party worked R on to the N ridge not far from the summit. This expedition is confused in recent mountaineering literature as a major variation of the N ridge and as part of the history of climbing on the NNE face. It really belongs to neither, and the climbing is unpleasant, dangerous and difficult.

64. Start from the Col de la Dent Blanche (3531m.) reached by

Routes 67 or 68. Go up the easy rounded ridge on mixed terrain to a rock wall (2 h.). Climb this direct, trending L then R on good holds (15m., III) to a zone of prominent snowy slabs. Make a rising traverse R for two rope lengths, delicate, often icy, IV, to a low-relief slabby spur, slanting R. Climb this in three pitches (III/III+). Continue traversing R below a wall towards the far end of the snowy slabs, now a mere band inclined at a steep angle. This section can be very delicate. Reach a chimney/crack in the wall above, and climb it (IV) to the ridge. Either climb on the crest (IV+), or below it on the R (III). So reach a gap at the foot of the main step and overhang. Climb on to a pedestal (3m., belay). Continue direct over two small overhangs (V, or IV+ and A1 with stirrup, combined tactics alternative) and after 6m. traverse R for 5m. (V-, peg runner) to a short overhanging chimney. Climb this awkwardly (5m., IV+) and exit R on to slabs. Follow these trending L to a stance (8m., III). This section of 25m. is extremely difficult in anything less than perfect conditions. The rock is excellent.

Now climb slabs and two short walls, trending L to reach the crest (III, IV, III). Follow the slabby crest, steep and interesting. Cross a couloir to the L and continue on clean rock (ice). After a further 200m. reach the summit (III, II) (6-12 h. from col).

North-West Face. Very little has been known about this side of the mtn. until 1969. The middle part of the face is quite narrow, being confined by a large rib on the L, rising into the NNW ridge, and the tall flank of the W ridge on the R. Below this a broad fan of mixed terrain and an ice slope run down to the upper plateau of the Dent Blanche glacier. Above the central rock wall is a large steep icefield, the most conspicuous feature of the face, overlooked by a headwall. Stonefall danger is considerable. Not a pleasant route and a candidate for climbing in the right winter conditions. 750m. TD, with pitches of IV and V. First ascent: K. Schneider and L. Steinauer, 17 August, 1934. Second ascent: Camille Bournissen and C. Pralong, 8 August, 1969. Third and first winter ascent: C. Bournissen, T. Brigger, S. Sermier and M. Siegenthaler, January, 1973, with two bivouacs on the approach, one on the face and one on the descent.

65. After crossing the bergschrund a snow/ice slope of 55° is climbed to its highest pt., just R of the L containing rib. A couloir and dièdre line rises directly up the central rockface to the lower edge of the icefield. Follow this line, sometimes taking pitches on walls to the R, difficult and sustained. On the top part of this section the first ascensionists followed a horizontal ledge line to the R, then climbed the wall in zigzags to the R-hand edge of the icefield. This route is reckoned to be slightly easier. The icefield is climbed directly, 50-55°, to its highest pt., and an exit made up steep snowy rocks trending L to the NNW ridge not far from the summit (10-15 h. from bergschrund).

North-North-East Face. Recent exploits on this broad ice face, while only successful on four occasions up to the end of 1973, have elevated it to the premier class of ice climbing. Some Swiss sources think it overrated and the ED grade accorded after the Vaucher ascent has been dropped. The main feature of the face is two large icefields slanting L to R. The upper is divided from the lower (called central) by a long, low but vertical rockband, and the central one is raised like an arch high above the bergschrund by a much larger crescent-shaped band. Above the icefields a wall of very steep rocks and snow/ice bands rises in the summit line and to the Viereselsgrat, while at the R side of the face rocks form a more continuous barrier extending to the NNW ridge. The upper wall is the steepest and most difficult part of the face. All routes are about 950m. and exposed to a fair amount of stonefall.

Dent Blanche   NE faces   Grand Cornier

Col de la Dent Blanche

66c

66b

66a

Japanese Routes

68 var.

68

Grand Cornier glacier

Durand glacier

3455

70

3623

69–70

74

74

74 var.

3455

70

Starting from the L, the original route, unrepeated, makes the most of snow and ice before taking an almost featureless line on the upper rock section. TD, initial section 55° with poor rock, icefields at 50° with the connecting pitches through the dividing rockband at 60°, upper wall on mixed terrain, steep, loose and difficult at 55-60°. Technical rock pitches probably not harder than IV. Snow and ice climbing problems are always more serious. Comparable with but not as pleasant as the Dent d'Hérens Welzenbach route: First ascent: K. Schneider and F. Singer, 26-27 August, 1932.

Direct route: This goes up more or less in the summit line, reaching the central icefield by a rock buttress, and the upper one where it has narrowed and depending on conditions gives as much delicate climbing on snowy rocks. The wall finish is somewhat R of the original route line. TD+, with pitches of IV+. Average angle 56°. Difficult or impossible pegging for security. Harder than the Dent d'Hérens Welzenbach route, about equal to the Nessi-Andreani route on Liskamm NE face. First ascent: Michel and Yvette Vaucher, 10-12 July, 1966.

Winter variation to direct route: This follows the Vaucher route to the central icefield then keeps slightly R, seeking rocks, and finishes just R of the summit line. First ascent: Camille Bournissen, solo, 28-29 February, 1968.

First British ascent (4th ascent of face) by direct route to upper icefield, then by a rising traverse on to the top section of the winter Bournissen line: R. Renshaw and J. Tasker, 15-16 August, 1973.

66. Reach the foot of the face on the Grand Cornier glacier at c. 3400m. by Routes 67 or 68 for the Col de la Dent Blanche.

(a) Original Route. Start below the L end of the crescent-shaped rockband. Cross the bergschrund and work L on to a steep ice curtain like a couloir with rocks on either side. This trends R to the lower L side of the central icefield. The rocks are bad and should be avoided wherever possible. Climb the icefield diagonally R, passing above a big outcrop, and higher up reach on the L a rocky ice groove cutting L through the rockband supporting the upper ice slopes. Climb this difficult groove and continue trending R towards a vague area of rocks descending in the slope of the icefield from the headwall. Go up the L side of these rocks on difficult mixed terrain and climb several horizontal snow and rock bands on to the upper face where a vague rib, generally snow covered, leads to the Viereselsgrat about 100m. from the summit (12-16 h.).

(b) Direct Route. Somewhat R of a centre line to the highest point of the crescent-shaped rockband a snowy buttress descends towards the bergschrund. A rope length above the bergschrund leads to its foot. Climb the buttress direct for 100m., then zigzag up and round a succession of smooth slabs and walls for 120m. to where the buttress narrows and becomes vertical. Move up L and climb two corners trending L (IV+). Finish up a third and easier open corner on to slabs leading to the central icefield. Rock and holds slope the wrong way on this section and placing pegs is difficult. Climb the icefield in six rope lengths to a break on the L not far from its highest point. This is at the R-hand end of the rockband extending down to the L and dividing the two icefields. Go through the break in the rockband on a bulge of steeper snow/ice to the upper snowbands on the face. Continue as directly as possible, slightly L of the summit line (stonefall), and climb the R side of the rock rib concealing the line of the original route further L. Continuously steep snow and rock bands, poor for pegging, lead to an exit on the Viereselsgrat at about the same place as the original route, and 100m. from the summit (30 h. climbing time on first ascent in poor conditions and bad weather).

(c) Winter Bournissen Route. As for the direct route to the central icefield. This is climbed directly to a small rock buttress descending from the R-hand end of the rockband dividing the two icefields. Climb the buttress on its L side by steep, difficult and loose snowy rocks to a snow rib which leads to the headwall directly below the summit. A large transversal rock wall extending from the NNW ridge is skirted on its L (exposed to stonefall), then characteristic snow and rock bands are climbed trending R to a large red tower. Go up this (III+) on unstable rock, easing towards the top, with the stonefall line to the L. Continue directly on easier ground to the N ridge which is reached about 30m. from the summit (20 h. climbing on first ascent, with the benefit of some preparation to a high point on the face following an attempt and retreat a month earlier).

Note: Two shorter routes at the L side of the face (L of the original route), on snow, ice and mixed ground which form an angle between the face proper and a NW facet containing a small hanging glacier under the ridge junction of the Viereselsgrat, were climbed in 1971 by Japanese parties.

PART II

Moiry group

Grand Cornier sub-chain

COL DE LA DENT BLANCHE 3531m.

Between the Dent Blanche and Grand Cornier. A fine glacier pass sometimes with complications according to conditions and season, not infrequently crossed from Ferpècle to the Mountet hut. A project exists for building a bivouac hut on the col. The W (Ferpècle) side is PD, the E (Mountet) is generally PD+. First traverse: J.J. Hornby and T.H. Philpott with C. Lauener and J. Vianin, 27 July, 1864. Crossed on ski by W.A. Moore and J.R. Dixon with L. and B. Theytaz, 28 January, 1909.

67. Ferpècle side. Approach as for Route 13 to Bricola Alp ($1\frac{3}{4}$ h. from Ferpècle). Continue by the main footpath to the second stream (before pt. 2512m.). Leave the path and ascend near this stream on its R side to the moraine lake at pt. 2857m. Continue up moraines to the edge of the Dent Blanche glacier, which is often badly crevassed. The best route is usually near the L(N) side, keeping away from the flanking rock wall. By bearing gradually R (SE) reach an upper snowfield and the col (3 h. from Bricola Alp).

68. Mountet side. From the Mountet hut take a small path S over scree and moraine to the Durand glacier. Cross it SW in the same direction as large crevasses, pass round the foot of the Roc Noir and reach snow on the lower part of the Grand Cornier glacier. Keeping close to the wall of the Roc Noir, ascend SSW towards the foot of the Viereselsgrat (3000m.), forcing a route through séracs above and to the R of this pt.

Reach the upper glacier basin, some large transversal crevasses, aim directly for the col, cross a bergschrund and climb a steep snow/ice slope or rotten rocks on the L to the pass (4 h.).

The glacier is intricate and the following alternative is usually better. Follow Routes 56 and 61 as for the Viereselsgrat. Climb on to the lower part of this ridge, not by the couloir/ramp used for Route 61, but by a similar couloir immediately below and to the R. This slants up from the R-angle snow bay mentioned in Route 61 and reaches the ridge at a small shoulder below the gendarme bypassed on the L by the higher couloir. From this point make a descending traverse over rocks and snow to the Grand Cornier glacier, above its icefall. Continue to the col (4 h.).

GRAND CORNIER 3961.8m.

A mtn. probably with more variety of climbing at a standard than any other in this guidebook. Owing to the fact that it just fails to reach a height of 4000m., and has a rounded, dome-like appearance, the ascent is not made as frequently as its taller neighbours. On the other hand it is the principal climb from the Moiry hut, while an ascent from any direction is strongly recommended. The mtn. has ridges of rock and snow of general mountaineering appeal, and at least one excellent face climb. The rock is generally compact.

First ascent: E. Whymper with Chr. Almer, Michel Croz and F. Biner, 16 June, 1865. First winter and ski ascent: Marcel Kurz with T. Theytaz and a porter, 10 February, 1914.

East Ridge. The ordinary route from the Mountet hut. A varied glacier expedition and climbing on a nice snow ridge. There is an important variation, to avoid the Grand Cornier glacier, whose icefall is often in bad condition after July. PD+. First ascensionists.

69. From the Mountet hut follow Route 68 (either approach, according to conditions) and reach the upper plateau of the Grand Cornier glacier (3 h.). Cross this NW to the foot of a large

snow slope rising towards the E ridge, L (W) of pt. 3300m.
Climb in the centre of the slope, cross a bergschrund and slant
R at the top to a rock rib at the edge of the snow. Climb this
to the snow ridge above, which is reached below where the crest
steepens ($1\frac{3}{4}$ h.). Climb the fine snow/ice ridge, broad at first
then narrow and steep, to where it may be corniced. If the
cornices are bad, move L below them and climb near a rocky
edge on sound holds to the summit ($1\frac{1}{2}$ h. , $6\frac{1}{4}$ h. from Mountet
hut, 3 h. in descent).

70. Variation, same standard. This is recommended when the
glacier is in bad condition (it is in full view from the Mountet
hut). Go up the glacier as for the usual approach for Route 68,
pass the foot of the Roc Noir, then slant NW to the N end of a
long low rock barrier marking the true L bank of the glacier.
This barrier comes down through pt. 3165 to pt. 2827.2m.
Immediately below the latter pt. climb polished rock at the N
end of the barrier and reach stones and snow which lie as a
broad band along its top. Follow the edge of snow along the top,
up to pt. 3165m. where an obvious rock ridge develops (3 h.).
From the highest snow, climb steep rocks between the crest of
this ridge and a couloir further R. Climb on to the ridge as soon
as possible and follow it easily on good rock to a snow dome
leading to pt. 3623m. , near the lower end of the snowy part of
the E ridge. Climb the broad ridge to join the previous approach
near its narrow upper part (3 h. to summit, 6 h. from hut).

<u>South-West Ridge</u>. The best of the three ridges and an excellent
rock scramble. It can be taken all the way from the Col de la
Dent Blanche (Mountet side), or from a point higher up the ridge,
to avoid the crevassed glacier approach to this col when starting
from Bricola Alp. Either way, PD+ with pitches of III. First
ascent: A. Barran and F. Corbett with J. Petrus and J. Langen,
18 August, 1879.

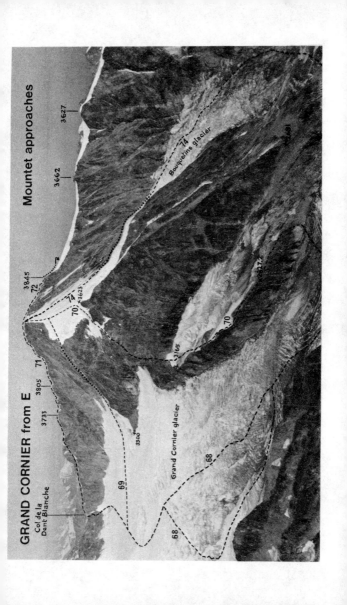

GRAND CORNIER from E

Mountet approaches

Col de la Dent Blanche

3733 3805 71

3300

69

68 68

Grand Cornier glacier

3845 72

74 3623

70

74

3165

3627

3662

Bouquetins glacier 74

1975

527.2

70

71. From the Mountet hut reach the Col de la Dent Blanche by Route 68 (4 h.). Climb the broad, easy snow ridge to a rock knoll (3592m.); turn the top of this on the L. A rock ridge now leads to pt. 3733m., where a branch spur descends towards Bricola Alp (1 h.).

From Bricola Alp this spur provides an approach which avoids climbing the Dent Blanche glacier to the col. From Bricola follow the big moraine marking the N side of a cwm formed within the spur, to below pt. 3102.8m. Now slant R into the stony cwm and climb it (snow) to a snowy ridge leading up to pt. 3733m. on the main ridge ($3\frac{1}{2}$ h.).

Continue along a short horizontal section of the ridge, which is crossed quickly by keeping to an edge of snow on the L. Soon reach the point where the ridge becomes very narrow. The slabs on the L are often verglassed, so climb on the crest, making the shortest turning movements possible; several gendarmes of excellent rock. Reach the top of a high red tower, nearly equal in height to the summit ($1\frac{3}{4}$ h.). Descend a chimney (4 m.). in the R flank and move R along a ledge to rejoin the crest. Now traverse three gendarmes, fine interesting climbing, to reach the summit (30 min., $3\frac{1}{4}$ h. from Col de la Dent Blanche, $7\frac{1}{4}$ h. from Mountet hut, $5\frac{3}{4}$ h. from Bricola Alp).

North-West Ridge. The ordinary route from the Moiry hut. Equally approachable from Bricola Alp. An interesting mixed climb. PD+. First ascent: T. Bornand with E. Peter, 18 July, 1873.

72. From the Moiry hut take a good path over stones to a moraine cwm coming down from the Col du Pigne. Below this col, continue over snow and stones towards the Pigne de la Lé, to where you can conveniently traverse R(S) to the W foot of this mtn., above the central icefall of the Moiry glacier. Work S and either climb a steep slope direct or turn it on the R, to reach the next plateau level in the glacier, close to its L side.

Continue parallel with the Bouquetins ridge on your L, pass pt. 3627m., then work up the steep triangular snow/ice facet leading to the end (3845m.) of the Grand Cornier ridge (2 h.). Move R as soon as possible and climb the R (W) retaining rock rib. The rocks are somewhat loose but not difficult. Alternatively, if the snow is good, cross a bergschrund and climb the facet to join the rib high up on the R, near pt. 3845m. (30 min.). This is the NW forepeak of the mtn.

From the forepeak at first climb precisely on the crest of the near horizontal and sharp rock ridge. Close to the summit turn a step on the L and reach the top. Fine scrambling in a good position ($1\frac{1}{4}$ h., $3\frac{3}{4}$ h. from Moiry hut).

73. Starting from Bricola Alp, climb beside the first stream above the chalets, then work towards the moraine cwm entrance marked pt. 2696m. Move on to the L-hand moraine and follow its crest to the top. Go on to the Bricola glacier just below the foot of a buttress marked pt. 2987m. Turn this buttress on the R. Pass behind and above the foot of it, and enter a large open couloir rising N and NE. Climb this, scree and snow, to a fork. Take the R branch, and as soon as possible climb rocks on the R (E) side, up to the Col de Bricola (3622m.). Stonefall in the afternoon ($2\frac{1}{2}$ h.). On the other side, cross the upper snow plateau of the Moiry glacier in a curve from E to S (pt. 3596m.) and soon join the Moiry hut approach (45 min. to forepeak, $3\frac{1}{4}$ h. from Bricola Alp, about $4\frac{1}{2}$ h. all told to summit).

North-East Face. A splendid ice climb, one of the best of a straightforward style in the Pennine Alps. Though short, it is very steep, not often in good condition, and the approach up the badly torn Bouquetins glacier is quite difficult, for which there is an alternative. There is virtually no objective danger. The line taken by the first ascensionists is less direct than that of most subsequent parties. Comparable with the Ober Gabelhorn N face. D+ in good conditions, 550m., average angle 54°. First ascent: L. Devies and J. Lagarde, 8 August, 1932. Direct line (third ascent and first descent): M. Brandt, A. and R. Voillat, 30-31 July, 1956. American ascent: P.R. Burgess and J.R. Sadler, 1957. First winter ascent: P. Feune, J.J. Hänggi and A. Herrmann, 3-5 February, 1967. First British ascent: R.J. Collister and R.I. Ferguson, 19 July, 1972. Climbed about 15 times to date.

74. From the Mountet hut, reverse the hut approach route from Zinal, cross the Zinal glacier and climb easily into the entrance of the Bouquetins glacier leading to the foot of the face. This glacier is almost a continuous icefall. Keep fairly close to the R side all the way up. The route will vary according to conditions. Reach the foot of the face near some rocks at its R-hand side (4-6 h.).

Alternative approach, much more sure. From the Mountet hut follow Route 70 to pt. 3623m. marking the foot of the snowy section of the E ridge of the mtn. (about 4¼ h.). Below this point, a steeply sloping glacier terrace slants down NW to the foot of the face. Descend it, soon cross a bergschrund and follow the line down below this bergschrund, crossing another bergschrund to reach the base (30-45 min., about 5 h. from Mountet hut).

The first ascensionists crossed the bergschrund well to the L, directly below a prominent sérac bulge high on the face and to the L of the summit. Then the line trends R, keeping the séracs up to the L, till a direct ascent on a corrugated ice slope leads to the summit. It is normally easier to slant R near the top and finish on the NW ridge about 50-100m. from the summit.

The direct route crosses the bergschrund near rocks at the R side of the face, somewhat R of the summit line. The bergschrund at this point can be very difficult. Either slant L and turn a snowy rockband on the L before resuming a direct ascent, or go up an ice groove through the rockband near its L end, with mixed climbing, normally very difficult. Follow a vague rib line on the face, becoming a plain slope, and finish directly at the summit (about 5 h. from bergschrund).

PIGNE DE LA LÉ 3396.2m.

75. An excellent viewpoint, climbed easily from the Moiry hut, either via the Col du Pigne (3141m.) and N ridge (1½ h. to summit); or by the snowy SW face (1¾ h., better in descent). Both ways are approached by Route 72. F/PD-.

COL DU PIGNE 3141m.

76. An easy pass from the middle basin of the Moiry glacier to Zinal. In this direction you need not descend to the Moiry hut, say after climbing the Grand Cornier, or go over its Zinal approach via the Col du Gardien. F+. First traverse: J. J. Hornby and T. H. Philpott with C. Lauener and J. Vianin, 28 August, 1864.

AIGUILLES DE LA LÉ

77. A broken rock ridge with several pinnacles, situated immediately behind the Moiry hut. The most northerly point (3179m.) gives a nice short climb and traverse on sound rock. A traverse of all the points is also short, II/III/IV, according to route.

POINTE DE BRICOLA 3657.6m.

78. Easily reached from the Col de Bricola (3622m.) (Routes 72, 73) by climbing the SE ridge in 15 min. (2¾ h. from Moiry hut). First ascent: C. Socin with E. Peter, 30 July, 1879.

DENT DES ROSSES 3613m.

79. From the Moiry hut the mtn. is approached by Route 72. Cross the crevassed glacier at c. 3540m. to a bergschrund below the SE flank. Reach a snowy gap on the L (S) of the summit, then climb easy rocks and snow to the top ($2\frac{3}{4}$ h. from hut). From the Col des Rosses (3498m.), the NW ridge is a fine scramble, III. You can also make a fairly easy traverse of the ridge between the Pte. de Bricola and Dent des Rosses in 1 h.

First ascent: C.G. and W.D. Munro and O.G. Jones with A. Bovier and P. Gaspoz, 2 September, 1891.

POINTES DE MOURTI 3563.8m. (E) 3529m. (W)

80. Frequently climbed from the Moiry hut. Starting by Route 72 the E peak is climbed from the Col des Rosses (3498m.) and SE ridge, turning a gendarme on the L (W) and finishing up a steep firm ridge (3 h. from Moiry hut). Or, in the same time and more directly by the NE ridge, reaching its crest above a large gendarme (3274m.). This NE ridge is also often climbed from its foot (pt. 2886.6m.), starting up on the R (W) side of the crest, turning the gendarme 3274m. on the L side, II/III. The ridge between the peaks can be traversed in 30 min. Attractive training climbs suitable for a day's outing from Ferpècle have been made by the guide Joseph Savoiz in 1968 on the W face of the E peak and S face of the W peak. These are small faces composed of excellent rock, reached from Ferpècle by a pleasant approach with a path on the lower steep section up the cwm below the adjoining faces, in 3 h. The W face route (III, IV and one pitch of V) is 300m., the S face about 200m. (III, IV+ and one pitch of V), and both ascend more or less in the summit lines. Good conditions are normal, 3 h. for each route. Descend to Ferpècle by the easy W ridge of the W peak.

First ascent: P. Montandon and E. Farner, 12 August, 1890.

COURONNE DE BRÉONA 3159.1m.

81. A useful training climb on good rock. It can be taken while crossing the Col de la Couronne from Les Haudères to the Moiry hut (Route 18). From the col, climb the SE ridge to the top of a subsidiary point. Descend from this a few m. on the L (W) side before traversing a wall to reach a gap between this point and the summit. Alternatively, turn the subsidiary pt. on the R, slight descent from col, and reach the gap without difficulty. From the gap descend on the L side for about 12m. before climbing along ledges which avoid a series of small gendarmes on the ridge above. Reach the crest above the gendarmes and follow fine slabs to the summit, II+ (1¼ h. from col). There are other climbs of similar standard or harder on the mtn.

NEUES WEISSTOR TO COL D'HÉRENS AND COL DES BOUQUETINS

Zermatt - Macugnaga - Breuil frontier ridge

Huts and other mountain bases

SWISS

<u>Monte Rosa Hut</u> 2795m.

Monte Rosahütte. An elaborate hut, situated on the Unter Plattje rocks at NW foot of Monte Rosa, and above the R bank of the Grenz glacier.   Warden and staff, restaurant service, places for 130.

82. Few if any parties walk all the way to the hut from Zermatt ($6\frac{1}{2}$ h.).   The Gornergrat railway is used to Rotboden station, which is the last stop before the upper terminus.

From Rotboden station (2815m.) a footpath descends S across a saddle (2775m.), then makes a long descending traverse down to the Gorner glacier at pt. 2657m.   Cross the glacier in a straight line, usually marked by flags, crossing a low central moraine. Then aim for the moraine below and L of the hut, which is in view but somewhat camouflaged by the rocks. Find the place where the glacier is left by moving towards the point where the path from the hut descends to it; large crevasses here. The path leads across a moraine and up rocks to the hut (2 h. from Rotboden).

<u>Gandegg Inn</u> 3029m.

Gandegghütte.   Really a small hotel, privately owned, which is not run like a hut.   There is dormitory accommodation as well as beds in rooms, places for about 35. Restaurant service.

83. From Zermatt the inn can be reached in about 30 min. from the top of the cablelift system at Trockener Steg (2920m.). The walk from Zermatt via Zum See and near Hermettji by mule path takes 4 h.

Monte Rosa Hut - Gandegg Inn connection

84. From the Monte Rosa hut take the most direct line in the centre of the Gorner glacier, to pass the corner of Triftji, directly opposite (S of) the Riffelhorn. Round this corner, cross a series of moraines and work up the centre then the R-hand side of the U. Theodul glacier, to about c. 2860m. on the R side of the glacier. From here a small track trends R up steep grass, scree and rocks to the inn ($3\frac{1}{2}$ h. from Monte Rosa hut).

Hörnli Hut 3260m.

Hörnlihütte. The new hut opened in 1966, next to the hotel owned by the Zermatt commune, at the foot of the NE ridge of the Matterhorn. Various drinks are sold, and hot water is available, but no meals are served. You go to the hotel to eat or cook on your own stove. Warden, places for 50.

85. From Zermatt either walk up the old mule path to Schwarzsee (3 h.) or take the cablelift. From here the continuation path is signposted and unmistakable. It leads finally to the famous series of endless zigzags on the shaly Hörnli buttress and to the hut (2 h. from Schwarzsee).

Solvay Hut 4003m.

Refuge Solvay. Situated on the NE (Hörnli) ridge of the Matterhorn, immediately above the lower Moseley slab pitch. See description of this ridge under heading of Matterhorn. After a fantastic wrangle with the sponsors, the CAS and the Zermatt commune, a new hut shell was placed on the site (1917) in 1966,

after attempts to have the bivouac transferred to the Ober Gabelhorn had failed. The hut is only a bivouac and emergency shelter
for up to 12 persons, and a fine is imposed for using it as a
stage to climb the Matterhorn.

Bertol Hut 3311m.

An important hut at the western edge of this guidebook area,
fully described in the Pennine Alps West volume. This base has
a glacier connection with the Dent Blanche hut (Route 15), and
is mentioned hereafter in the traverses of two of the most westerly passes within this Central region, namely the Col d'Hérens
(in Route 14, and in a separate entry) and the Col des Bouquetins.

ITALIAN

Eugenio Sella Hut 3029m.

Rifugio Eugenio Sella. Situated on the Italian approach to the
Neues Weisstor pass, on a platform at the top of a promontory dividing the Jazzi and Roffel glaciers. The hut has been
prone to damage by avalanches in the past. Warden, simple
restaurant service, places for 50.

86. From the square in Macugnaga (Staffa) go down the main
road (bus) to Pecetto di Sopra (1362m.). Keep R and follow
a lane through the last houses to a fork (1378m.). Keep R
again (L for the Belvedere), cross some pastures and climb
a moraine cwm between the stream and the mountainside.
When the path leaves the stream, climb a rock spur (cut steps)
and descend a little to reach the foot of a grassy gorge with
a waterfall on the R (1 h.). Climb zigzags in the gorge (cut
steps); in the upper part cross the gorge to a grassy knoll
where the path forks. Take the L branch and ascend another
grassy gorge (waterfall) to reach the Roffelstafel huts (1905m.)
(45 min.). It is not necessary to pass the huts which stand

100m. to the L, below a rocky bank.

Now the path climbs grassy slopes in zigzags, passing to the L of two waterfalls and going up some rocks. More grass then stony slopes and scree lead to snow under the promontory on which the hut stands. Work up to the lower L (W) side of the promontory and ascend under the rocks to the foot of a buttress forming a corner. Slant R (N) round this and climb snow and scree to the hut ($2\frac{1}{2}$ h., $4\frac{1}{2}$ h. from Macugnaga. In descent, 2 h.).

Starting from the Belvedere, at the top of the chairlift, the glacier can be crossed to Alpe Fillar, and a path followed down to a junction with the Macugnaga path at a point slightly above Roffelstafel ($3\frac{1}{2}$ h. from Belvedere to hut).

Belloni Bivouac 2509m.

Bivacco Valentino Belloni. Not shown on LK25, but marked on LK50, 284. Situated exactly at the crest-foot of the E ridge of the Gr. Fillarhorn, directly above the Belvedere of Macugnaga. No cooking facilities, take your own stove, places for 9, door unlocked.

87. From Pecetto (Macugnaga) follow Route 86 to Roffelstaffel. Ignore the R fork for the Eugenio Sella hut and follow a slightly descending path into the moraine valley below Alpe Jazzi, and along to Alpe Fillar (1974m.), directly opposite Belvedere ($2\frac{1}{4}$ h.). This point can be joined from the top of the Belvedere chairlift in 30 min. by crossing the moraine covered Belvedere glacier.

From Alpe Fillar follow a continuation path SW and cross the stream coming down from the Castelfranco glacier. After this, climb rough ground in the same direction, above the main path, and reach a second stream descending under the S side of the E ridge and spur of the Gr. Fillarhorn. Follow this stream with increasing steepness to the W, climb round a bluff to the

R where the stream gorge narrows, and continue by slopes above the stream, on its N side till you can reach the crest of the rocky spur on your R and at the foot of the ridge where the hut is found ($1\frac{3}{4}$ h., 4 h. from Pecetto, or $2\frac{1}{4}$ h. from Belvedere chairlift).

Alpe Pedriola Huts (Zamboni and Zappa) 2065m.

Two adjoining huts now forming one establishment under CAI direction, providing between them dormitory and bedroom accommodation with restaurant and other services. Places for about 80. Situated in a grassy hollow on the E side of the Belvedere glacier, directly opposite the E face of Monte Rosa.

88. Reached from Macugnaga (Pecetto) by chairlift to the Belvedere, and from there by good path in 45 min. ($2\frac{1}{4}$ h. all the way on foot).

Paradiso Hut 2271m. TCI

A privately run hut on the N side of the Lago delle Loccie (2223m.), situated directly above (S of) Alpe Pedriola. Restaurant service, places for 30.

Marinelli Hut 3036m.

Rifugio Damiano Marinelli. This small hut is situated in an important position on rocks of a buttress (Crestone Marinelli) forming the true L bank of the famous Marinelli couloir in the face of Monte Rosa. It is advisable to take your own food and stove, although in recent years a calor gas cooker has been installed. Warden sometimes present. Door unlocked, places for 12, snow melt nearby.

89. From the huts on Alpe Pedriola (see above) cross by a small track the big moraine forming the R bank of the Belvedere glacier, then cross this stone covered glacier towards the foot of the large rock buttress on the R-hand side of the Marinelli couloir. Go over the lateral moraine then more moraine forming the R bank of the Nordend glacier above you. This is the R-hand of two parallel moraine crests. A path (not marked on maps) goes up this moraine to its top. Keep to the R (N) of the foot of the Crestone Marinelli and climb scree and snow to its crest on the L, at a grassy saddle (2621m.). Follow a path across the L side of the buttress, over rocks and grass to a short rockface. Climb this, then a snow slope above and slightly L of the crest. Finally the path moves further L (SW) and descends slightly to reach the hut (3¼ h. from Alpe Pedriola).

Gallarate Bivouac 3969m.

Bivacco Città di Gallarate. An important high altitude shelter, situated immediately below the twin rock prongs forming the summit of the Jägerhorn, on the side facing the Jägerjoch, and looking at the Cresta di Santa Caterina ridge of the Nordend. The shelter is painted bright orange and has places for 9. Take your own cooker, door unlocked.
In fact the approach from Macugnaga is long and not easy. It involves climbing the Jägerhorn, normally by staying first at the Belloni biv. Therefore the logical and more straightforward approach from the Zermatt side is described below. PD.

90. From the Monte Rosa hut climb the large dome of rounded rocks to the E (small path), then make a slightly rising movement ESE to reach the L lateral moraine of the Monte Rosa glacier. Cross the moraine and reach the glacier at c. 2900m. Climb up the crevassed glacier to the E, then more steeply ENE and reach the other side near the upper end of the moraine (3074m.). Before getting there a cairn can be seen on a rock rib above the moraine, which marks the easiest way across the next section; 400m. higher up, this rib is capped by pt. 3263.9m. Reach the rib by crossing scree and easy rocks (1½ h.). On the other side descend snow N then NE to the Gorner glacier. Climb its R side to the foot (pt. 3197m.) of the NW spur of the Nordend

133

(large crevasses). Keep L and continue up the glacier cwm with crevasses to the bergschrund below the Jägerjoch. This can be quite difficult and it is preferable to cross it well to the R. Above, a steep snow/ice slope leads to the col (3913m.) (3 h.). Turn up an easy snow slope to the N and scramble up rocks to the hut just below the summit of the Jägerhorn (15-30 min., about 5 h. from Monte Rosa hut).

91. The most direct approach from Zermatt is to take the Gornergrat train then the cable car to the Stockhorn terminus (3405m.). From here go along the ridge easily to the Stockhorn (3532m.), and continue in the same direction to the Stockhornpass (3394m.) (1 h.). Now keep to the broad glacier hump rising SE towards the Torre di Castelfranco. At c.3540m. below this contour easy snow slopes to the S, which form a broad plateau below the Altes Weisstor, Fillarhorn-joch and Jägerhorn. So reach the bergschrund below the Jägerjoch and join the previous route ($2\frac{3}{4}$ h., $3\frac{3}{4}$ h. to hut from Stockhorn cable car terminus).

Resegotti Hut   3624m.

Rifugio Luigina Resegotti. This small hut is situated about 800m. to the E of Colle Signal, which marks the foot of the Cresta Signal (E) ridge of the Signalkuppe. The hut is placed about 5m. below the snow crest of the ridge, on the S side. It serves as a high level starting point for the latter climb, or for more difficult routes on the flanks of this mtn. No warden, places for 16, small stove - but it is better to take your own. Door open.

92. From the Alpe Pedriola huts (Macugnaga) follow a small path up the moraine cwm to the S, pass above the W side of the Loccie lake and go on to the N Loccie glacier, near pt. 2343m. Aim for the Colle delle Loccie (3334m.) at its head, which is a broad saddle between the Punta Grober (3497m.) and Punta Tre Amici (3425m.). Follow the crevassed depression in the centre of the glacier, and pass close to pt. 3146m., while keeping a safe distance from the rocks of Punta Tre Amici. From there slant SSE to the col (5 h.). Follow the broad easy ridge to the WNW, up to a step in front of Punta Tre Amici. This can be turned on the R (N) by snow slopes (generally icy), but it is usually preferable to turn it on the L by climbing straight up steep rocks on the crest of the step for about 12m., then by a traverse L along a ledge parallel with and about 25m. below the crest. This ledge line leads directly to the hut. PD+ ($1\frac{1}{2}$ h., $6\frac{1}{2}$ h. from Pedriola huts).

93. From Alagna the road up the Sesia valley is motorable to the S. Antonio oratory (1391m.) and across a bridge and up to the start of the old military and mines road leading to the Colle del Turlo. The latter should be ignored. Continue along the unmade valley road to Bitz (1603m.) and the Blatte chalets. Further on the road ends at more chalets (1695m.) below Safejaz (45 min.). Ignore to the R paths mounting to Fonkegno and lower Vigne, and take a well marked path climbing NNW over wooded moraines, up to a tributary stream. So reach after numerous zigzags a signpost at the L (W) end of the rock band below the upper Vigne pastures (45 min.). Without crossing the stream on the L, a good path works R above the rock band to upper Vigne (2230, 2247m.) where the Città di Vercelli hut is found (30 min., $2\frac{1}{4}$ h. from motorable roadhead, $3\frac{1}{4}$ h. from Alagna). Thus far all signposts have pointed the way to the Valsesia hut.

Now take a track in zigzags to the N, which soon becomes faint. Continue in the same direction to the big moraine above (2791m.), on the R side of the Sesia glacier. More to the R, reach the plateau of the adjoining Vigne glacier, cross it to the N, then climb steeper slopes NE, in the direction of the Colle delle Loccie. Keep to the R of a large rock island (Rocce Vigne) and climb NW, up the arm of the S Loccie glacier between the island and the Punta Tre Amici. The hut is visible from a distance. Reach the ridge slightly L(W) of the Tre Amici and follow it to the hut ($3\frac{1}{2}$ h., about 7 h. on foot from Alagna).

Margherita Hut 4554m.

Rifugio Regina Margherita. Situated on the summit of the Signalkuppe (Punta Gnifetti), this hut is the highest in the Alps. Only part of the building, an observatory for scientific studies, is open to climbers. Warden in summer, 30 places, some food available but always take your own. Charges for cooking and accommodation are dear. Most climbers will need aspirin to get a good night's sleep. The approach from Switzerland up the Grenz glacier is often badly crevassed. PD.

94. From the Monte Rosa hut follow the good path over glaciated rocks then moraine in the cwm to the L of the lateral moraine of the Grenz glacier. Reach a not very obvious fork where the more prominent track climbs L towards Monte Rosa. Keep R and continue in the same direction to reach the glacier just beyond pt. 3109m. (1 h.). More or less follow the L side of the glacier all the way. The first section is usually badly crevassed, to beyond where a side branch enters the main glacier. Pass near the foot of pt. 3472m., then either climb the cwm between pt. 3696m. and the icefall to the R, or, if the crevasses are bad, ascend a steep snow slope to the L, and so pass below the rock ridge coming down at pt. 3753m. as the W spur of the Dufourspitze. Another steep snow cwm between two icefalls leads to a small plateau. Cross this keeping L(E), and at 4200m. turn an ice barrier on the R. Now climb NE into an open snow cwm between the Zumsteinspitze and Signalkuppe, aiming for the col at its head. Near this climb SE up a plain snow slope and finally by a few rocks to finish just R of the summit of the Signalkuppe and the hut (5-6 h. from Monte Rosa hut, $2\frac{1}{2}$ h. in descent).

95. From the Gnifetti hut descend E to the snow slopes and turn the upper end (3648m.) of the rock rib on which the hut stands. Then climb N and pass close to the foot of the islet called the Balmenhorn (4167m.). Ahead is the Lisjoch with the Dufourspitze rising behind. Aim to the R of the lowest point (4151m.) and cross a shoulder to the R of pt. 4252m., which is NW of the Ludwigshöhe (1¾ h.). On the other side continue in the same direction, hardly losing height before contouring into the open snow cwm between the Zumsteinspitze and Signalkuppe, where the previous route is joined. There is usually a big trail in summer (1½ h., 3¼ h. from Gnifetti hut).

Balmenhorn Hut 4167m.

Bivacco Cristo delle vette. A simple unoccupied emergency shelter on the rock islet called the Balmenhorn, passed by the trade route (95) between the Gnifetti hut and Margherita hut.

Valsesia Hut 3312m.

Rifugio Valsesia. A small hut with no warden, placed on the large broken rock promontory which divides the Piode and Sesia glaciers coming down from the Parrotspitze. The condition of the hut is not guaranteed, places for 10, door unlocked.

96. From Alagna follow Route 93 to the signpost below the L end of the rock band below the upper Vigne chalets (about 3 h. from Alagna).

The signpost indicates cross the stream for the Valsesia hut. A track goes up the moraine above. Later it leaves the crest and slants L through a hollow close to the Piode glacier. Finally it works along the top of a rock barrier overlooking the glacier, to near a waterfall further L (2 h.). Scramble up rocks to the R on to a snow patch which extends to the R as a large ledge system. Follow this line to a broad crest and go up this to the

hut further N (1 h. , 6 h. from Alagna on foot, about 45 min.
less from roadhead).

Città di Vercelli Hut 2247m.

Rifugio Città di Vercelli. Situated on the upper Vigne pasture,
a bunkhouse looked after in summer by the shepherds. Self
catering, places for 20. Reached from Alagna in $3\frac{1}{4}$ h. by Route
93.

Gnifetti Hut 3611m.

Rifugio Giovanni Gnifetti. A large building, new in 1967, situated on the upper rocks of the long rib separating the Lis and
Garstelet glaciers. One of the most frequented huts on the
Italian side of the Pennines, in a classic site near where the
former hut was situated. Warden, restaurant service, places
for 200.

97. From Alagna there is a cableway system in three stages to
Punta Indren (3260m. TCI), not shown on LK. This terminus
is on the ridge dividing the Valsesia (Alagna) and Gressoney
valleys. If approached on foot the usual route is via Colle
d'Olen, part jeep road and mule path (Alagna to upper station on
foot, 5 h.).

From the upper station walk out on to the Indren glacier and
cross this to the NW, usually by a deep trail in the snow (crevasses possible). Reach the foot of the rock barrier separating
the Indren and Garstelet glaciers. At one point (3481m. IGM)
these rocks are capped by a cross. Climb a steep slope to the
L(SW), up to the Garstelet glacier, on the L of the cross, where
a signpost is found. The hut lies a short distance to the NNW
and is reached in a few min. ($1\frac{3}{4}$ h. from cableway terminus,
about 7 h. on foot from Alagna).

98. From Gressoney-la-Trinité there is a cableway to Alpe

Gabiet (2354m.), two huts here, on the path to Colle d'Olen. Ignore the latter. To the N a well marked path is followed to Lago Verde (2609m.), then by many zigzags to the ruined Linty hut on the crest of a ridge. The path works across the side of this ridge to moraine and stones leading on to the Garstelet glacier and to the Gnifetti hut a little higher to the L (5 h. from cableway terminus).

Città di Vigevano Hut 2864m.

Rifugio Città di Vigevano. Situated on a terrace adjoining the E side of Colle d'Olen (2881m.), the trade route across the main divide from Alagna to Gressoney-la-Trinité. Restaurant service, places for 80.

99. From Alagna the shortest route to the hut consists of using the Punta Indren cableway to the second intermediate station of the Bocchetta delle Pisse (2396m.). From here a large footpath works up the Pisse valley under the top stage of the cableway towards the Colle delle Pisse. From the top of the cwm just below this pass a track is followed S up to the plateau with small lakes on the E side of the main ridge,   past the saddle of the Pso. d. Salati and so to the hut ($1\frac{3}{4}$ h. from cableway station).

Walking all the way from Alagna by a jeep road and large mule path up the Olen valley, 4 h. First stage of the cableway reaches the path in this valley at 1825m.

100. From Gressoney-la-Trinité, by cableway to Alpe Gabiet (2354m), and from there by mule path to Colle d'Olen (2881m.), which is crossed in a few min. to the hut ($1\frac{3}{4}$ h. from cableway terminus. On foot all the way from Gressoney, $3\frac{1}{4}$ h.).

<u>Gastaldi Bivouac</u> 2531m. TCI

Bivacco Carletto Gastaldi. As one of the Laghetti tarns just below the hut is measured 2542m., the height of this biv. seems likely to be c. 2560m. Situated in the Netscio cwm directly above and E of Gressoney-la-Trinité. Standard pattern CAI aluminium biv. with 4 bunks, small stove for which you take your own wood, and mini-table. Door locked, keys at Gressoney municipal office and tourist office.

101. From Gressoney-la-Trinité cross the road bridge from the village centre to the outer E road, and from the hamlet opposite the bridge take a path rising NE and N through forest above the stream coming down from the Lago Gabiet. After 20 min. a path to the R is followed to Spilmansberg (2098m.). From here continue due E by a path rising up the R side of the Netscio valley, making two big zigzags before crossing its stream to the L side. Continue by zigzags on a small path to the entrance of the upper cwm containing the small Laghetti lakes. The biv. is situated above the furthest N lake ($2\frac{3}{4}$ h. from Gressoney).

<u>Rivetti (Staval) Hut</u> c. 1845m.

Rifugio Carla Rivetti. Shown on TCI map only. A privately owned hut, open to all, at the roadhead in the Gressoney valley, about 5 km. above Gressoney-la-Trinité (1 h. on foot, or by car). Situated on the E side of the loop roadhead, behind a chapel adjoining the Gaval bridge, 1848m. TCI (1825m. LK). Restaurant service, places for 24. A good valley base.

<u>Quintino Sella Hut</u> 3585m.

Rifugio Quintino Sella. Situated at the top of the ridge which divides the Gressoney and Ayas valleys, near the point where the ridge merges with the Felik glacier below Castor and Pollux. Resident warden, restaurant service, places for 60.

102. From Gressoney-la-Trinité by motor road to Betta hamlet at the foot of the mule path to the Colle di Bettaforca (2672m.).

140

Follow this large path to the col (3 h. from Gressoney-la-Trinité on foot, save 45 min. by car). From here the path, which is good all the way, more or less follows the R-hand side of the ridge, under the Bettolina mtn. and pass and in a cwm normally with snow up to a stores depot for the hut situated on the ridge crest. After this the ridge becomes quite rocky and exposed and has four sections with fixed cables before the hut is reached by a series of zigzags and another crest (3 h. from Colle di Bettaforca, 6 h. all the way on foot from Gressoney).

103. From San Giacomo in the Ayas valley follow the large mule path up the Forca valley to the E, via Resy (2072m., now almost reached by a road), to the Colle di Bettaforca (2½ h.), then as for the previous route (5½ h. from San Giacomo).

However, a small road has been completed from San Giacomo to Alpe Pian di Verra Sup. (2382m.), called simply Alpe di Verra. At the time of writing this road is shown only on the TCI and KK maps. Nearly all parties bound for the Quintino Sella and Mezzalama huts drive or use a taxi to this point. From the Alpe di Verra roadhead keep R of the stream (you go up L to the Mezzalama hut) and follow a small but well marked track with red and white paint flashes (not shown on any map) up steep rough ground to the SSE, passed a lake (2775m.), and eventually reach the ridge just L of the stores building of the previous route at c. 3120m., and just below the exposed rocky ridge with fixed ropes as followed on the Gressoney approach (Alpe di Verra to hut, 4 h.).

<u>Fiery Inn</u> 1878m. TCI

This is a classic valley base site, frequented since the 19th century by climbing parties working from the head of the Ayas valley. It is situated just above the village of San Giacomo (roadhead), at the fork in paths leading to the Valtournanche and the Mezzalama hut. Reach from San Giacomo by a jeep road

(On foot, 15 min.).   The inn has beds for 20 and a restaurant service.

Mezzalama Hut   3004m.

Rifugio Ottorino Mezzalama.   This hut is located high up on a moraine ridge dividing the two branches of the Verra glacier, above the head of the Ayas valley, warden in summer, restaurant service, places for 27.

104. From San Giacomo by motor road to Alpe di Verra (2382m.). Details about this new road are given in Route 103. From Alpe di Verra cross the streams to the N by footbridges, where the original path from the valley is joined. Now climb a steep zigzag path due N and eventually reach the moraine crest which is followed to the hut ($1\frac{1}{2}$ h. from Alpe di Verra).

Cozzi Bivouac   2800m.   TCI

Bivacco Vittorio Cozzi.   Not marked, nor its path indicated, on LK. Situated at the top of the steep nameless hanging valley overlooking and due W of Gressoney-la-Trinité, and under the E face of the Testa Grigia mtn.   No personal record and no communication received from any correspondent.   Not described to date in any Italian guidebook. Presumably built and opened after 1961. Places for 16, door possibly locked, inquire at tourist office in Gressoney.

105. A clearly marked path is traced on the TCI map (a vaguer version is shown on KK). It starts from the road at Gressoney a little N of the cemetery and zigzags steeply up the wooded and rocky mountainside to Schelbete (2093m. TCI), then NW across a ravine to Hoggene Stein (2313m.). From here the path climbs a short rock barrier SW to enter a steep narrow valley with rocky sides. Higher up the path crosses to the L (S) side of the stream and continues to the hut which is situated on the L enclosing spur, rising into the E face of the Testa Grigia (about

$3\frac{1}{4}$ h. from Gressoney).

Cesare e Giorgio Bivouac c. 3750m.

Bivacco Cesare e Giorgio.   After Cesare Volante and Giorgio
Rossi. Only shown at present on TCI map, confusingly as Biv.
Rossi e Volante. Standard pattern CAI biv. shelter with bunks
for 4, no other facilities, door unlocked. Situated on a lateral
rock barrier at the SW base of the terminal mass of the Roccia
Nera (Schwarzfluh on older maps) at the SE end of the Zermatt
Breithorn ridge massif. This shelter is perhaps more used by
spring ski touring parties doing the Italian High Level Route
than by summer climbers for whom it serves as a useful emergency shelter in a remote high glacier setting. On the Italian
side in this part of the frontier ridge the Mezzalama hut   seems
high enough to make all the popular ascents comfortably without
having to resort to the biv. hut. However, for Italian routes
on Castor and Pollux, Zermatt based parties will find it a convenient starting point by coming up from the Theodulpass and
over the easy Breithornpass.

The biv. hut is reached from the Mezzalama hut up the Verra
glacier in 3 h. PD-. From the Theodulpass by the trade route
across the Breithornpass and a traverse of the upper plateau
of the Verra glacier in $2\frac{3}{4}$ h. F+ (save 30 min. from Testa
Grigia cableway terminus). Also practicable, but probably
rarely done, by crossing the Schwarztor (pass), starting from
the Gornergrat railway or Monte Rosa hut. PD. About $4\frac{1}{2}$ h.
to pass plus 30 min. to biv.

These routes are others passing near the biv. hut are described in more detail in various climbing routes. See Routes
161, 164, 165 and 166.

Testa Grigia Restaurant 3479.6m.

Adjoining the cableway terminus from Breuil, on the frontier
ridge above the Theodulpass. Meals served all day, no accommodation.

Theodul Hut 3317m.

Rifugio del Theodulo. Situated on the low rock step immediately
above the Theodulpass (3290m.). Warden, restaurant service,
places for 67. Tends to be overrun by skiers all year round.

143

106. Swiss side: From the Gandegg inn there is a snowcat service to the pass. On foot follow the line across the glacier as indicated on the map, alongside skitows. There are some crevasses, sometimes quite large, marked by flag poles (1½ h. on foot).

107. Italian side: From Breuil very few people walk to the pass and hut. The path is in a bad state but can be followed from the map without possible error (4 h.). From the Testa Grigia cableway terminus descend snow slopes and ski pistes to the pass in 15 min. and follow a short path up rocks to the hut.

<u>Furggen Station Restaurant</u> 3491m.

Cableway terminus of this branch of the Breuil-Plan Maison system, on the highest point of the Furgggrat. No overnight accommodation.

<u>Bossi Bivouac</u> c. 3345m.

Bivacco Oreste Bossi. Situated about 100m. distance NW of the Breuiljoch (3323m.) and a few m. below ridge pt. 3352m. on the Ital. side, at the foot of the Furggen ridge of the Matterhorn. Places for 9, blankets, cups, utensils, etc., but take your own stove. Door unlocked.

108. The shortest route from Zermatt, and the one taken by most parties, is from the Trockener Steg cableway terminus (2920m.), some distance below the Gandegg inn. From the cableway contour rocky ground SW to the edge of large snowfields of the Oberer Theodul glacier, merging into the Furgg glacier. Cross the glaciers due W, without losing height, a few crevasses, for about 4 km., to the foot of the steep broken snow slope and ice walls under the E face of the Matterhorn. The opening to these slopes is marked on the R side by pt. 2982m. Start at the opposite L side and climb snow near the lower edges of three rock ribs to a small semi-circular snow plateau immediately below the Breuiljoch. Continue up the final snow slope or sometimes by rocks further L to the pass, then move R along the easy ridge to the hut. PD-. (2 h. from cableway terminus).

109. Alternative from Hörnli hut. From here follow a slightly descending track in scree SW (not the one at a higher level going up the Matterhorn) to the glacier below the E face of the mtn. In the same direction cross a large and obvious glacier terrace at c. 3220m. between two ice cliff bands, then slant L along the semi-circular terrace to the final slope of the Breuiljoch, as in the previous route (1 h. from Hörnli hut to biv. hut).

110. From the Breuil side, the shortest route is from the Furggen station cableway terminus. From here traverse the Furgggrat over its minor summits on snow and a few rocks to the Furggjoch (3271m.), 45 min. At the far end of this saddle is a red rock tower about 50m. high, separating you from the Breuiljoch. Go up the tower with the aid of a fixed rope and traverse its summit (La Madonnina, 3348.6m.). A short descent to the Breuiljoch is along a small path in the ridge, then to the biv. hut a little further. F+ (30 min., 1¼ h. from cableway terminus). The merit of this route is the superb close-range view of the Matterhorn.

111. For those who cannot afford the cableway (much lire!) the best way is as follows. From Breuil get a ride on the new private road to the Duca degli Abruzzi hut (2802m.). Now go up the good path taken for the Italian ridge of the Matterhorn, as far as the rock barrier called the Grand Escalier (Croce di Carrel, 2920m.). From here traverse R (NE) below the barrier, over scree, moraine and snow, and continue to the E at c. 2900m. below the Sup. del Cervino glacier. Descend a little to cross a moraine, and on the far side of this traverse again then climb NE to the Inf. del Cervino glacier, a large snowband lying below the S face of the Matterhorn. Follow the lower edge of the glacier, with rocks and debris, and eventually traverse R to the snow and rock slope directly below the Breuiljoch. Climb this without difficulty to the pass. F+ (2¼ h. from Duca degli Abruzzi hut). A direct ascent to the biv. hut on the mixed slope L of the Breuiljoch is quite steep with a rock pitch of II.

Duca degli Abruzzi (Oriande) Hut 2802m.

Rifugio Duca degli Abruzzi. A privately-run inn, open to all, situated above Breuil on the approach to the Italian ridge of the Matterhorn. 40 beds and restaurant service. The inn is now reached from Breuil by a small motor road, somewhat L(W) of the original mule path. The owners describe the inn and their jeep service vehicles are marked "Rifugio Oriande".

112. On foot from Breuil the way cannot be missed. Follow the road then mule path branching R(N), which leads in turn to the Batze, Crot de Palet (junction) and Eura chalets. From the last continue in two wide zigzags to the hut (2¼ h. from Breuil).

Carrel Hut 3830m.

Rifugio Jean-Antoine Carrel. Previous hut (in this series!) correctly marked on current maps Rif. Luigi Amedeo di Savoia, 3835m. New Carrel hut opened in 1969, while the nearby Savoia hut serves as an overflow (very rough). Situated on a platform some distance up the Italian ridge of the Matterhorn, below the Great Tower. Places for 50, calor gas cooker and kitchen equipment complete, radio telephone, snow melt for water. No regular warden, provisioned by goods transporter cable from the Duca degli Abruzzi hut, door always open. The hut approach is PD, allowing for fixed ropes, etc. in place.

113. From the Duca degli Abruzzi hut (q. v. above), at roadhead from Breuil, follow the zigzag path up scree or snow to the rock barrier of the Grand Escalier del Leone (Croce di Carrel,

2920m.). Climb a broad terrace line up R through the rocks to more scree and broken rock walls (3076m.), to below a larger barrier. The track becomes faint. Keep L along the edge of a small snowfield, and up to the L climb an easy slanting rock couloir which finishes over a rocky, stepped knoll. This leads to more scree and snow lying on the SSW side of the Testa del Leone. This slope is steep and exposed to stonefall, so cross the foot of it to the R as quickly as possible, using an edge of rocks, then climb straight up the R-hand side of the facet by a vague rock rib, to below the summit wall of the Testa del Leone, and level with the Colle del Leone further R. Now make a more or less horizontal traverse to the col (3580m.) over snowy ledges and shallow snow/ice couloirs, gritty and loose but not technically difficult (stonefall) with fixed belaying stanchions in places. This "gallery" is well shown on the map (2½ h.). The Italian ridge proper of the Matterhorn rises above.

Climb the ridge keeping to snow and scree on the R side of the crest and so reach the first belt of slabs. Make a rising traverse R across the slabs using a crack system (delicate with fresh snow, II+, fixed ropes and pegs), followed by more slabs and rock steps going straight up to another fixed rope. This leads horizontally R to the Seiler Slab, often snow covered and verglassed. At the top of this pitch is the famous chimney where Whymper fell. Climb it, 12m. , vertical, with a fixed rope, strenuous. More slabs and fixed ropes ensue, on or near the crest, and lead to the hut (1½ h. , 4 h. from Duca degli Abruzzi hut).

Benedetti Bivouac   c. 3490m.

Bivacco Nino Benedetti. Situated almost exactly at the head of the S spur coming down from the end of the E ridge of the Dent d'Hérens. This junction of ridges is found about 100m. W of the Colle Tournanche (3479m.). The biv. is located near a sharp rock knoll. When visited a few years ago by correspondents its condition was reported as poor and uncomfortable. Standard pattern CAI shelter with 4 bunks. Take your own cooker, etc. Door open. Both the Italian and Swiss approaches are those for Colle Tournanche itself.

114. Italian side. By far the best approach is from the roadhead at the Duca degli Abruzzi hut. From here follow the path towards the Matterhorn for a few min., as in the previous route, then leave it and traverse grass and scree to the L (W and NW) at c. 2850m. Continue at this level across the broken rock hump under the Leone glacier and reach the E side of the S spur coming down from near the Colle Tournanche at pt. 2897m. To the R of this is a short couloir. (A longer, more continuous one to the L, also more obvious, should be avoided, especially in descent, which is a blind approach from above). Climb the couloir and after 40m. move R up a gangway to scree and snow forming a slope on the E side of the spur. This slope was bare scree in 1974. By a rising traverse L across this reach a ramp going up steep rocks on to the crest of the spur which is reached just below and L (S) of pt. 3200m. Follow the crest on easy slabby rocks, over pts. 3200m. and 3322m. to the upper snowy section which leads to the junction with the E ridge of the Dent d'Hérens. Colle Tournanche is below to the R. The biv. hut is in a hollow to the R, just behind a sharp rock knoll. PD- (about $3\frac{1}{2}$ h. from Duca degli Abruzzi hut).

115. Swiss side: From the Schönbiel hut go down a vague track to the SW, to the edge of the cliff overlooking the Zmutt glacier junction. There is a complicated route down the cliff, slanting R, short walls, open chimneys, slabs and scree, to reach loose moraine at the bottom. Examine in daylight.

If in doubt start as follows. From the hut follow the main path NW for 10 min., then scramble down moraine to the glacier and descend it round below the cliff under the hut.

Now cross the Zmutt glacier tediously to the S and skirt R of the foot of the Matterhorn. Then keep L and climb a small

COLLE TOURNANCHE S (Breuil) side

Punta Cristina

– Dent | d'Hérens Cresta E –

Testa del Leone

col

Benedetti biv.

3322

309S×

Leone glacier

×2897

114

branch glacier to the SE, towards the Zmutt ridge of the Matterhorn. Go up this to an obvious break on the R, pass through this opening, which is situated immediately L (E) of pt. 2974m. (Sattelti), and descend slightly to the glacier slopes leading to the snowfield of the Tiefmatten glacier. Cross this glacier plateau to the SW and reach the foot of a rock rib at c. 2970m. on the R of the Colle Tournanche. This rib goes up via pt. 3078m. to a flattish glacier spur rising to near the foot of the E ridge of the Dent d'Hérens, i. e. slightly above the Colle Tournanche. Reach the crest of the rib from its L side, at pt. 3078m., and climb the rocks to the longer snow/ice section where conditions can be variable. Trend slightly L to finish on a steep snow/ice slope, and arrive on the ridge in a small saddle to the R of pt. 3547m. Descend over this pt. towards the col and soon reach the biv. hut (4 h.). PD+.

If coming directly from Zermatt, leave the Schönbiel hut path at the foot of the last zigzags and go over the moraine (small track) on to the Zmutt glacier (Zermatt to biv. hut, 7-8 h.).

Albertini Bivouac c. 3325m.

Bivacco Gianno Albertini. Situated on the Cresta Albertini, the prominent S ridge of pt. 4039m., called Spalla, on the E ridge of the Dent d'Hérens. The hut position is not precisely indicated on any map. Places for 4, door open.

This biv. was erected for the purpose of making it easier and more popular to climb the Dent d'Hérens direct from Breuil, via the Col des Grandes Murailles (3827m.) to reach the ordinary SW side route. Due to the difficulty of getting to the biv. hut itself the object is somewhat defeated, while the ensuing ascent of the E side of the Col des Grandes Murailles is steep and liable to bad stonefall. The approach from Breuil is either up the Montabel glacier, normally blocked side to side by séracs and ice walls, though reasonable in a good season (AD), or by the lower part of the Albertini rock ridge, which is always sure but has pitches of IV/IV+, sometimes found with ropes left in place. Above the biv. hut, the Cresta Albertini as an alternative route to the Dent d'Hérens, which is practical and direct, also has pitches of IV.

As no route on the Dent d'Hérens is described in the guide from these approaches, more details about the biv. hut route from Breuil are omitted. From accounts received, seldom used except by two or three guided parties each year.

Aosta Hut 2781m.

Rifugio Aosta. A notorious hut! both for its tedious approach and battered condition in which it is so often found. Visited by the writer and no less than four independent correspondents/ parties in the six years following publication of the 1968 guide. All reports differ in their degree of depreciation but all concur on the importance of the site, the magnificence of the lonely setting, and the topographical misfortune that this base should provide the starting point for the easiest route up the Dent d'Hérens (q. v. for more precise comments).
   Situated at a relatively low altitude at the foot of the W ridge of the Tête de Valpelline, and above the E bank of the Tsa de Tsan glacier. Places for 18 (4 or 5 more at a pinch), wood and gas stoves, kitchen utensils, etc., but safer to take your own stove. Water from snow melt about 100m. away. No permanent warden, door always open. When the roof has been holed and snow is piled inside, blankets and wood (if any) have normally been stored away in a dry quarter of the hut.

116. In the Valpelline the approach has changed and is much longer and tiring than it used to be. From the roadhead (carpark) at Place Moulin (Albergo below), c. 1850m. , walk along the new path now constructed along the N side of the barrage and at the far end reach the deserted hamlet of Prarayer (2005m.) (1 h.). From here follow the clearly marked path on the L side of the Buthier river to a bridge somewhat above the junction bridge (2021m.) with the stream coming down from the Braoulè glacier cwm to the N. Do not cross this second bridge to the other side of the river (old route), despite the fact that all paths shown on maps indicate you should. A few m. before the bridge turn L up a small but clear track with red waymarks which takes you up the L side of the stream, as before. The path is later followed with numerous cairns which peter out on moraines higher up. The hut is soon visible a long way off. Continue by a vague track which later works further away from the river. Gradually in barely recognisable zigzags it climbs L across several streams coming down from the rock barrier supporting the higher Alpe de Tsa de Tsan. Keep working up to the N, tedious, till the huge moraine crest is reached. Follow this to nearly its end (2715m.) against rocks. Now traverse R, steep and loose at first below these rocks and contour R on to the Tsa de Tsan glacier, which is crossed, icy and loose stones, to the opposite W side. Above, the moraine on which the hut stands is reached at an obvious gap a short distance below the hut, by climbing a loose and unpleasant gully containing a stream (4 h. from Prarayer, 5 h. from Place Moulin).

The original approach by crossing the bridge mentioned above and following terraces above the R side of the river is still waymarked with paint and cairns. However it is impossible to recross the river, either at pt. 2250m. or near pt. 2318m. (original bridges washed away once too often to be replaced). Therefore by this route you must climb on to the lower tongue of the Grandes Murailles glacier up to the R (E). Crossing this in 1971 involved about 50m. of steep ice climbing, requiring crampons and step cutting, in order to rejoin the original moraine track on this R side of the river.

PART III

Weissgrat

Neues Weisstor to Jägerjoch

WEISSGRAT

General name for the frontier ridge contained between the Neues Weisstor (pass) at the N end and the Jägerjoch at S end. The highest and easily the most frequented summit in the first sec- tion is the Cima di Jazzi (3803m.). See below. Contrasting with the huge glacier snowfields covering the W (Swiss) side, the E (Italian) side is mostly rock in prominent spurs divided by small glaciers. This side is altogether more serious for climbing than the Swiss.

NEUES WEISSTOR (PASS) 3499m.

In the Weissgrat, between the Neue Weisstorspitze (Punte del Neues Weisstor) and the Cima di Jazzi. The most direct and easiest pass between Zermatt and Macugnaga, at the lowest point in this section of the frontier ridge. The Zermatt side consists of huge uneven glacier slopes with several but not ser- ious crevasse zones, F+. The Italian side is blocked by a large cornice, below which is a somewhat dangerous couloir. This "direct" route is not used today, for which there is a conven- ient variant (Passage Jacchini), PD-.
    First tourist traverse: Walters and Blomfield with J. and S. Zumtaugwald, 29 August, 1856.

117. Zermatt side. Start either from the Fluhalp hotel or from the top of the Stockhorn cableway. The former is longer and bedevilled by masked crevasses between 3000-3200m. Other- wise it is straightforward and with intelligent use of the map requires no special directions. In good snow conditions one of the finest glacier tours in the Alps, recommended. Reach the frontier somewhat L(N) of the lowest point of the pass, at the top of the first low shoulder on the ridge rising to the Neue Weisstorspitze (about 4h. from Fluhalp, $2\frac{1}{4}$h. in descent).

From the Stockhorn terminus follow the easy ridge to the Stockhorn and continue down to the Stockhornpass (3394m.) (1 h.). Continue up the broad glacier spur to the SE, and only at c. 3500m. leave it and contour slopes to the E and N in order to round the NW glacier shoulder of the Cima di Jazzi at c. 3600m. This high contouring movement avoids large crevasses lower down. On the N side snow slope of this mountain, drop down before turning E(R) to reach the pass ($1\frac{1}{2}$h., $2\frac{1}{2}$h. from Stockhorn terminus, about same time in reverse direction).

118. Italian side. Passage Jacchini. From the Eugenio Sella hut return along the hut approach for c. 50m. to a track forking R and leading on to a buttress overlooking the hut to the WNW. This buttress marks the S edge of the Roffel glacier and the track on it is clearly marked on map. Climb along the shoulder crest of the buttress, beside the glacier, to where the track is lost in rocks and snow. Continue in the same direction, either on the buttress or glacier slopes just to the R. A steeper snow slope leads to a snow shoulder, which is climbed to mid-height. Now slant L in the direction of the pass; cross a natural break in the rocks and using ledges and terraces reach the frontier ridge immediately above and to the R of the lowest point of the pass. From here descend a short snow slope to the pass ($1\frac{1}{2}$h., 1 h. in descent).

CIMA DI JAZZI 3803m.

Ital: Cima di Iazzi. The highest mtn. on the frontier ridge

between the Strahlhorn and Monte Rosa, formerly a popular training exercise from Zermatt but now climbed less frequently. A fairly popular spring skiing expedition. The Ital. side provides better climbing and has a larger following among climbers visiting Macugnaga.

First recorded tourist ascent: G. M. Sykes with M. Zumtaugwald, August, 1851. First winter and ski ascent: V. de Beauclair and A. Weber with guides, January, 1902.

<u>Swiss (North-West) Side.</u> From Zermatt, approaches up the Gorner or Findelen glaciers can be made almost anywhere, starting from the Fluhalp hotel or Monte Rosa hut. However, these give lengthy glacier excursions, crevassed but generally free of obstacles, and the shortest approach with cableway assistance is described below. F. First ascensionists.

119. Zermatt - Gornergrat - Stockhorn cableway terminus. From here go along the ridge easily to the Stockhorn (3532m.), and continue in the same direction to the Stockhornpass (3394m.) (1 h.). Now keep to the broad glacier hump rising SE towards the Torre di Castelfranco, to about the 3500m. contour. Now cross the N side of the glacier hump, contouring at this level to the E and N in order to reach the broad NW glacier spur of the Cima di Jazzi. To this point the way corresponds with Routes 91, 117. Now climb straight up the NW spur to the summit (3 h. from Stockhorn cableway terminus).

<u>North-West Spur (from Italian side).</u> A popular climb from the Eugenio Sella hut. More ascents or descents of the mtn. are made by this route than all others put together. PD-.

120. From the Eugenio Sella hut reach the Neues Weisstor (pass) by Route 118 (1½ h.). Contour the almost level glacier due W and after 15 min. rise SW and make a circle round R (SE) so as to reach the broad back of the NW spur (crevasses). Continue up the spur to the summit (1¼ h., 2¾ h. from E. Sella hut).

121. <u>North-East Ridge</u>. A rarely followed but more direct alternative to Route 120. This snow ridge rising above the Neues Weisstor (pass) is easy except for a step at 3660m., which is often steep ice and broken by the sérac barrier which extends to its R. PD-/AD. 1-2 h. from pass.

<u>East-North-East Side</u>. The classic Italian route, quite direct, giving steeper climbing on snow or ice than the normal routes. Interesting but some stonefall danger. PD+. First ascent: A. A. Pearson with A. Lochmatter and a porter, 16 August, 1874.

122. From the Eugenio Sella hut descend the hut approach path for a few min. until it is possible to traverse W under the rock barrier towards the couloir of the Neues Weisstor. Pass the foot of a rock rib (2984m.) and climb towards the couloir entrance. On your L is the sérac barrier forming the lower edge of the hanging Iazzi glacier. Climb on snow and loose rock to the rib marking the L side of the couloir above its entrance, then move L (SW) along the base of rocks which start to form the upper edge of the Iazzi glacier. A little further up the glacier, climb R above the lower rock base and keep close to the rock wall under the NE ridge of the mtn. Now the glacier becomes a narrow and often icy terrace, possibly cut by crevasses, suspended between the retaining wall and a fairly large rognon/barrier with séracs below, to your L. Cross this sloping glacier terrace keeping close to the rocks on the R. At its upper end continue up a fairly steep snow/ice slope to the narrow summit rock band which is surmounted by a steep-sided corniced ridge. Cross a bergschrund and slant L up steep snow, utilising rocks on the L as necessary, in order to reach the summit snow cap at the extreme L(S) side, where the cornice is usually negligible (3 h. from hut).

123.<u>South-East Ridge.</u> Topographically an enormous promontory, rising for approx. 1600m. above Alpe Fillar. Its long crest was followed direct for the first time in 1959 and gives uneven climbing from II to IV with pegs over many steps up to pt. 3347m., above which the climbing is fairly easy. All ascents have taken two days. Climbed in winter, January, 1967 (3 days). The promontory has a secondary branch running E from pt. 3347m. on the main crest. This secondary ridge and the upper part of the main crest above pt. 3347m. was first climbed to the summit by C. E. Mathews with Melchior Anderegg, 11 August, 1872.

<u>South Face Ramp.</u> The S face of the mtn. is entirely of rock, cut by narrow slanting snowband ledges. A direct route, crossing the ramp high up, was made by G. Vitale and A. Bonacossa in 1946 at about grade III+. The rock is fairly good. The ramp line crosses the face from L to R to join the SE ridge not far above pt. 3347m. The Macugnaga guides say it is the best route on this side of the mtn. PD+. First ascent: F. and G. Spezia with J. B. Andenmatten and G. Burgener, 27 August, 1874.

124. From the Belloni biv. cross grass and stone slopes to the NW and pass through a break in a low rock barrier to reach the S edge of the Castelfranco glacier. Traverse the glacier (crevasses possible) to the foot of the large rock island dividing the glacier into two branches. Climb the N branch which is a large glacier couloir, narrowing higher up where it is known as the Tuckett Couloir, leading to the frontier ridge depression of the Altes Weisstor N pass (3632m.). Only go up the glacier to a point level with the top of the rock island, then traverse up R to the foot of the S face at this point, where a small snow inlet is formed. Just above the inlet a large snow/scree terrace rises diagonally R into the face. Follow this to where it narrows and becomes vague. Continue in the same line across the face, below steep rock rising towards the summit. Climb from one narrow ledge running R to another with short pitches between them, and by an almost horizontal line finish more steeply on the SE ridge at a small snow shoulder (c. 3450m.) (3 h.). Now go up the L side of the SE ridge on snow until it is better to follow the crest on rocks to a junction with the frontier ridge (3705m. IGM) due S of the summit. Continue up the latter ridge on mixed ground to the summit (2 h., 5 h. from Belloni biv.).

TORRE DI CASTELFRANCO 3628.8m. 3632m.

This snow cap (3632m.), as seen from the snowfields of the Weissgrat on the Swiss side of the frontier ridge, is fairly insignificant and corresponds with the adjoining N col of the Altes Weisstor (see below). From the snow cap, across the slightly lower saddle marking the actual N col, lies the head of the rock ridge (3628.8m.) which the Italians call the Torre. The ridge is in fact the safest and surest way of crossing the Altes Weisstor. The rock island on Route 124 is a prelude to this ridge which is about PD+.

ALTES WEISSTOR (PASS)

Three poorly defined cols in a semi-circular section of the frontier ridge. On the Swiss side all three can be reached easily over the snowfields of the Weissgrat. On the Italian side the approaches are separate and lie in distinct couloirs with something of a reputation. All are dangerous.

From N to S the topography can be defined as follows: N col, adjoining the snow cap of the Torre di Castelfranco (3632m, 3595m. TCI). Its Italian side is marked by the Tuckett Couloir which divides into two branches high up. Normally the R-hand one has been climbed. Steep snow or ice, quite exposed to stonefall, AD. Next, Central col (3684m.) whose Tyndall Couloir marks the L(S) side of the Torre di Castelfranco ridge (see above). The couloir is a narrow ice gutter which in good conditions becomes entirely rock. Serious stonefall. The Central col is followed by a snow hump on the main ridge, called Cima Brioschi (3642m.). Its conspicuous Italian E spur at the L side of the E face gives a modern rock climb at grade V. S of this comes the S col (3560m.), the lowest depression of the three and the one marked on most maps as the true pass.

Yet it is probably the most dangerous crossing point of the three. The Italian side is approached from the foot of the central Tyndall Couloir, L-wards up a large snow ramp into a narrow sinuous gutter (Ellerman Couloir).

None of these cols is used much if at all today. N col: F. F. Tuckett and C. H. and W. F. Fox with J. J. Bennen, P. Perren, J. A. Andenmatten and B. Burgener, 20 June 1861. Central col: John Tyndall with J. J. Bennen and J. B. Andenmatten, August, 1861. S col: J. R. Ellerman with L. Zurbriggen, 10 July, 1882.

GROSSES FILLARHORN 3676m.

Ital: Gran Fillar. A prominent snow cap on the frontier ridge just S of the Altes Weisstor passes. The Italian side is marked by a huge E spur and its S side in the summit line forms an impressive rockface. Several routes of D and TD have been made in recent times on the latter face, while the E spur is normally approached up its N flank from the Belloni biv., giving climbing at AD standard.

KLEINES FILLARHORN 3621m.

Ital: Piccolo Fillar. A smaller snow cap on the frontier ridge S of the Grosses Fillarhorn. An exceptionally fine climb on good rock at TD+ was made up its well defined E spur (500m.) by M. Bisaccia and M. Bramanti, 30 August, 1959. This route is reached from the Belloni biv. directly up the Piccolo Fillar glacier.

FILLARJOCH 3586m.

Ital: Colle Fillar. Between the Kl. Fillarhorn and Jägerhorn. The rock wall on the Ital. side gives climbing at grade III and and IV. Not used as a pass as such. Crossed by W. M. Conway with L. Zurbriggen, 3 July, 1882.

JÄGERHORN 3969.6m.

In this direction the last and highest summit of the Weissgrat but dwarfed by proximity to the Nordend of the mighty Monte Rosa. Rarely if ever climbed for itself from the comparatively easy Swiss side although its summit must be visited not infrequently by parties using the Gallarate biv. (q. v.) which is situated just below the summit. The summit consists of twin rock prongs, separated by a deep gap. The most northerly, furthest from the biv., is the highest and quite awkward to attain from the lower. The mtn. has a following on the Italian (Macugnaga) side. See Route 90 for easiest approach from Swiss side (Jägerjoch). First ascent: C. E. Mathews and F. Morshead with Chr. Almer and A. Maurer, 17 July, 1867.

Jägerrücken (Italian) Route. This is the huge E spur of the mtn. which bends NE in its lower section. The route corresponds exactly with the approach on this side to the Jägerjoch. It is climbed from the Belloni biv. fairly often. The top part of the spur is very steep and is normally avoided by traversing L on to the S ridge (normal Swiss route to Gallarate biv.) between the Jägerjoch and summit. PD+. First ascensionists.

125. From the Belloni biv. descend a little to the S then cross scree and rocks to reach rubble at the bottom of the Piccolo Fillar glacier. Climb the R side of the glacier, sometimes with complications in getting past this N side of the icefall at c. 2700m. Continue up the R-hand glacier trough till above the level of the central crevasse zones then turn S and cross the glacier snowfields at c. 2850m. Contour round and rise to join the L enclosing ridge of the Jägerrücken at the point where it is level with the glacier snows, c. 2980m. Now climb the ridge of the Jägerrücken, keeping to the rock crest where possible and turning a few short steps on the L side. Higher up is mixed ground and short narrow snow crests. About 100m. below the summit climb out L and make a rising traverse across a shoulder into a couloir. Cross it and continue the traverse on steep mixed ground, either joining the Jägerjoch straight ahead or climbing more directly to reach the S ridge of the mtn. above the col. Then continue as for Route 90 past the Gallarate biv. to the summit (about 6 h. from Belloni biv.).

JÄGERJOCH 3913m.

Between the Jägerhorn and Nordend. Rarely used as a pass from Zermatt to Macugnaga but both sides are climbed often enough to reach the Jägerhorn and Nordend. For Swiss side see Route 90. For Italian side see Route 125. First traversed by Jägerhorn (q. v.) first ascensionists party.

STOCKHORN 3532m.

Many years ago one of the traditional training walks from Zermatt, now almost reached by the Stockhorn cableway (3405m.), from which the summit is a mere 30 min. walking away. Climbed by Gottlieb Studer, 11 July, 1840.

RIFFELHORN 2927.5m.

Due to many protests LK has put the double "ff" back into the spelling on all editions of the 25m. and 50m. maps dated after 1970. Undoubtedly the most climbed upon hunk of rock in the Zermatt neighbourhood, an elongated spur of serpentine situated above the Gorner glacier and behind Rotboden station on the Gornergrat railway. All the main routes are well scratched.

Nowadays the mtn. is not used for training purposes in the accepted sense, rather for teaching people the art of rock climbing. The N side (Rotboden) climbs are short, up to 150m., the S side (Gorner) are quite long, up to 400m., but only the upper part of the face is continuously steep.

The normal route takes the short Skyline (E) ridge (III, direct), or an easier variant on its flank (30 min. to 1 h. according to the pitches you fancy). The W ridge is dull (II). There are face climbs on the N side (III), not particularly interesting, and a great variety of routes on the S side, in a series of gullies and on dividing buttresses. You can reach this face easily from the Riffelberg hotel (station) by a traverse path SW and SE, across the W ridge, then by ledges leading across the face at the base of the steep part.

The important routes on the S face are from L to R (some starts are paint-marked with their names): Matterhorn Couloir (IV), Grogan Couloir (III+), Über das Eck (III+), Glacier Couloir (III+), Über die Kante (IV), Biner Couloir (IV+), Thermometer Couloir (III+).

First known tourist ascent: J. Barwell, W. and V. Smith and Lushington with guides, 8 August, 1842.

PIZZO BIANCO 3215m.

A huge and fairly complex mtn. standing directly above Macugnaga and opposite the Monte Moropass. It commands the most superb view of the E face of Monte Rosa. Very much the training peak par excellence for Macugnaga, climbed frequently, and facilitated today by the new cableway to the grassy terraces (2093m.) above Alpe Rosareccio. The mtn. has several good and hard technical rock routes involving starts from remote points. The description below is of the normal and easiest route from Macugnaga.

First ascent: not traced. Attempted by H. B. de Saussure as early as 1789. The highest pt. was certainly reached before 1870.

North Side. A rough walk, on snow to finish. F. Recommended.

126. From the P. Bianco cableway terminus (2093m.) follow a small track S and SE over grass then scree towards the NE ridge of the mtn. The track eventually disappears. Aim for a large gangway slanting R up a rock barrier at c. 2500m. Climb this then bear L along the top of the barrier on a large sloping scree terrace which leads to the NE ridge at c. 2750m. This pt. is some distance further along the ridge than its butt end marked pt. 2750m. which precedes the minor P. Nero (2738m.). Now climb the broad easy ridge on scree and rocks to below a shoulder at c. 3100m. From here make a slightly rising traverse on scree or snow to the L and so turn this shoulder and the higher forepeak (3180m.) of the mtn. on the E. side. Then scramble over rocks and snow to the R and reach a saddle in the ridge between the forepeak and summit. Finish up the L side of a short snow ridge to the top (4 h. from cableway terminus, 2 h. in descent).

PART IV

Monte Rosa

Jägerjoch to Lisjoch

MONTE ROSA GROUP

The limits of this group are the Jägerjoch (N) and Lisjoch (S).
It is the most complex mtn. group in the Pennine Alps guidebook region. Besides revealing the second highest peak in the
Alps, this group embraces a number of peaks of similar altitude so that it really forms the highest massif in Europe. Seen
from the Gornergrat above Zermatt, the group is oversimplified
and is one of the most picturesque and photographed sights in
the Alps. From Macugnaga it presents an impressively beautiful
E face which offers the climber some of the longest mixed
routes and ice climbs of a high standard in the Alps. The
southern flank, above Alagna and S. Giacomo, is less outstanding, with rounded profiles but the climbing is nonetheless
popular and good.

From N to S the main peaks are: Nordend (4609m.), Grenzgipfel (4596m.), Dufourspitze (4634m.), Zumsteinspitze
(4563m.), Signalkuppe or Punta Gnifetti (4554m.), Parrotspitze
(4432m.), Ludwigshöhe (4341m.) and Pyramide Vincent
(4215m.). There are other lesser summits of 4000m.

Several peaks are often climbed together as simple traverses.
Only the Nordend and Dufourspitze are frequently climbed for
themselves although the Signalkuppe is often visited in the course
of staying a night in its summit hut. For this guidebook special
climbs of all grades and traverses are selected on a wide basis
of popularity, and on the whole they represent the best combinations among many routes and variations available in the
entire group.

NORDEND 4609m.

After the Dufourspitze this is the most important peak of the
Monte Rosa group, although the Italians and keen ice climbers
might contest this in favour of the fine collection of climbs on
the Signalkuppe. It forms a glacier shoulder from which the

N end of the group plunges to the Jägerjoch. Owing to its detached position, the peak is not often included in a traverse with other summits in the group. Well worth climbing on its own account. The frontier ridge, running to a junction with the Dufourspitze spur, is a fine snow crest with huge cornices. All the routes are attractive and in a magnificent setting.

First ascent: T. F. and E. N. Buxton and J. J. Cowell with M. Payot, 26 August, 1861. First ski ascent: A. Mazlam with J. Knubel, May, 1913. First winter ascent: J. Dubois and A. Schaller, 4 March, 1920.

<u>South-South-West Ridge (from Silbersattel)</u>. The ordinary route on the Swiss side of the mtn., a popular climb which can be combined with the Dufourspitze without incurring an unduly long day. In this case always climb the Nordend first because the descent from the latter can be tricky. The bergschrund below the Silbersattel can be a serious problem in descent and some parties have only got over it by driving in a wooden stake for abseiling. The frontier ridge can be icy and normally has a huge cornice. PD. One correspondent in 1972 reported, remarkably, no cornice at all. First ascensionists.

127. From the Monte Rosa hut follow Route 131 as for the Dufourspitze to a riser in the Monte Rosa glacier at c. 4000m. The route to the Dufourspitze slants R up the riser. Instead, cross the broad glacier basin to the L (SE) and work towards the large rock buttress of the Nordend, base pt. 4200m. Pass this about 200m. to the R and climb the steeper section of the glacier between the Nordend and Dufourspitze. Avoid several big crevasses and reach an upper plateau which is crossed SE to the foot of the Silbersattel, under the rocks of the Grenzgipfel. Cross a large bergschrund (see preamble comments) and climb a short snow/ice slope to the saddle (4515m.) (5 h.). Now follow the fine snow/ice ridge with big cornices on R to some rocks below the summit. Keep L on a steep slope, delicate, to avoid the cornices, and finish up the rocks (1-2 h., 6-7 h. from Monte Rosa hut).

MONTE ROSA from NW

Lisjoch

Grenz glacier

94

Dufourspitze sattel

131

127

Nordend

M. ROSA HUT

90

3074

Riffelhorn

3995

Gorner glacier

Matterhorn Couloir

North-East Ridge (Cresta di Santa Caterina). Above the Jägerjoch this ridge seems to leap in one step to the glacier shoulder
(4355m.) of the Nordend. The ridge is a superb route on excellent rock, classic, fairly short in itself but at great altitude
and in a remote setting. There are short delicate sections on
snow or ice. Climbing the upper glacier shoulder is longer
and steeper than it looks. The ridge is in four sections, of
which the first and third are near-vertical. Peg belays in place,
and pegs in place for peg moves which are not strictly necessary.
D+, pitches of IV, IV+ and one of borderline V. Col to shoulder,
450m., climbing fairly sustained. 700m. total to summit.
Climbed about a dozen times up to 1945 and frequently since
then. The ridge is a favourite with Zermatt guides if they can
find the clients. Descended by W. Flender with H. Burgener
and F. Furrer, 5 September, 1899. Climbed by V. J. E. Ryan
with F. and J. Lochmatter, July, 1906. Climbed guideless by
several British parties in the early 1950s. First winter ascent:
L. Bettineschi, C. and F. Jacchini, M. Pala and N. Pironi,
10-11 February, 1967. First solo ascent: R. Bex, 17 August
1973.

128. From the Gallarate biv. descend to the Jägerjoch (Route 90)
(15 min.) and from this col climb snow and broken rocks to
the foot of the first vertical step. Climb on the R side of the
ridge by a series of obvious cracks and ledges in a couloir
formation trending R (IV, delicate). These lead in the same
line, R-wards, to two large open chimneys with bulges. Climb
them turning the bulges on the R (V-) and reach an easy gang -
way running R. Follow this to continuation slabs and cracks at
a high angle. Climb these for 30m. (IV+), stance, and continue
up a wide chimney/crack for 25m. (IV+) till you can move R
across and up a slab (IV+) to a large ledge where the angle
eases. This first section is steep and exposed throughout,
100m. Do not move L to the ridge crest.
Straight above the ledge climb a wall of 15m. from L to R,

using toe ledges (IV) and reach broken rocks which are taken up the L side of a couloir (IV) to a band of icy slabs rising for 120m. to an overhang. Climb this section (IV in good conditions) with little protection and very difficult when badly verglassed to a stance below the overhang. Now trend L up cracks to the ridge crest (III+). Climb the crest strenuously up the obvious prow (25m., IV), finishing with a crack on the R (10m., (III+). An easy angled ice crest and rocks leads in 120m. to the last pitch which is climbed from L to R then straight up by cracks (III). Finish on a ledge which runs L to the top of pt. 4355m. (5 h.).

Now climb the long upper snowfield to the top of the Nordend ($1\frac{1}{2}$-2 h., $7\frac{1}{2}$ h. on average to summit from biv. hut).

129 North Pillar. This broad buttress above the Gorner glacier, passed by Route 90, is marked at its top by pt. 3985m. It has a well defined pillar edge slanting down R (NW). The extreme L side of the buttress was climbed by T. Graham Brown with Alex. Graven and A. Aufdenblatten, 14 July, 1933 at little more than AD standard. A more direct line on this side, finishing up the easier upper section of the pillar edge (TD) was made in 1944. This somewhat unimportant buttress came into the news again when a Polish party climbed the pillar edge directly from the bottom, giving a route, not entirely new, of 550m. at TD+ standard with pitches of V+ and A1. H. Furmanik, A. Tarnawski and A. Zysak, 21-23 August, 1969 (two bivouacs).

East Face (Via Brioschi). On the whole this is the safest of all routes on the E face of Monte Rosa, being the least exposed to long-run avalanches. However small avalanches on the route are not uncommon even in good conditions. Whereas it is a fairly good line it is not particularly elegant. The technical difficulties are not great (II+ max on rock), but the snow/ice problems are sometimes very serious and time consuming.

About 30 ascents per annum at present, which is something less than half the number recorded for its more famous and neighbouring Marinelli Couloir route. Macugnaga guides rate the lower rock section as only a little harder than the key pitches of the Matterhorn Hörnli ridge, but then these guides regard the latter pitches as grade III, when they are II by modern British standards. One British party correspondent who made the ascent in 7 h. in excellent conditions rated the route as AD- .

Looking at the face below the Nordend the line of the route is marked by a rock rib which borders the L side of a long couloir, coming down from a point about 150m. R (N) of the summit. This rib is above and slightly R of the Crestone Marinelli, itself R of the Marinelli Couloir. Optimum conditions are a fine cold night and a good covering of frozen snow on the icy upper sections of the climb and snow-free rocks on the lower section. Virtually used as a "voie normale" by some Italian parties. Serious, AD+, 1100m. from bergschrund to summit.

First ascent: L. Brioschi with F. and A. Imseng, July, 1876. One of the most notable Alpine accomplishments at this date. First British ascent: C. S. Houston and T. Graham Brown with Alex. Graven and T. Biner, 25 July, 1935. First British guideless ascent traced: R. L. B. Colledge, D. Davis and F. A. Smith, 31 July, 1953. First winter ascent: T. Micotti, G. Rognoni, P. Sartor and P. Signini, 11-13 February, 1967.

130. From the Marinelli hut go a few steps along the little track leading to the Marinelli Couloir, then climb straight up rocks to reach a couloir which leads to the tiny Nordend glacier. Climb this glacier, easy-angled and narrow but crevassed by its L side. Near the top slant R and arrive below the main rock rib which marks the general line of ascent ($1\frac{1}{2}$ h.). Cross the bergschrund, often large and awkward, somewhat R of the lowest rock toe, then slant L up snow or ice to reach the crest of the rib. Continue up the rib by climbing on its L(S) flank,

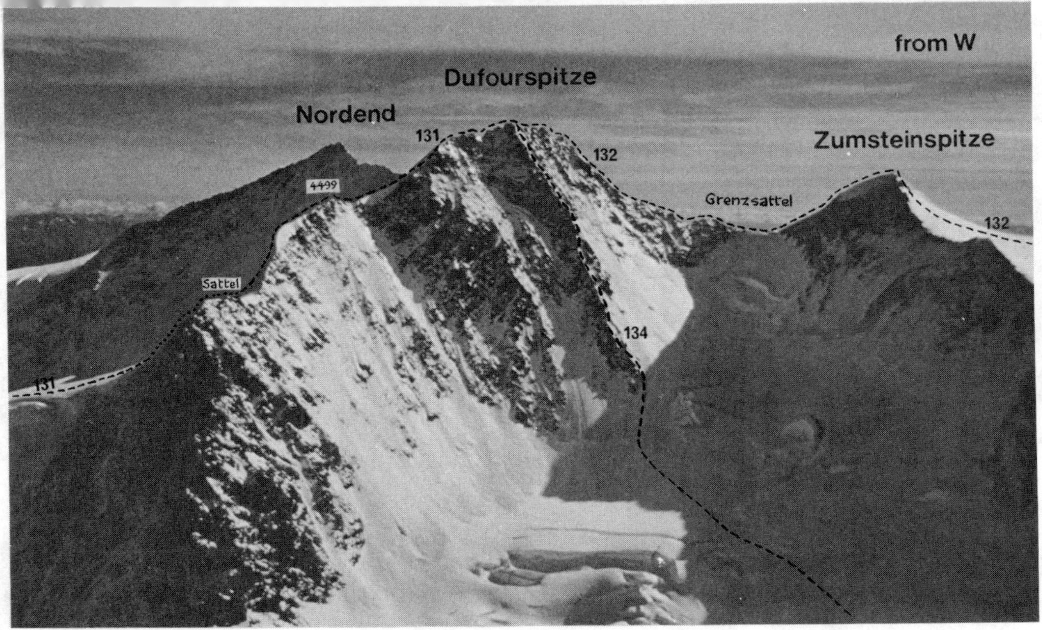

from W

Zumsteinspitze

Dufourspitze

Nordend

Grenzsattel

132

132

131

134

131

4499

Sattel

131

then follow the crest which becomes vague and featureless. This gives monotonous climbing with a few steeper pitches in cracks. Reach a sloping snow shoulder, above which the rib merges into the face of the mtn. Trend R up snow and a steep wall to reach a large, steep and L slanting snow slope (45°) called the Linceul. Climb the L edge of the slope, using a narrow snow crest. From the highest point of the Linceul, climb a sometimes near-vertical snow/ice funnel and enter a very steep and narrow couloir (crux). Go up its icy bed with rocks to help to the N ridge, about 10 min. (cornices) from the summit (7-8 h.). Allow 8-12 h. from hut to summit.

East Face. Other routes. To the L of Via Brioschi are the two so-called direct routes. Both start up the main rib in the summit line above the L edge of the Nordend glacier. At mid-height the original route, Via Restelli, bears R away from steep rocks into a couloir to continue higher up by a narrow rock ridge before joining steep mixed ground on the summit slopes to finish on the ridge where Via Brioschi exits. Exposed to falling stones and ice. D. C. Restelli with M. Zurbriggen and L. Burgener, 10 September, 1893. Rarely repeated. Still more difficult and direct, Via Diretta climbs the steep rocks avoided by Via Restelli along the summit rib line, with pitches of V and very difficult mixed terrain to finish exactly at the summit. TD-. E. Ranzoni, F. and C. Jacchini, 18 September, 1949. Second ascent (solo): A. Gardin in 10 h. from Marinelli hut, 24 October, 1971.

Two routes have also been made to the R of Via Brioschi, which are very dangerous.

SILBERSATTEL 4515m.

Ital: Sella d'Argento. The snow saddle between the Nordend and Grenzgipfel. Its W (Swiss) side is reached by Route 127.

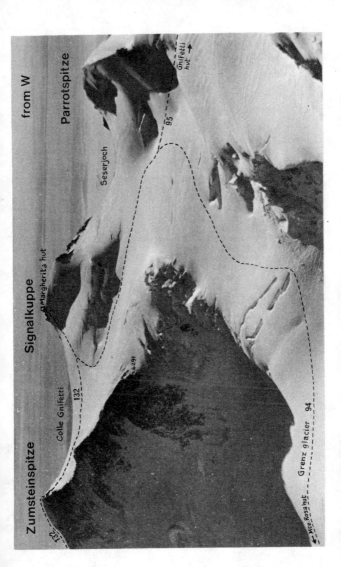

Zumsteinspitze   Signalkuppe   from W

Parrotspitze

Colle Gnifetti

Margherita hut

Seserjoch

Gnifetti hut →

132

133

95

94

Grenz glacier

Mte Rosa hut

The Italian side is essentially the same as the Marinelli Couloir route (q. v.), although the final slope section below the saddle is steeper than most other parts of the couloir and has not been tackled on this line often.

DUFOURSPITZE 4634m.

The highest point in Switzerland, situated on a rock spur extending W from the backbone of the Monte Rosa group. The spur meets the ridge at a mere shoulder, the true Grenzgipfel (4596m.). Here the spur rises to the false Grenzgipfel (4618m.), then to the Ostspitze (c. 4630m.) and finally to the Dufourspitze. Further W the spur drops to a prominent saddle, called Sattel (4359m.), before it drops down steeply (rock) to the Grenz glacier. This spur is a mtn. in itself and the one regarded as Monte Rosa by Zermatt clientele. Even so we have to consider other parts of the Monte Rosa group which are often climbed before the Dufourspitze is reached. In practice, the topography is fairly simple. In the following descriptions traverse connections are given separately with appropriate cross references. Probably the most frequented big mtn. in the Pennine Alps.
 First ascent: J. G. and C. Smyth and E. J. Stephenson with U. Lauener, J. and M. Zumtaugwald, 1 August, 1855. First winter ascent: V. Sella with J. J. and D. Maquignaz, 26 January, 1884. First ski ascent: O. Schuster with H. Moser, 23 March, 1898.

<u>North-West Flank and West Ridge (Swiss Route)</u>. One of the most frequented snow climbs in the Alps, a beaten trail in summer and indicated as such on the map. The final rock ridge is welcome after the long snow slopes below. Crevasses should not be underestimated. F+. First ascensionists.

131. From the Monte Rosa hut follow the main footpath winding among rounded rocks in the open valley behind the lateral moraine of the Grenz glacier. Shortly after 3000m. (large cairns) the path forks. Take the more prominent L branch and climb scree and rocks to snow patches beside the Monte Rosa glacier. So far lots of cairns and false trails! ($1\frac{1}{2}$ h.). Climb snow between two low relief rock arms (3303m. and 3277.3m.), up to a vague snow spur which is a feature of the R side of the

from S

Dufourspitze

Zumsteinspitze

131

4499

134

132

1491

132

Zumsteinhütte

94

Monte Rosa hut

Monte Rosa glacier. It is really the curved edge of a long escarpment above the Grenz glacier, and in ascent one should keep to the L of it. Climb E and SE through a crevassed zone, then in a steeper glacier cwm, passing pt. 3827m. on your L. Then go up steeper slopes in a continuation cwm and keep to the general line of its bed. Arrive at the foot of a riser (4000m.), which is climbed slanting R to a gentle slope (crevasses) then a steeper one approaching the Sattel. Cross a bergschrund, usually easy, and reach the saddle somewhat L of its lowest point by a steep snow/ice slope (4359m.) ($2\frac{3}{4}$ h.). Climb a narrowing snow slope to where the ridge develops, snow and rocks at first, then rocks with teeth and gaps. In good conditions these can be climbed or turned at will. The final rock crest is narrow. Avoid a step by moving L into a short couloir, from the top of which (gap) a few rocks lead to a chimney then the summit ($1\frac{1}{4}$ h., $5\frac{1}{2}$ h., allow 6 h. from hut).

<u>Ridge to Grenzgipfel, Zumsteinspitze and Signalkuppe (Italian Route).</u> This constitutes a traverse of Monte Rosa, the most popular of all, from the Monte Rosa hut to the Margherita hut on the Signalkuppe. In reverse it is the normal Italian route. A pleasant outing. PD-. First done in two parts between 1872 and 1882.

132. From the summit of the Dufourspitze (about 6 h. from Monte Rosa hut) climb over various teeth and small towers of good rock on the ridge, without difficulty in good conditions. Drop down and rise a little to the false Grenzgipfel before reaching the Grenzgipfel proper (30 min.). Turn half R (SE) and descend a fairly steep rock crest dropping to the Grenzsattel (4453m.). Lower down avoid the crest by using a loose rock/ice slope on the R. Near the bottom reach an easy snow ridge and the col (30 min.). Now climb the snowy N ridge of the Zumsteinspitze (4563m.), steep and narrow, with a rock outcrop at midheight (30 min.). Descending from this summit towards the

Colle Gnifetti (4452m.) you must take care in cloud to bear R(S). There are large cornices at the snowy edge to the L (SE). From the summit climb down a few rocks to an easy snow slope, safe glissade, running into the head of the snow cwm under the Signalkuppe (15 min.). Then climb a similar slope to the rocks and hut on top of the Signalkuppe (15 min., 2 h. from Dufourspitze, 3 h. in reverse direction).

<u>Nordend - Dufourspitze Ridge</u>. To reach one peak from the other you follow the frontier ridge over the Silbersattel (4515m.) (Route 127) and Grenzgipfel. PD to junction with the first part of Route 132. First ascent: W. Penhall, G. Scriven and F. T. Wethered with F. Imseng, P. J. Truffer, U. Almer and F. Andenmatten, 10 August, 1878.

133. From the lowest point of the Silbersattel climb snow to the R of rocks forming the ridge rising to the Grenzgipfel. This snow becomes a steep icy slope. Climb it to equally steep but sound rocks which lead directly to the Grenzgipfel (45 min.), then as for Route 132 in reverse to the Dufourspitze (30 min., $1\frac{1}{4}$ h. from Silbersattel, $2\frac{1}{4}$ h. from Nordend).

<u>South-South-West Ridge (Cresta Rey)</u>. This ridge is well defined and rises from the glacier bay between the Dufourspitze and and Zumsteinspitze. It finishes exactly at the summit. The ridge gives excellent climbing on steep sound rock with good belays. It is a pity that the approach from the Monte Rosa hut is tedious, but the quality of the climbing when you get there compensates for the glacier trudge. The ridge provides the most direct route from the Gnifetti hut to the Dufourspitze. PD+ with pitches of III. About 500m. from bergschrund to summit. First ascent: E. Hulton with P. Rubi and J. Moser, 20 August, 1874.

DUFOURSPITZE
S face

Ostspitze

False Grenzgipfel

Grenzgipfel

131

134

132

135

134. From the Monte Rosa hut follow Route 94 to c. 4000m. on the Grenz glacier, not far below where you bear R and turn a sérac barrier. Instead, turn N and contour crevassed slopes into the bay below the S side of the Dufourspitze. Go up to the bergschrund (c. 4150m.) directly below the toe of the ridge (4 h.).

Starting from the Gnifetti hut follow Route 95 across the frontier to the head of the Grenz glacier and descend Route 94 to reach the same place ($2\frac{1}{2}$ h.).

Care is required to identify the correct start. The foot of the rib lies somewhat L of a straight line to the summit. Cross the bergschrund and go up an ice slope to the rocks. These are climbed as far as possible on the crest, steep slabs and cracks with plenty of holds and no special difficulty, to the summit (3 h., 7 h. from Monte Rosa hut, $5\frac{1}{2}$ h. from Gnifetti hut).

<u>Marinelli Couloir (East Face)</u>. A famous ice climb with a big reputation largely built on the avalanche risk. Apart from this it is technically interesting and the sort of climb which in good conditions can be done quickly. The face is one of the highest in the Alps, and although you start at 3000m. the vertical interval of serious climbing up to the Grenzgipfel is nearly 1600m. It was during an attempt to make the third ascent in 1881 that the Marinelli party was swept down. The route is less interesting, less difficult in good conditions, less steep and more dangerous than the Via Brioschi on the Nordend. While the couloir itself is merely crossed, the rocks called Imsengrücken, which form the L side in the lower part, are exposed to falling rocks and ice, and to a lesser extent so are the slopes immediately above these rocks. Considering the lack of shelter there is probably no other route in the Alps where the potential objective danger appears to be great which is climbed as frequently as this one. About 80 ascents per annum at present.

Technical difficulties can be greater than the grade applied and the route requires sound judgement in estimating prevailing conditions and above all prudence in setting out not later than midnight under a clear and very cold night sky. The Imsengrücken rocks are not difficult to scale by torchlight. The angle varies between 47 and 55°. AD+, exposed and very open. The upper rocks of the Grenzgipfel are sound (III+) but very difficult when covered with fresh snow.

First ascent: R. and W. M. Pendlebury and C. Taylor with F. Imseng, G. Spechtenhauser and G. Oberto, 22 July, 1872, by a big circuit to the L not followed today. First descent: O. Stein with H. and A. Burgener, 1 September, 1911. First solo ascent: A. Taveggia, 1924, and climbed many times since in this fashion. First winter ascent: L. Bettineschi, F. Jacchini, M. Pala and N. Pironi, 5-6 February, 1965. Climbed previously in winter to the Silbersattel by E. Amossi and O. Elli, 9-11 March, 1953. Descended from the Silbersattel on ski right down to the Belvedere glacier 2300m. below in $2\frac{1}{2}$ h. by Sylvain Saudan, 11 June, 1969. Best time traced from Marinelli hut to summit of Grenzgipfel in normal summer conditions, 5 h. 50 min. Some faster solo ascents have been reported.

135. From the Marinelli hut a small track rises slightly to the edge of the couloir (15 min.). It is advisable to examine this approach and the point at which to cross the couloir in daylight. Generally you should aim to cross in the continuation line of the small track, passing just above a small rock island. The couloir is about 50m. wide and 40° steep at this point. Its slightly convex slope is often corrugated by icy grooves. In normal conditions it can be crossed in 15 min. On the other side climb the Imsengrücken rocks (Crestone Imseng on new maps), easy, in four steps (partial shelter from avalanches), keeping to the R flank near the edge of the couloir. A useful snow/ice rib can be found here and in excellent conditions some

178

parties have made rapid progress in crampons by climbing this edge of the couloir. The rocks gradually merge with the face and peter out (c. 3540m.). It is here that the avalanche danger is greatest. Climb direct, and as quickly as possible, keeping in a line L of the couloir and R of a group of séracs. At this point the slope is very steep and often icy. Reach a point level with the top of the highest séracs, then traverse L and work up a snowband where the angle is more reasonable and where on both sides of it there are steeper ice slopes. Later trend R towards the lowest rocks of the Grenzgipfel, cross two or three bergschrunds, the largest one appearing between 3800-3900m. Above the last one climb an ice slope, 55°, rarely snow, to the rocks (7 h. on average from hut). This section is exposed to stonefall and you should reach the lowest rocks not later than 9 a.m.

Finishing up the rocks which higher up form a buttress to the summit of the Grenzgipfel is the classic exit. It is also the most difficult way, technically. The lower section, a sort of wall, is very steep and quite difficult, but the rocks are sound. It soon leads to the crest of a well defined buttress, and this is climbed direct to the top, 300m. (2 h.). The direct finish is recommended when the rocks are free from snow and when the slopes on either side of the buttress are ice. In excellent snow conditions it can be much quicker to climb slopes L of the buttress. Some distance up, traverse R and reach the crest of the buttress in its upper part. You can also finish by slopes to the R of the buttress and later move L to the Grenzgipfel buttress near its summit - usually much more difficult (9 h. to Grenzgipfel, and another 15-30 min. to Dufourspitze. Average time, 10-12 h.).

Piramide Vincent

Punta Giordani

Parrotspitze

Signalkuppe

S side

P.Vittoria 3435

192

143

139

Indren glacier

Bors glacier

Punta Indren cableway terminus

GRENZSATTEL 4453m.

Between the Grenzgipfel and Zumsteinspitze. Not of any value
as a pass. The Italian side corresponds with most of the Marinelli Couloir. First traverse: Achille Ratti and L. Grasselli
with J. Gadin and A. Proment, 31 July, 1889.

ZUMSTEINSPITZE 4563m.

Ital: Punta Zumstein. A mtn. occasionally climbed for itself
but more often traversed as part of an expedition to reach or
leave the Dufourspitze. See Route 132. The Marinelli Couloir
has sometimes been climbed to reach its NE face which comes
to hand across steep snow/ice slopes below and to the L of the
lowest Grenzgipfel rocks encountered on Route 135. By this
line from the summit, K. Lapuch and M. Oberegger made a
descent from the Zumsteinspitze down the couloir to the Marinelli hut on ski in 2 h. on 20 July, 1969.
  First ascent: J. Zumstein and a large party, 1 August, 1820.
First winter ascent: E. Allegra and guides, 30 March, 1902.

COLLE GNIFETTI 4452m.

A broad snow saddle between the Zumsteinspitze and Signalkuppe. Not of any value as a pass. The Swiss side corresponds
with Route 94 to the Margherita hut. The Italian side corresponds
with the NE face of the Zumsteinspitze (q.v. above). This
side is also an exit for variations to serious routes on the NE
face of the Signalkuppe (see below).

SIGNALKUPPE (PUNTA GNIFETTI) 4554m.

An important mtn. of the Monte Rosa group. The Margherita
hut is on the summit. See Routes 94, 95 and 132. Climbed
frequently for itself by both the easier and harder routes. Its
E ridge is a classic route, still rarely done because of the
long approach. The SE face is one of the least known walls on
a major summit in the Pennine Alps. The NE face is a continuation of the E face of Monte Rosa and provides one of the
finest climbs of its class in the Alps.
  First ascent: G. Gnifetti, J. Farinetti, C. Ferraris, C.
Grober, J. and J. Giordani and porters, 9 August, 1842. First
winter ascent: C. and G. Sella with guides, 18 January, 1886.
On ski: P. Preuss and party, 1912.

<u>East Ridge (Cresta Signal).</u> A route of character in a fine
position forming the L edge of the imposing E face of the Monte
Rosa group. A classic expedition. You have the advantage of
a hut at both ends of the ridge but the Resegotti hut takes some
reaching in the first place. AD, rock fair to good. First
ascent: H. W. Topham with A. Supersaxo and a porter, 28
July, 1887.

136. From the Resegotti hut follow the crest of the easy ridge
to the Colle Signal (3769m.), where the Cresta Signal rises
steeply (30 min.). Climb steep rocks on the crest, turning
difficulties on the L. After a section of whitish rock the ridge
becomes mainly snowy though still mixed with rocks, till another
whitish section leads to a gendarme. Turn this on the L, using
slanting ledges and rejoin the crest behind the gendarme by a
chimney (15 m.). Finish in a small snow gap (1¼ h.). The
gendarme can also be turned on the R. Continue up the steeper
and more difficult rock ridge, over a thin snow/ice crest, then
along a razor edge with a few difficult bits on good rock. Move
to the R side of the ridge, along a series of longitudinal cracks,
then climb a dièdre/chimney to reach a small shoulder on the
ridge at the foot of a large and near-vertical step (2 h.). You
can climb the step direct but it is easier to turn it on the L;
descend slightly along ledges to where you can move on to a
steep snow/ice slope leading to the ridge above the step. The
rocky ridge eases off gradually. Near the top move on to the
glacier plateau adjacent to the Colle Gnifetti and climb an easy
snow slope to the top. Otherwise the last bit of the ridge proper
has a thin gendarme, which is climbed or turned before the top
is reached (2 h., about 6 h. from Resegotti hut).

<u>South-East Face.</u> Several routes have been made on this mainly
rocky wall of 700m. which is contained between the frontier
(S) ridge and Cresta Signal (E) ridge. On the whole the climbing
is exposed to bad stonefall except for the Terazzi route up the

Monte Rosa group E

Ludwigshöhe
Parrotspitze
Signalkuppe
Margherita hut
Zumstein-spitze
Grenzgipfel
Nordend
130

Sesiejoch
Colle Gnifetti
Silber-sattel
Hinter

Canale Sesia
136
135
3806
3480

Terazzi Raduelland
Cresta E (Signal)
Passo Signal
Crestone Imseng
Crestone Zapparoli
137

Roccia
3286
92
Resegotti hut
93
Rocce
Vignè

Roccia (Imseng) Sesia
Vignè glacier
1570

Sesia glacier
(note)

Coolidge 76

MONTE ROSA
NE - E side

Signalkuppe

Zumsteinspitz
Colle Gnifetti

136

Colle Signal

RESEGOTTI
HUT

137

3806

3286

Monte Rosa glacier

Tosengrücken

137

Marinelli

Crestone Marinelli

92

Belvedere

Pedriola
ZAMBONI HUT
Alp

Dufourspitze
127-133
Nordend
128
Linceul
4355
128
GALLARATE
BIVOUAC
130
90
Jägerhorn
3621
Jägerrücken
125
Piccolo Fillar gl.
HUT
Nordend glacier
Belloni
biv.
87
BEDERE
FFA
Collomb 1968
revised 1974

great snow couloir/ramp at the R side of the face (D). Climbs
on this face have only been done a few times.

North-East Face (French Route). A magnificent route at the
L-hand side of the great E face of the Monte Rosa group. The
most important ice climb on this face, the longest and on the
whole the most serious. A prestigious climb comparable in
position, length and difficulty with the Dent d'Hérens North
face. The nearest hut is the Zamboni on Pedriola Alp. Whereas
some parties have started from here most have remarked that
it is normally essential to start from a bivouac on the lower
rocks of the face. Somewhat L of a line directly below the
Signalkuppe summit are two long narrow rock spurs. The foot
of the L-hand one is marked pt. 3286m. The R-hand one is
called the Promontory. R of these is an equally long and parallel
glacier couloir, rising like a ramp in a near-perpendicular
plane towards the summit. It is bounded on the R by a rib of
rocks and ice. Above the ramp, and extending R, is a rock
wall through which the top of the ramp continues as a deep
rock and ice couloir. The rock wall is crowned by a line of
séracs which extends from just below Colle Gnifetti to below
the Zumsteinspitze.

The route followed varies according to conditions. Major
and minor variations have been made on either side of the
original route line, though mostly to the R, and criss-crossing
it. Some of these have been claimed as independent routes,
but only the following can be regarded as separate: the solo
climb by A. Gardin, 19 September, 1971 which keeps more or
less completely L of the original line, and the R-hand face
route by M. Maglioli and G. Mosca with Z. Zurbriggen and
P. Pironi, 24 July, 1933, which starts from the Marinelli hut
and traverses below rib pt. 3806m. to climb the next rib leading to the Colle Gnifetti. The Italians call the French route
(L) and last named 1933 route (R) confusingly the Left and Right

Ribs of the face. In this examination it is worth noting that the first British ascensionists (see below) finished by a central line trending R up the séracs between the two, thereby avoiding the entire upper half of the French route, and near their finish even crossed the 1933 route and exited further R.

In permissible conditions the main part of the face is climbed on one side of the ramp or the other, but if started up the R side the couloir/ramp itself should be crossed L if at all possible to join the original route line. Several variation finishes have been made. There is a fair amount of danger from stonefall and ice avalanches which are the only demerit of the climb. TD, variable and serious snow/ice difficulties and mixed terrain with rock pitches of III/IV, sustained. 1250m. from bergschrund, average angle 52°. Climbed about 30 times to end of 1973.

First ascent: J. Lagarde and L. Devies, 17 July, 1931. First British (7th) ascent: C. J. Mortlock, C. W. F. Noyce and J. R. Sadler, 15-16 August, 1959. First winter ascent: A. Chio and D. Vanini, 26-27 February, 1965. First solo ascent: A. Gogna, 17 June, 1969, in 14 h. to summit from Zamboni hut, and solo in $10\frac{1}{2}$ h. by R. Bez, August, 1972. Climbed by Madame F. Zani with D. Vanini, 3-4 September, 1971.

137. From the Zamboni hut reach the Monte Rosa (Belvedere) glacier as for the approach to the Marinelli hut (Route 89). Climb in the centre of the glacier. There are some large crevasses and wide detours can be necessary. Generally speaking better progress can be made near the R side but here you are exposed to avalanches from the E face above. Higher up keep to the centre where the glacier narrows and steepens. Reach a sort of cul-de-sac (3 h.), trend R over often troublesome crevasses and multiple bergschrunds to the foot of the rocks forming the toe of the double rock spur (stonefall) and climb diagonally R beside the rocks. Cross a double bergschrund and slant R or L to the rock band which extends R from the toe of the Promontory (the R-hand rib of twin spur). Above this band is the foot of the couloir/ramp. You can find a bivouac place on these rocks, somewhat exposed to stonefall ($1\frac{1}{2}$ h., 4 h. from hut). The British party bivouacked safely on rocks below the bergschrunds, at the foot of the Promontory proper, i. e. 150m. lower.

Climb the rock band by a large open couloir (icy) to the R side of the couloir/ramp, somewhat above its foot which hangs above the slanting rock band.

Two possibilities. Make a rising traverse L across the couloir slope to the L side, beside the rocks of the Promontory (stonefall). There climb an ice and rock rib on this L side to reach a steep hump back snow crest rising to the R, which marks the top of the couloir ramp. Or, if the couloir slope is completely ice, climb snow, ice and mainly rocks of a rib marking the R side of the couloir/ramp.

If conditions are good traverse R from the first line up the couloir and to the L of the second line, to reach the central and direct exit couloir. This is steep and difficult with icy rocks and possible ice pitches. You finish up an ice slope to the glacier plateau above the terminal rock wall, from where an easy snow slope leads to the summit. It is possible to descend to the Monte Rosa hut in 3 h.

The first alternative finish, alleged to be easier in the right conditions, is to move L from the hump back snow crest and climb steep snow or ice towards the Cresta Signal ridge. You can then turn the upper rock wall on the L and continue up a snow/ice couloir to the glacier plateau. However, when you have climbed the R side of the couloir/ramp slope another alternative is to climb the rock wall to the R of the central direct finish and find a way through the séracs above. For this at least two lines up the rock wall have been taken, the one furthest R being followed by the British party (10-15 h. from bivouac on rocks).

COLLE (PASSO) SIGNAL 3769m.

A saddle at the foot of the Cresta Signal (E) ridge of the Signal-kuppe. No value as a pass. On the S side access from Alagna is easy but long and corresponds for the most part with Route 92 to the Resegotti hut.

PUNTA TRE AMICI 3727m. IGM

Cima Tre Amici. Valid objections have been raised against the map term "Punta". Great confusion may be caused by this mtn. when consulting LK. For this reason the description of Route 92 to the Resegotti hut ignores the fact that only the lowest of the three summits (3425m.) is mentioned and by implication suggests (as on LK) that this is the highest pt. From pt. 3425m. two further summits are formed along a rising ridge to the W, one before the Resegotti hut (3624m.) as pt. 3620m., and one after as pt. 3727m. before the Colle Signal (3769m.). The whole of the L side of this ridge from below pt. 3425m. is traversed by the aforesaid approach to the Resegotti hut. First ascent: G. Farinetti, A. Grober and G. Prato, 2 September, 1867.

COLLE DELLE LOCCE 3334m.

Between the Pta. Tre Amici and Pta. Grober, a classic glacier pass from Macugnaga to Alagna-Valsesia. In the same scenic class as the Mischabel passes from Saas to Zermatt. Virtually all the ground is covered by approaches to the Resegotti hut, see Routes 92, 93. PD. First traverse: J. A. Hudson and W. E. Hall with F. and A. M. Lochmatter, 12 August, 1864.

PUNTA GROBER (MONTE DELLE LOCCE) 3497m.

A fine secondary mtn. with some following at Macugnaga as a training climb. Fine regional view. Numerous fairly difficult routes of quality have been made on the mtn., very much the preserve of Italian climbers. First ascent: G. Necer and G. Curtonelli, 3 September, 1874.

<u>North-West Ridge (from Colle delle Locce)</u>.   An easy climb reached by a more complex approach up glaciers amid fine scenery, q.v. Routes 92, 93. F. First ascensionists.

138. From the Colle delle Locce (3334m.) climb the broad snow ridge to a rather steeper, short, narrow rock band which is taken direct to a forepeak snow cap. Continue along the almost level snow ridge to the top (20 min. from col).

SESERJOCH 4296m.

Ital: Colle Sesia. A snow saddle between the Signalkuppe and Parrotspitze. No value as a pass. The Swiss side is easily reached from the Monte Rosa and Gnifetti huts approaches to the Margherita hut on the Signalkuppe, and from the col a slightly more sporting way and easy scramble can be made up the frontier ridge to the Signalkuppe summit. The Ital. side of the pass is marked by the Canale Sesia, a huge couloir battered by stonefall and avalanches.

PARROTSPITZE 4432m.

Ital: Punta Parrot. A mtn. of some significance in the Monte Rosa group, easily climbed by a slight diversion of 15-30 min. up the narrow snowy frontier ridge adjoining the approaches from the Monte Rosa and Gnifetti huts to the Margherita hut on the Signalkuppe. By any route thus, F+. The most direct routes from the Valsesia hut are the E spur (British Route), which is reached by a traverse N over mixed ground. The spur is steep and interesting, PD+ (A. W. Moore and H. B. George with Chr. Almer and M. Zumtaugwald, 11 July, 1862). Equally varied and popular from this hut is the S and E spur (Italian Route) which is a L-hand and more direct approach to the British Route, the latter being joined and followed to the frontier ridge which is reached between the Seserjoch and summit, PD+ (E. Canzio, G. Gugliermina and G. Lampugnani, 18 July, 1906). These routes take 7-8 h. from hut. As the Moore party of 1862 did not bother to complete the last 60m. to the summit and crossed the frontier directly into Switzerland the first ascent proper was made by R. J. S. Macdonald, F. C. Grove and M. Woodmass with M. Anderegg and P. Perren, 16 August, 1863.

COLLE DELLE PIODE 4283m.

Marked but not named on LK, a snow saddle between the Parrotspitze and Ludwigshöhe. Not of any value as a pass.

LUDWIGSHÖHE 4341m.

The most westerly summit formed on the frontier ridge of the
Monte Rosa group. Climbed in a few min. by a snow slopes
detour from the Gnifetti - Margherita huts approach, Route 95.
First ascent: Ludwig von Welden and several companions, 25
August, 1822.

ZURBRIGGENJOCH 4272m. IGM

Ital: Colle Zurbriggen. Not marked on LK. A small col between
the Ludwigshöhe and Corno Nero. No value as a pass.

CORNO NERO 4321m.

Schwarzhorn. The name is eclipsed on current LK50 map. A
minor summit formed as the first point on the important ridge
running S into Italy from the Ludwigshöhe. Reached easily by
snow slopes and a short ridge from the Gnifetti-Margherita
hut approach, Route 95. First ascent: M. Maglioni and A. de
Rothschild with P. and N. Knubel, E. Cupelin and porters,
18 August, 1873.

COLLE VINCENT 4087m.

Marked but not named on LK. A prominent saddle between the
Corno Nero and Piramide Vincent. No value as a pass. See
Piramide Vincent below.

PIRAMIDE VINCENT 4215m.

An important and imposing southerly summit of the Monte Rosa
group, climbed frequently from the Gnifetti hut. Piste in season.

NORDEND E side

Grenzgipfel

127

135

R-hand headslope of Marinelli couloir

The face routes and ridges are also climbed regularly and it is an excellent and varied practice ground with steep and serious terrain. First ascent: J. N. Vincent and three others, 5 August, 1819. First winter ascent: A. Mosso and A. Sella with guides, 14 February, 1885. On ski: A. Bonacossa and C. Franchetti, 3 August, 1916.

<u>South-West Ridge</u>. The normal ascent route but not entirely the easiest way up the mtn. Interesting mixed climbing, recommended. PD-. First ascent:: C. Perazzi with P. Maquignaz and A. Welf, 22 July, 1882.

139. From the Gnifetti hut cross the hut promontory NE by a path to the Garstelet glacier and cross the snowfield in the same direction, above and R of the piste leading N to the frontier. Then climb the snowy flank of the SW ridge to its broad crest which is reached below a rocky narrowing. Follow the nice crest on alternate rock and snow to a steep finish best taken direct (2 h. from hut).

<u>Descent by Colle Vincent</u>. Invariably used to return to the Gnifetti hut. F. First used by: A. and H. Schlagintweit with P. Beck, 15 September, 1851.

140. From the summit go down the large rounded snow slope N to the broad saddle of the col in 15 min. From the col continue over snowfields W to join the piste from the Gnifetti hut to the frontier. Descend this without incident to the hut, 30-45 min. (1 h. in descent to hut, 2 h. in ascent to summit).

141. <u>South-West Facet</u>. This facet gives three excellent and varied practice routes for serious climbing. All are about AD+, 350m. from bergschrund (generally easy) to summit, approx. 3 h. climbing. The foot of the face is reached in 20 min. up the snowfield from the Gnifetti hut. From L to R across the narrow facet. (1) Via della Spalla. In the L corner, steep snow/ice to a rock rib marking R edge of big broken buttress

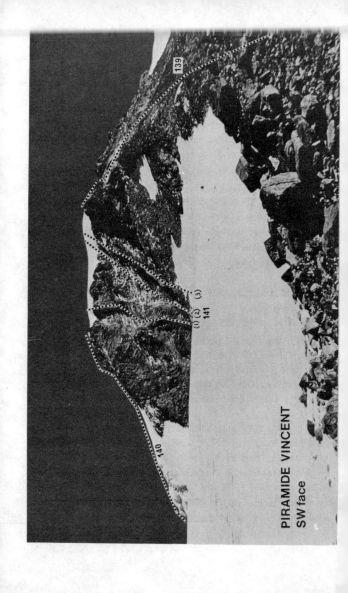

PIRAMIDE VINCENT
SW face

enclosing facet on L. Up this and traverse up R on snow/ice across broad shallow couloir to terminal rock wall. Take this near its L side, close above the snow/ice couloir just quitted and near the top finish diagonally R to summit. (2) Central Couloir. Obvious and steep. Needs good conditions and crampons. (3) Direct Route. A well defined rock rib with snowy bits at R side of facet. Nice slabs and rock step pitches, well protected.

<u>East-South-East Ridge (from Punta Giordani)</u>. The classic route, recommended. PD-. First ascensionists.

142. From the Pta. Giordani (q.v. below) follow the fine snow ridge with cornices on R, turning an outcrop on the L. The ridge soon rises with more rock outcrops to the summit. Climb in a direct line to the top (1-1¼ h.).

PUNTA GIORDANI 4046m.

A prominent and quite individual shoulder of Piramide Vincent. Combed with routes on all sides, as might be expected. First ascent: P. Giordani, 23 July, 1801.

<u>South-West Flank</u>. The normal route from the Gnifetti hut. Piste in season. F. First ascent: G. Calderini and V. Zoppetti with G. Gugliermina, 10 August, 1877.

143. From the Gnifetti hut follow Route 139 to the SW ridge of Piramide Vincent and a little higher traverse R off the ridge and over a scree and rock band with snow which cuts an horizontal line on to the uppermost snow slopes of the Indren glacier. Continue in the same direction directly towards the summit and climb a slightly steeper slope to the top (2 h. from hut).

CORNO BIANCO 3320m.

After leaving the Monte Rosa group along its southern arm, this is the most important summit on the great ridge dividing the Valsesia (E) and Gressoney (W) valleys. The summit lies on the ridge in a direct line between Alagna and Gressoney-la-Trinité. It is one of the finest viewpoints in the Western Alps and provides a number of technical rock climbs, somewhat remotely situated, as well as easy but generally rough and long scrambles to the top on the E and SE sides. The usual route, mostly grade II, from the Gastaldi biv. is up the Netscio valley to the Bocchetta di Netscio (3107m. IGM) at its head ($1\frac{1}{2}$ h.), then along the secondary ridge to the main one NW of the summit, where this junction is marked by the Pta. di Netscio (3280m. IGM) (1 h.). From here up the NW ridge on which there are gendarmes and gaps, pitches of II/III to the top ($1\frac{3}{4}$ h., $4\frac{1}{4}$ h. from biv. hut).

PART V

Liskamm – Breithorn group

Lisjoch to Theodulpass

LISJOCH 4151m.

Between the Ludwigshöhe and Liskamm, a feasible and superb glacier pass between the Monte Rosa and Gnifetti huts with obvious connection to the Margherita hut. However the frontier ridge hereabouts is usually crossed well to the E of its lowest pt. over the easy snow saddle (4246m.) much nearer the Ludwigshöhe, used by hut approach route 95. For climbing the Liskamm (see below) it is necessary to reach the slopes beside the col proper. First recorded traverse: W. and G. St. John Mathews with J. B. Croz and M. Charlet, 23 August, 1859.

LISKAMM 4527.2m. (E) 4479m. (W)

A magnificent snow mtn., one of the most beautiful in the Alps and Himalayan in character. Its complex structure reveals a variety of routes in all grades of difficulty, none of which is dull. The mtn. is huge, with an elongated NE face and a tri-angular NW face overlooking Switzerland. The Italian (S) side is marked by a number of short rock spurs between large areas of snow and ice, giving a different style of climbing. Foremost with the Liskamm is the traverse of its two summits by the frontier ridge, a route feared at one time because of its difficult double cornice which nowadays rarely forms (Lewis, Paterson, Knubel accident, 1877). Apart from two small rock outcrops this ridge is snow and one of the finest expeditions of its class in the Alps. This traverse has often been continued to Castor and Pollux, and even to the Breithorn. These links can be pieced together from descriptions which follow. The imposing NE face provides ice climbs of outstanding interest, often dangerous but nevertheless climbed fairly often.

First ascent, E and highest summit: J. F. Hardy, A. C. Ramsey, F. Gibson, T. Rennison, J. A. Hudson, W. E. Hall, C. H. Pilkington and R. M. Stephenson with J. P. Cachet, F. Lochmatter, K. Herr, S. Zumtaugwald, P. and J. Perren, 19 August, 1861.

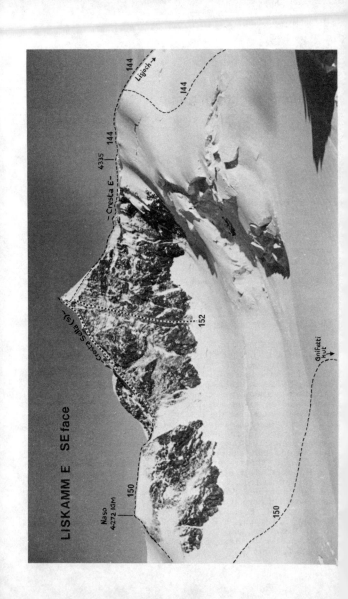

LISKAMM E   SE face

Naso
4·272 IGM — 150

Cresta E — 4335 — 144

Cresta Sella (s) —

Lisjoch →
144

144

152

150

Gnifetti Hut →

W summit and first traverse of both summits: Leslie Stephen and E. N. Buxton with J. Anderegg and F. Biner, 16 August, 1864.

First winter ascent: A., C. and V. Sella with J. J. and D. Maquignaz and P. Gugliermina, 22 March, 1885.

On ski: E peak, A. Mazlam with J. Knubel, May, 1913. W peak, Hofmeier, Wien and von Kraus, 7 April, 1926.

East Ridge (from Lisjoch). The usual route from the Monte Rosa and Gnifetti huts. Access from the Margherita hut is the easiest of all. Cornices on this ridge can be very large and great care should be taken. A delicate snow climb, PD. First ascensionists.

144. From the Monte Rosa hut follow Route 94 to where you turn a sérac barrier near the top of the Grenz glacier (c. 4150m.). Instead, make a rising traverse R (SW) and contour the snow shoulder pt. 4252m. above the level of the Lisjoch, then go down to the col (allow $5\frac{1}{2}$ h. from Monte Rosa hut). Alternatively, if the rumpled glacier directly below the Lisjoch is in good condition, go straight for the Lisjoch instead of making the detour L, which can save 20 min.

From the Gnifetti hut follow Route 95 till you are level with the Lisjoch, lying NW. Now either cross easily to the col, or contour W just below it, cross a large bergschrund and reach a shoulder above the first riser in the ridge but lower and to the R (E) of pt. 4335m. ($1\frac{3}{4}$ h.).

From the Margherita hut descend by Route 95 to the frontier snow shoulder (4246m.) and follow this easily, down to the Lisjoch ($1\frac{1}{4}$ h.).

Climb straight up the first riser in the ridge to a shoulder, a steep and narrow snow crest. From here you can examine the state of cornices higher up. The next section, over the snowy knoll pt. 4335m. rises and falls. The crest is sharp and large cornices appear on the L. Make low traverse movements on the steep N side. The next section rises steeply with a rock wall on the Italian side. The cornices are less serious

199

but you should still keep to the R flank. A few rocks lead to the E summit ($2\frac{1}{2}$ h., $1\frac{1}{4}$ h. in descent; 8 h. from Monte Rosa hut, $4\frac{1}{4}$ h. from Gnifetti hut, $3\frac{3}{4}$ h. from Margherita hut).

<u>Main ridge between summits</u>. A magnificent airy snow crest, from the E summit to the W. This is the best direction for making a traverse. More delicate on the whole than either the E or SW ridges, by which the summits can be approached separately. PD+. First ascensionists of W summit.

145. From the E summit descend keeping to the R (Swiss) side of the crest (cornices on L). Reach a broad easy section which goes into a saddle (4417m.) marking the lowest point between the summits. The next section is very narrow and particularly delicate, with a regular cornice on the L. At the end of it cross a hump, then climb snowy rocks to a knoll. From here an almost level horizontal ridge leads to the W summit (2 h. on average).

<u>South-West Ridge (from Felikjoch)</u>. This ridge leads to the W and lower summit. PD-. The approach to the Felikjoch (4063m.) from the Monte Rosa hut is frequently awkward because of the bad state of the Zwillings glacier, and the best line up it is exposed to avalanches from the Liskamm. PD. The Italian approach is simple. This pass is much simpler in spring for skiers. First ascensionists.

146. Swiss approach. From the Monte Rosa hut descend the approach route to the Grenz glacier and cross it SW to reach the double glacier torrent flowing over the surface of the bare glacier, about 300m. E of the Schalbetterflue. Follow the torrent upstream (S) and reach a zone of complex crevasses at the junction of the Grenz and Zwillings glaciers. Slant WSW, to the W of pt. 3097m., and find a route through the crevasses - not an easy matter in the dark. Reach the first plateau of

the Zwillings glacier, cross it S, and above 3400m. stay close to the central rock barrier. The plateau is cut by huge crevasses, making big detours necessary. The best line is close to the W face of the Liskamm, but here you are exposed to avalanches. Climb steeper slopes SE, then reach an upper plateau (3800m.) by moving R (SW). Cross this due S and climb a glacier cwm with more large crevasses to the flat slopes leading to the col (5 h. on average from Monte Rosa hut, $2\frac{1}{2}$ h. in descent).

147. Italian approach. From the Quintino Sella hut a small track in rocks and scree leads to the Felik glacier where there is generally a beaten trail. Climb N on gentle slopes under the E flank of the Pta. Perazzi, then trend NE to a steep slope at the foot of the col. Climb this without difficulty ($1\frac{1}{2}$ h., 45 min. in descent).

148. From the Felikjoch climb easy slopes of a snow spur up to pt. 4201m. which can be crossed or turned on L. The next section is narrow but not corniced. Reach a broader, steeper section where it is usual to bear L up to near a bergschrund, then move L again to a snow rib which is followed back to the main ridge at a shoulder (4447m.). This shoulder can be reached by a direct ascent. From here follow an almost level snow ridge to the summit (2 h., 1 h. in descent; 7 h. from Monte Rosa hut, $3\frac{1}{2}$ h. from Quintino Sella hut).

<u>West-South-West Ridge (Cresta Perazzi)</u>. In practice this is the normal route from the Q. Sella hut to the E peak. A good climb, interesting and sure. PD. First ascent: F. Morshead and C. E. Mathews with Chr. Almer and A. Maurer, 22 July, 1867.

149. From the Q. Sella hut follow a small track N for a min. or so, then slant R and cross the Felik glacier NE, aiming for the foot of the rock spur descending from near the Felikjoch where the glacier flows through a broad sloping corridor above pt. 3744m. Reach the foot of this spur (c. 3845m.), at the R (E) side of the glacier. Now cross the corridor and make a short descent to the Lis glacier. Climb its L side, then curve NE and E, well above some large crevasses, and cross the glacier terrace to the foot of the WSW ridge. This has séracs at its L (W) foot. Cross a bergschrund, climb rocks R of the séracs and reach a snow slope above, to the N (2 h.). Climb snow till the ridge on the R steepens. Follow the crest which is irregular and alternately snow and rock. Turn short steps on the L. There are no particular difficulties. Reach an upper step, the Signal Perazzi, cross it and continue up a fine snow crest to the summit ridge, about 15 min. from and to the W of the E peak (3 h., 5 h. from hut).

South Ridge (Cresta del Naso or Cresta Sella). Some very academic arguments have been put forward for disclaiming "Cresta del Naso". The ridge rises above a snowy dome called the Naso (4272m. IGM). Below it is the Passo del Naso (c. 4100m.), which is the easiest passage, not a col, from one branch of the Lis glacier to the other; therefore between the Q. Sella and Gnifetti huts. A reliable direct route to the E summit from either of these huts. PD. First ascent: P. W. Thomas with J. Imboden and J. Langen, 1 September, 1878.

150. From the Gnifetti hut follow Route 95 to near the "Balmenhorn". Now slant L in the direction of the Liskamm, descending slightly, and cross the Lis glacier in a big circle to below the SE side of the Naso dome. Cross a bergschrund at c. 4050m., sometimes quite difficult, climb a steep snow/ice slope, then go up an easy snow shoulder to the dome. Cross this and descend a snow ridge with a few rocks to a saddle at the foot of the ridge. Climb on the crest which has a number of small rock knolls, steps and towers. Some of these can be turned on

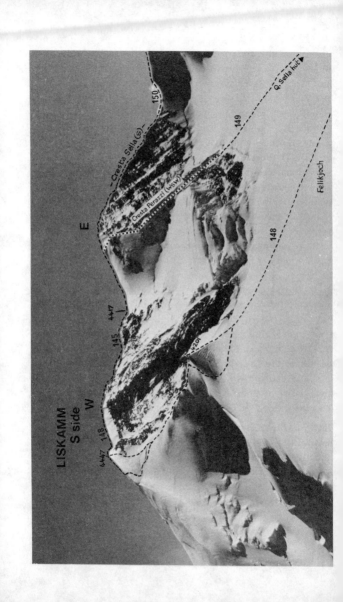

LISKAMM
S side

W   E

4447   118

145   4447

150

Cresta Sella (s)

Cresta Perazzi (w/sw)

101

149

148

Q. Sella hut ▶

Felikjoch

reasonable rock, but it is better to traverse them. Reach the summit ridge R of the E top and about 15 min. from it ($4\frac{1}{2}$ h. from Gnifetti hut).

151. From the Q. Sella hut follow Route 149 to the large central terrace of the E branch of the Lis glacier. Continue crossing it horizontally E, below the Cresta Perazzi, and reach the W foot of the Naso dome, just above some sēracs. Climb the steep flank and slant L (NE) to reach the top of the dome, where the previous route is joined (3 h. , about 6 h. from hut to summit).

152. South-East Face of E peak. A triangular wall about 350m. high, cut by alternate couloirs and dividing rock buttresses/ ribs. It has been climbed by several routes, all approx. AD/ AD+, but is exposed to stonefall. The buttress which descends from the apex of the face (not actually the summit) to the lowest middle point above the large bergschrund gives the best and safest line, up its R side on a secondary crest. The face is easily approached from the Gnifetti hut.

North-East Face

This impressive glacier face overlooking the L bank of the Grenz glacier is more than 3 km. long and is counted among the finest ice walls in the Alps. A prominent rock barrier slants steeply R from the centre foot of the face (3663m.) towards the W summit and this feature divides it in two sections. Each has rock buttress and rib features which are particularly complex in the W section, but also several enormous sērac barriers and ice cliffs which threaten most of the routes. The E section is about 700m. high. The W section, which is slightly steeper, is about 1000m. high. Climbs on the W section are much more serious and difficult. The routes are described from L (E) to R (W).

East Summit Direct (Norman-Neruda Route).

The route of the face, classic, relatively safe and sure. It follows a low relief rock rib which descends from just R of the summit down to pt.

4000m. Its foot. Below this is a snow/ice slope in the same line, sometimes marked by a few outcrops. When the rocks are verglassed, a long parallel couloir slope L of the rib can be climbed as a variation (Welzenbach, 1925). There is a similar variation on the R side of the rib. D, delicate and sustained. Poor resting places, carry rock and ice pegs, crampons essential. 700m. with an average angle of 52°, steeper in places. With a lot of good snow and little ice, and snow-free rocks, the climbing is quite straightforward. Objective danger is negligible. Climbed about 15 times up to 1935 and frequently since then. First ascent: L. Norman-Neruda with Chr. Klucker and J. Reinstadler, 9 August, 1890. First winter ascent: G. C. Fosson and O. Frachey, 11 March, 1956. Solo ascents have been reported as far back as the 1950s but no one seems to have recorded them properly.

153. From the Monte Rosa hut follow Route 94 up the Grenz glacier to the vicinity of pt. 3699m. Now cross the glacier due S and reach the foot of the face directly below the E summit ($2\frac{1}{2}$ h.). Cross the bergschrund and climb direct on a steep featureless snow/ice slope for 250m. to reach the toe of the rock rib ($1\frac{1}{2}$ h.). Climb the rib as directly as possible, delicate riblets and cracked slabs with little protection except where you can put an axe in snow patches. The lower part of the rib has pitches of III/IV while the upper part is mainly II/II+. The rib peters out and you climb in the same line up a snow/ice slope, less steep, to finish a few m. R of the summit (5-6 h., 7 h. on average from bergschrund in good conditions).

By the Welzenbach variation, L of the rib, the face has been climbed in $3\frac{1}{2}$ h. Some parties have climbed snow/ice on the R side of the rib. In both cases it is usual to join the rib about half-way up or a little higher.

<u>Central (Blanchet-Mooser) Route</u>. The original line approaching the W summit, finishing on the frontier ridge at a rock

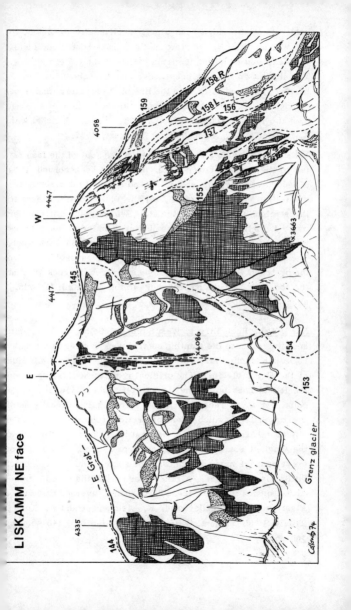

LISKAMM NE face

knoll where the ridge runs almost horizontally for 300m. to the W summit. Not as steep as the Neruda route but somewhat exposed to falling ice from séracs at the top of the face. The line is an obvious one, above and L of the central rock barrier, slanting L to R in the line of the barrier. Snow/ice throughout, D, sustained, 700m. Climbed much less often than the Neruda route. First ascent: E. R. Blanchet with K. Mooser and J. Aufdenblatten, 5 August, 1927.

154. Start as for Route 153 and reach the foot of the face not far to the R of the latter route. Cross the bergschrund, then a second one straight above. Trend R and climb directly towards the summit ice cliffs, all the while drawing closer to the straight rock edge on the R. Below the ice cliffs either move L (delicate) and traverse upwards on ice to find a break in the cliffs, or find a break on the R, near the rock band. The séracs vary and can sometimes be impassable. Above them, trend R on an easier slope and reach the rock knoll at the top (5 h.). Go along the ridge to the W summit (15 min., about 8 h. from Monte Rosa hut).

<u>North-East Face Direct, West Summit.</u> Below the W summit and fairly close to the slanting central rock barrier is a broken rock spur which, lower down, forms a rognon above the R side of the Grenz glacier. The original route turns this rognon on the R and goes up the next rock tier from its lowest R-hand point. A more recent variation starts up the L-hand side of the rognon itself, which offers protection from falling ice, then climbs the L-hand crest of the next tier. The variation joins the original route in the next ice slope section. The rocks of the variant are more difficult but the route is safer. The chief difficulties are on ice. All the lower part of the face is somewhat exposed to falling ice. TD-, 900m., average angle 54°. First ascent (original route): K. Diemberger and W. Stefan, 23 July, 1956. Variant: W. Gross and T. Hiebeler, 7-8 August,

208

1960. First British and first solo ascent: J. Taylor, 1972.

155. From the Monte Rosa hut follow Route 94 up the Grenz glacier to c. 3400m., just below the first considerable icefall. Cross the glacier to the foot of the face ($1\frac{3}{4}$ h.). The original route start is ignored.

From the glacier start from a point below and 50m. L of the rognon. Climb straight up for c. 100m., then make a rising traverse R to reach the L-hand rib of the rognon at its lowest point. Climb precisely on the crest for about 400m., rock pitches of III and IV, with a section on snow half-way up. Finish on a hanging ice slope where the rock rib disappears. Climb the slope trending R for 35m. to a rock outcrop. Continue still trending slightly R, and after four rope lengths reach the R-hand end of the ice cliffs situated half-way up the face; junction with original route. Alongside the upper R-hand edge of the ice cliff, climb a vague ice couloir for 200m. to reach the upper ice slope, which has no obstacles. Climb this directly to the W summit (10 h. on average from bergschrund).

<u>North Face Route, West Summit</u>. The E(L) side of this part of the face is marked by a rock spur which rises to within 150m. of the summit. The spur is in a line slightly R of the summit. It is well marked on the map, finishing below with a triangular rock formation about one-third distance up the face. The climb follows ice slopes and associated obstacles on the R (W) side of the spur, and continues on the slopes above it. A magnificent ice climb, 54° average angle with several steeper ice pitches, etc. TD, sustained, 900m. First ascent: T. Hiebeler and H. Pokorski, 30-31 July, 1961. First winter ascent: A. Schlick, F. Jäger and W. Nairz, 5-7 January, 1971.

156. Start as for Route 155 and go down the L bank of the glacier to below the foot of the spur. Start below a large couloir coming down between the spur (L) and a large sérac barrier (R). Climb an ice slope and trend L to a short narrow couloir at the base of the spur. Climb this couloir and reach the big ice slope R of the spur. Trend L and in three rope lengths reach a rock islet, good resting place and belay. From here continue in the same direction, with the spur on your L, to where the slope meets rocks. At this point abseil and tension traverse 10m. across an overhanging ice wall, to the R facing in. Continue up an ever-steepening slope to a little gap between a large ice tower and a wall. Traverse 4m. R on a near-vertical ice wall, then continue the ascent diagonally L as soon as possible, where the slope is easier, to reach the lower edge of a huge crevasse. Follow this edge to its L extremity, climb a little to the R, then diagonally R up to the L-hand edge of a rock barrier, which is turned on the L. Continue diagonally R towards a rock islet, then bear away L and eventually reach the snow crest above the top of the rock spur.

Climb the R side of this indefinite crest, then up a little rock couloir, short and steep, followed by three rope lengths to reach a small rock platform situated just below the final ice walls. Bivouac of first ascensionists.

From the platform turn the first ice wall by moving L up a very steep ice slope, then traverse R for 35m. on an ice ramp below the overhanging second wall to reach the upper slopes which are less steep. So to the summit (18 h. climbing time on first ascent).

157. North Spur, West Summit. This route uses the rock spur which separates the NE and N faces (a vague separation), which is turned on the R by Route 156. It starts and finishes as for Route 156 and is independent for the height of the spur. The climb is the most serious undertaking on the mtn. There are equal rock and ice difficulties involving, unusually, artificial techniques. 950m., A1 and A2, rock pitches of IV and V, TD+. 25 h. climbing time on first ascent: G. Andreani and P. Nessi, 4-5 August, 1961. The route is unrepeated at the end of 1973.

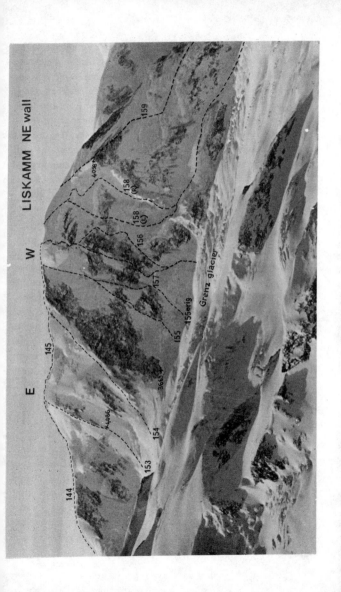

E W LISKAMM NE wall

144 153 *4086 3665 154 145 155 155erig 157 156 158 (2) 158 (1) 4986 159

Grenz glacier

158. North Face Routes. This facet rises to shoulder pt. 4447m. on the SW ridge of the W peak. It is more or less a very steep snow/ice slope cut by a small ice cliff band one-third way up, and a larger one two-thirds way up. The base rests on a long rock band above the Grenz glacier, through which there is an entrance on tumbled ice at the L side, near the start of Route 156, or the ice shelf along its top can be followed. Two routes have been made up the face, one passing L of the two ice cliff bands, the other R, but both involve getting through marginal ice cliffs on their respective sides. D+. Left-hand route: L. Herncarek and W. Welsch, 9 August, 1963 (15 h.). Right-hand route: M. Jagiello, G. Malaczynski, J. Poreba and N. Tarnawski, 4 August, 1972 (12 h.). Ski descent, H. Holzer, 20 June, 1974 in 55 min.

North-West Spur, West Summit. The R-hand (W) edge of the N-NE face, overlooking the junction of the Grenz and Zwillings glaciers, is a complex glacier spur with a conspicuous triangular rock facet (4058m.) at mid-height. The original route, described below, is the longest climb on the mtn. There is an important but somewhat dangerous variation to its L, which is ignored. An ice climb of character, interesting, with minimal objective danger but sometimes impassable bergschrunds, climbed quite frequently. AD+, 1150m. First ascent: Mrs. R. Thomson with Chr. Klucker and C. Zippert, 19 July, 1902.

159. From the Monte Rosa hut follow Route 146 as far as the lower end of the first plateau of the Zwillings glacier ($1\frac{1}{2}$ h.). Above the séracs, cross it E to near pt. 3300.6m. (30 min.), then climb a glacier spur SE, which forms the top of a sérac barrier above some rocks, to reach a terrace below another sérac barrier. Make a slightly rising traverse L (E) across the steep terrace (falling ice), cross a bergschrund and climb trending somewhat R, up the L (E) edge of the terrace towards the triangular rock buttress. Cross another bergschrund and climb a steep snow/ice slope to the R (NW) corner/crest of

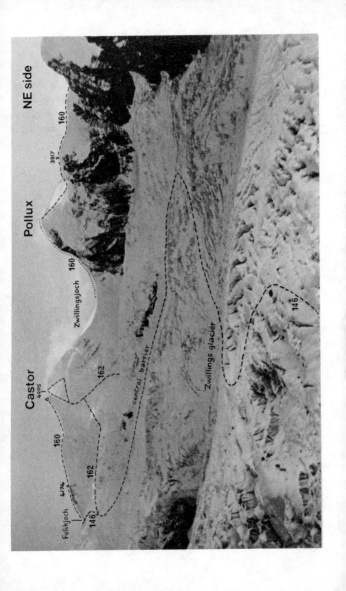

the buttress ($2\frac{1}{2}$ h.). Start up the ridge somewhat R of the crest, which is followed sometimes on the R side to the top of the buttress. Fairly good rock, II/II+ (4058m.) (1 h.). Continue up a fine snow/ice crest to an upper terrace. Now either trend L and reach the W summit directly, or, rather easier, climb straight up to the shoulder pt. 4447m. on the SW ridge not far from the top ($1\frac{1}{2}$ h., about 7 h. from Monte Rosa hut).

FELIKJOCH 4063m.

Ital: Colle di Felik. Between the Liskamm and Castor, an impressive glacier pass, PD, but complicated glacier terrain, leading from the Monte Rosa hut to the Quintino Sella hut. See Routes 146, 147. First crossing: W. Mathews and F. W. Jacomb with J. B. and Michel Croz, 23 August, 1861.

CASTOR 4228m.

POLLUX 4092m.

Zwillinge, The Twins. Ital: Castore e Polluce. Both mtns. can be considered together for climbing purposes. They lie prettily between the Liskamm (Felikjoch) and Breithorn (Schwarztor pass) and are separated by the Zwillingsjoch (3845m.). As an approach to either summit this latter pass is guarded by a badly crevassed glacier on the Swiss Monte Rosa hut side; rarely if ever used. A traverse of both peaks is normal. Pollux is really a large rock and ice knoll on the frontier, where its ridges are poorly defined, and care is needed to take the correct way down. Two routes on Castor merit separate consideration.

First ascent of Castor: W. Mathews and F. W. Jacomb with Michel Croz, 23 August, 1861. Pollux: J. Jacot with P. Taugwalder and J. M. Perren, 1 August, 1864. First winter and ski ascents of both mtns: A. von Martin, K. Planck and H. von Roncador (in combinations), 5 and 7 March, 1913.

<u>Pollux-Castor Traverse</u>. Several combinations are possible. Either peak can be climbed for itself without much difficulty, but Pollux is rarely done so. Access routes for starting from Switzerland and Italy are given. The complete traverse must

POLLUX NW side

Schwarztor

Schwärze glacier

160

164

be rated PD+, but the mtns. can be reached especially from the Italian side by access routes which are only F. Climbed much more frequently from the Italian side.

160. From the Monte Rosa hut the best plan is to climb Pollux by its long N (Schwärze) ridge. This ridge is flanked on the E side by the rock band of the Schalbetterflue. PD/PD+.

Start by descending the path to the Grenz glacier and cross it losing height gradually to the NW corner near pt. 2554m. of the Schwärze (30 min.). Climb scree, grass, snow and a glacier slope, keeping to the R (W) side of the broad promontory, to a snowy saddle near pt. 3282m. ($1\frac{3}{4}$ h.). Now follow the broad snowy promontory towards the summit of Pollux, first up a steep and usually icy slope to pt. 3659.7m., then down to a saddle and up an easy slope to pt. 3817m. Above is a steep snow/ice spur protected by an enormous bergschrund. This is sometimes impossible to cross. The slope above leads directly to the summit of Pollux (4 h., $6\frac{1}{4}$ h. from hut).

There is a shorter route to the first saddle, 3282m., by taking Route 146 up the Zwillings glacier to where you fork R on to its W branch. Reach and climb a snow couloir and rocks leading straight up the Schalbetterflue to the saddle, 2 h.

From the summit of Pollux follow the snow ridge towards the Zwillingsjoch. First reach steep rocks and continue down the vague line of the ridge for a few min., then trend R, through a couloir and over snow patches and broken rock to a bergschrund at the bottom. Move L to reach the col (30 min.). PD. Above is Castor and it is rarely climbed by the frontier ridge in front of you.

From the col climb diagonally R (S) till you are directly below the summit. Trend L up a snow/ice face to reach the summit ridge between a forepeak (4205m.) and the top. Some avalanche danger if the snow is poor (1 h., about 8 h. from Monte Rosa hut).

From Castor, descend the SE ridge, possibly corniced in the

POLLUX W side

Castor

Zwillings-
Joch

161
var.

161

Schwarztor

Mezzalama hut

lower half, to the Felikjoch (45 min.). Return to the Monte Rosa hut by Route 146 ($2\frac{1}{2}$ h., say 12 h. for round trip).

The easiest way up Castor from the Q. Sella hut is by Route 147 to the Felikjoch ($1\frac{1}{2}$ h.), then climb the SE ridge, PD- (1 h., $2\frac{1}{2}$ h. from hut). Very popular with piste in season.

161. From the Mezzalama hut you can reach the Schwarztor (3731m.) or Zwillingsjoch by crossing scree and glaciated rocks to the Verra glacier, which is climbed in its centre where the crevasses are least troublesome (route indicated on LK), N then ENE to the Schwarztor ($3\frac{1}{2}$ h.), or over a glacier terrace under the Pollux cone to reach the Zwillingsjoch in much the same time. Either way, join the usual traverse. However, if you reach the Schwarztor, slant well R (SSE) to the foot of a steep snow/ice slope between the main ridge (overhead) and WSW ridge. Cross a bergschrund and climb this slope directly to the summit, PD.

Castor, North Face. A fine, interesting snow/ice climb, reached from the approach to the Felikjoch. Multiple berg-schrunds, crevasses and séracs present some access problems depending on conditions and route chosen. 500m. or less for the face, depending on the point at which you reach it. AD/AD+. Descended by Miss K. Richardson with Emile Rey and J. B. Bich, 10 August, 1890. Climbed by G. I. Finch and H. A. Mantel, 16 August, 1909.

162. From the Monte Rosa hut follow Route 146 to the upper plateau of the Zwillings glacier at c. 3800m. Move easily R (W) on to the face above its first tumble of broken walls and crev-asses. Cross a bergschrund and climb towards the glacier ridge becoming more defined near the summit. Below another bergschrund traverse R again above ice cliffs into the centre of the face. Climb this crossing at least one more bergschrund. Turning movements are best made on the R. So reach the Castor

CASTOR WNW face

4205

163

160

Zwillingsjoch

163

Colle del Castore

163 note

163

Grande Verra glacier

forepeak (4205m.), then go along the frontier ridge to the summit. The route can be varied considerably according to conditions (7 h. from Monte Rosa hut). The lower part of the face, coming down to the W section of the Zwillings glacier, gives a longer and more complicated entry through séracs and low ice cliffs, but this is nevertheless the proper way to start the climb.

<u>Castor, South Buttress and South-West Ridge.</u> A good rock climb up to pt. 3992m., above which the ridge forms a saddle called locally the Colle del Castore (c. 4020m.), being the easiest pt. at which the SW ridge of Castor can be crossed to avoid its summit in moving between the Felikjoch and Schwarztor on the Italian side of the frontier ridge. Above the saddle the ridge continues with general mountaineering interest on snow and some steep rocks to the summit.

This buttress is favoured by some Italian guides as a spicy way up the mtn. It is quite direct from the Mezzalama hut. An enjoyable route with short and well protected pitches, peg belays, etc. in place. D, with pitches of IV/IV+. First ascent: C. Fortina with A. Welf, 4 August, 1911. First winter ascent: G. Gualco with E. and O. Frachey, 20 March, 1955. First British ascent: A. K. Rawlinson and M. P. Ward, 29 July, 1971.

163. From the Mezzalama hut descend diagonally E over scree and boulders to the Piccolo Verra glacier. Cross this in the same direction to the Castore glacier branch (not named on LK) on the R side of the large rock promontory below pt. 3992m. The entrance to this glacier branch is broken by séracs and crevasses. Climb up it keeping L and higher up reach the foot of a large triangular rock buttress on the L, at c. 3400m. (2½ h.). The crest of the buttress gives the general line of ascent though most of it lies a little R of the edge.

Start just round to the R of the corner. Go up an obvious

easy ramp rising R to L to the crest. Follow the crest with good climbing (II,III) to near the top of the first step. Turn the top on the R by a short easy descent, then climb an easy couloir to a gap behind. Move R, just below a light coloured band of rock, then climb to a steepening. Take a scoop on the L of an overhanging wall. When it steepens escape L and upwards to a stance (IV, pegs). Continue in the same line, keeping a little R of the edge, climbing several pitches with easier ground between them (III and IV), including a wall with pegs which is taken diagonally R to L (IV+). Above this section easier climbing leads to an exposed position on the crest. Climb direct and just R of the crest with pegs in place (IV+). At the top of this section slant L and go up easily to pt. 3992m., large cairn ($3\frac{1}{2}$ h.). Continue on mixed ground on the ridge over the Colle del Castore saddle and climb a fine snow crest to a rock band running right across the ridge. Climb this on rather smooth slabby rocks to a continuation mixed ridge then the final snow cap ($1\frac{1}{2}$ h., about $7\frac{1}{2}$-8 h. from Mezzalama hut).

ZWILLINGSJOCH 3845m.

Ital: Passo di Verra. Between Castor and Pollux, a fairly difficult pass on the frontier ridge due to badly crevassed slopes on the Swiss side. Not of any special interest. First traversed: S. Winkworth with J. B. Croz and J. J. Bennen, 31 July, 1863.

SCHWARZTOR 3731m.

Ital: Porta Nera. An old glacier pass between Pollux and the Breithorn (Roccia Nera), from Monte Rosa hut to Mezzalama hut. Not often used as a pass but useful for reaching or leaving the vicinity of the Cesare e Giorgio biv. hut (q.v.), which is on the approach to several climbing routes just below the Italian side of the pass. First traverse: John Ball with M. Zumtaugwald, 18 August, 1845.

164. For the Swiss side, the approach corresponds with Route 160 to the second saddle near pt. 3659. 7m. at the foot of the N ridge proper of Pollux ($3\frac{1}{2}$ h.). From this saddle slant R (SW) on to the upper snowfields of the Schwärze glacier and climb in the same direction avoiding a few large crevasses to the broad saddle of the col. PD- (1 h., $4\frac{1}{2}$ h. from Monte Rosa hut).

165. For the Italian side all the approach from the Mezzalama hut corresponds with the first part of Route 61, passing below the Cesare e Giorgio biv. PD- ($3\frac{1}{2}$ h.).

Theodulpass - Breithornpass - Schwarztor - Zwillingsjoch connection. Known as the Italian High Level Route, being a major variation of the more famous High Level Route which comes into Zermatt and finishes at Saas Fee. It is a high glacier traverse below the S side of the Breithorn, favoured by spring skiers but used just as much in the summer by climbers, and links the Gandegg or Theodul huts with the Castor and Pollux traverse, leaving choices of descent to the Mezzalama, Q. Sella or Monte Rosa huts. From the Mezzalama or Q. Sella huts the high level route can be continued to the Gnifetti and Margherita huts. In poor visability it is notoriously difficult to find the way but a lot of the route is usually a beaten trail in summer. F+. You pass immediately below the Cesare e Giorgio biv. hut.

166. From the Theodulpass (hut) climb the open glacier cwm on the L of the frontier ridge, pass the Testa Grigia station, and reach the Breithorn plateau. This section is normally churned up with tracks and ski trails. Cross the plateau ENE in the direction of the Rocca Nera. Reach a vague saddle on which it is almost impossible to ascertain the lowest point: Breithornpass (3816m.) ($1\frac{3}{4}$ h.). At this pt. you should keep some distance to the L, where pt. 3824m. is marked on map. From the saddle work across the more complicated Verra glacier on the Italian side, contouring and descending slightly, keeping above the rognons, till you can round a glacier spur under the Roccia Nera. This spur is traversed just above pt. 3675m. The Cesare e Giorgio biv. is situated on the next group of rocks higher up this spur. By ascending a snowfield to the NE the Schwarztor is soon reached ($1\frac{1}{2}$ h. from Breithornpass).

To continue to the Zwillingsjoch, cross a glacier terrace slightly below the level of the Schwarztor and under Pollux, where you rise a little (30 min.). To reach the Felikjoch the best plan is to traverse Castor (Route 160), or you can try the traverse below its summit as mentioned in the preamble to Route 163. Descent to the Mezzalama hut is by Routes 161, 165.

TESTA GRIGIA 3315m.

Not to be confused with the cableway station above the Theodulpass. This is the highest summit on the long ridge running S from the vicinity of Castor which divides the Gressoney (E) and Ayas (W) valleys. It is an excellent training walk/scramble from Gressoney-la Trinité or Champoluc. In either case you reach by good footpath the Colle di Pinter (2777m.) at the foot of the S ridge ($4\frac{1}{2}$ h. from either resort) and follow a rough path, steep in places on broken rock, to the summit in another 2 h.

The approach to the Colle di Pinter from Champoluc can be shortened by 1 h. by using the cableway to Crest (2000m.) from where the path up the valley to the col is joined. Above this cableway rises a continuation chairlift to slopes (c. 2300m.) below Monte Sarezza. With this mechanical assistance the unnamed saddle (3004m.) at the foot of the N ridge can be reached in 2 h. The ridge is climbed to the summit in another $1\frac{1}{2}$ h. (pitch of II).

The most direct approach from Gressoney-la Trinité is facilitated by the Cozzi biv. hut (q.v.). From here a small track with steep scrambling leads SW on to the S ridge above the shoulder of Monte Pinter (3132m.) where the track from the Colle di Pinter is joined (2 h. from biv. to summit). There is a more direct route from the biv. nearly straight up the E face to the summit, on snow and in couloirs.

The summit panorama is exceptional and stretches from Monte Viso to the Ortler Alps. First recorded tourist ascent: A. Laurent, L. Delapierre, B. Rignon, J. and J. C. Pinney, 7 August, 1858.

BREITHORN 4164m.

Probably the easiest 4000m. mtn. in the Alps but also a majestic massif, $2\frac{1}{2}$ km. long, with some of the best climbing of a standard in the Zermatt district. Extremely popular, 200 ascents a day being not uncommon on a fine day in summer. The wild N wall offers a crescendo of routes, increasing in difficulty from W to E. Two climbs on this face are classics. Along the frontier ridge the W peak is highest (4164m.). Moving E the other notable points are the Central summit (4159m.), E summit (4139m.), Gendarme (4105.8m.) - these last two being called Breithornzwillinge (twins) on LK25, and finally the Roccia Nera (4075m.). With regard to this last summit, it is usually considered to be an independent mtn. and the Swiss have finally dropped the German name of Schwarzfluh and given in to Italian precedent. A traverse of this frontier ridge is a magnificent expedition, still rarely done (only one report received since the 1968 guidebook was published).

First ascent: H. Maynard with J. M. Couttet, J. G., J. B. and J. J. Erin, 13 August, 1813. First winter ascent: J. Seiler, A. Bürcher and M. von Stockalper, 21 January, 1888. First ski ascent: R. Helbling, E. Wagner and H. Biehly, 6 January, 1899.

South-South-West Flank. The ordinary route, for walkers and skiers, and a quick way down after making a better climb on the N side. A deep trail in summer. F. First ascensionists.

167. From the Theodulpass (hut) follow Route 166 to the Breithornpass ($1\frac{3}{4}$ h.), then climb easy snow slopes almost due N to a final steep slope which can be icy after mid August and the summit (1 h., $2\frac{1}{2}$ h. from Theodulpass). A few crevasses might be encountered.

East - West Traverse. This great ridge is mainly snow with large cornices, except at the end of the season. It also has rocky sections which are fairly difficult. You can escape from

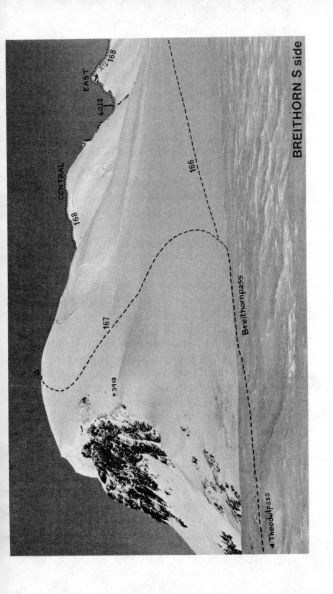

EAST

6022

168

168

CENTRAL

166

167

3418

Breithornpass

Theodulpass

BREITHORN S side

the ridge, down to the approach route, at several places. PD+ with pitches of III/III+. Delicate. First traverse: J. Stafford Anderson with U. Almer and A. Pollinger, 16 August, 1884.

168. From the Theodulpass (hut) follow Route 166 across the Breithornpass and contour the Verra glacier at a higher level than this high level route. Go round the foot of a rock island (c. 3800m.) and the base of the Central summit (c. 3800m.), then reach a long terrace forming the upper snows of the glacier. Large crevasses. Cross the terrace ESE to reach the glacier spur formed on this W side of the Roccia Nera, still at c. 3800m. Climb the spur to the frontier ridge, cornices, and move R to reach the top of the Roccia Nera (4075m.) ($4\frac{1}{2}$ h. from Theodulpass).

Starting from the Mezzalama hut reach the snowfields just below (SW of) the Schwarztor (Route 161) ($3\frac{1}{2}$ h.). Now climb NW up a steep snow slope and reach the glacier spur coming down from the Roccia Nera at c. 3800m. At this point the spur is only moderately steep, and you join the Theodulpass approach. The Cesare e Giorgio biv. is a short distance below ($1\frac{1}{2}$ h., 5 h. from Mezzalama hut).

From the Roccia Nera follow the main snow ridge W then NW, nearly horizontal and easy but with a huge cornice on the R side. The ridge steepens and leads to the top of Gendarme 4105. 8m. (30 min.). Keeping L, descend rocks and reach a snow saddle. Continue along the snow ridge, corniced, to a few rocks and the E summit (4139m.) (45 min.). Descend rocks on the crest to the point where the Younggrat route reaches the ridge, then go along an easy snow section to the lowest point in the ridge (4022m.) (15 min.). The ridge can be left here fairly easily. Carry on along the ridge to the foot of the first of three rock steps leading to the Central summit. Climb the first one direct (III+), or turn it on the L across the rocky flank before reaching the second step, and climb to the foot of the third step (III). Climb the latter as close as possible

226

to the crest, after which the ridge becomes snowy, narrow and corniced, and leads to the Central summit (4159m.) (2½ h.). Descend to a large snow saddle (4076m.) followed by an easy slope to the W summit (1 h., about 5½ h. from Roccia Nera). Descend by Route 167 to the Theodulpass (1½ h., about 12 h. for round trip).

For returning to the Mezzalama hut, descend by Route 167 to the Breithornpass, and continue by Route 166 to below the Schwarztor, then by Route 161 (4 h., about 15 h. for round trip).

North-West Face. An ill-defined face rising directly above the Triftji glacier and adjoining the much better known N spur situated to the E (Triftjigrat, Route 170). It gives a high standard ice climb with some difficulty on rock according to route, unfortunately marred by serious avalanche danger. It has been climbed as many times in winter as in summer, and in good winter conditions the route can be considered relatively safe. The rectangular shaped lower part of the face, forming a heavily crevassed headslope to the Triftji glacier below pt. 3696m., has an exit couloir slanting steeply SE near its top L-hand corner, below which extends an irregular rock band down the L(E) side of the headslope. This L side marks the general line of ascent to the upper section consisting of an ice slope and rocks leading to the Triftjigrat near the summit. 1000m., 50° average angle with pitches of 60° or more, TD, serious objective dangers except in ideal cond···ons. About 20 ascents to date.

First ascent: D. von Bethmann-Hollweg with O. and O. Supersaxo, 3 September, 1919 (by diagonal approach across headslope of Triftji glacier). Second ascent: W. Welzenbach, F. Rigele and O. Bachschmidt, 1926 (by more direct start up L edge of headslope). Lower rib variation start: H. Maeder with R. Arnold and P. Etter, 9 June, 1964. First winter ascent:

C. Mauri and E. Peyronel, 20 March, 1955. Solo ascent, 1973.

169. From the Gandegg inn descend the track to the Unterer Theodul glacier and cross the glacier SE to pass above the R (upper) side of a rock pile (2982m.). Now traverse the glacier E and turn L(S) into the upper bay of the Triftji glacier. Climb this to a bergschrund at the L side, under a steep broken rock band marking the L side of the crevassed and tumbled glacier headslope above ($1\frac{1}{2}$ h.).

Cross the bergschrund, generally quite large but not too difficult, and climb a steepening snow ramp immediately under the rock band to a very steep narrowing, just below the fan-shaped entrance to the exit couloir leading to the upper face. The original start makes a diagonal traverse across the headslope from R to L to join this point.

The narrowing is formed in ice by a rupture between the rocks and the edge of the headslope, into which runs a bergschrund from a diagonal line above, across the bottom of the couloir slope. Climb L up a corner ice pitch generally very serious and get on to the rocks above the end of the bergschrund. By rocks and ice continue up a riblet marking the L side of the broad entrance to the couloir, delicate and difficult, on to more continuous rocks above. Climb these rocks overlooking the couloir, trending L, which ease off towards the top, where ice intrudes again and bad stonefall can be experienced from the rock wall above and to the R. At the top of this section is a rock outcrop on the L with a good resting place. Now trend L to the end of a bergschrund running L across the base of the upper part of the face. The further L you keep the less danger from stonefall, but all the face above is now exposed to falling ice from the summit sérac barrier. Climb or turn the bergschrund according to judgement and climb trending L up an ice slope, passing R of a lower rock band and L of a middle one, between the latter and rocks further L. Continue slanting L, using rocks on the L according to conditions, and reach the

228

spur of the Triftjigrat below its final steepening to the summit snow cap. At this point the spur is a fine snow/ice crest which is followed to rocks. Either climb these icy rocks direct or traverse delicately L to another rock rib which leads more easily to a steep snow slope and the summit plateau (6-9 h. from bergschrund).

Lower rib variation start. Immediately after crossing the bergschrund climb L up steep ice and rocks on to the end of the rock band overlooking the L side of the Triftji glacier head-slope. Pass along the top of the band on snow and rocks with increasing steepness to a big rock pitch which must be climbed direct. Continue up ice ramps, icy rocks and bulges, trending L. With difficulty you can either break L on to the plain ice slope just below the second bergschrund, or work ahead to the rock outcrop providing a good resting place, where the original line is joined. This variation avoids most of the lower stone-fall danger, leaving the hazards of the summit sérac barrier.

North Spur (Triftjigrat). A very classic climb over a series of glacier steps and plateaux to the highest point of the mtn. There is some avalanche danger and the best time for an ascent is early in the season. One of the most varied climbs of its standard on snow and ice in the Zermatt district, very popular. It has the merit of being easily reached and the descent could not be easier. AD-. Slopes of 50-53° for two or three rope lengths. First ascent: R. Fowler with P. Knubel and G. Ruppen, 15 September, 1869.

170. From the Gandegg inn descend the track to the Unterer Theodul glacier and cross the glacier SE to pass above the R (upper) side of a rock pile (2982m.). Now traverse E across the Triftji glacier, above a group of crevasses, to the foot of a large rock band capped by pt. 3335m. Continue by a traverse movement E at c. 3000m. to a glacier hollow which is climbed to the Triftjisattel (3220m.), situated immediately S of pt.

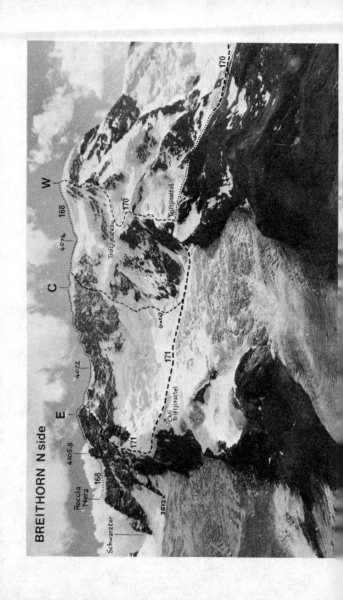

BREITHORN N side

3250.6m. (2 h.). Mid season and later the latter part of this approach can be badly crevassed. In this case descend about 100m. after passing the rock pile, reach the glacier hollow at its lowest point (c. 2860m.), then climb its L-hand edge on snow and scree to the saddle.

From the saddle climb the rock ridge direct, or work up snow on its R flank, to the first snow shoulder. This shoulder can also be reached without going to the Triftjisattel by a direct ascent on a steep snow/ice slope. Continue up a snow ridge to where it merges into a riser leading to higher glacier slopes. Climb this riser at its weakest point, generally somewhat R with parts on rock, and reach the glacier above. Cross this, keeping to its L-hand (E) edge, and at c. 3650m. continue up a snow ridge on this side, which avoids a broken glacier zone more in the previous line of ascent. Arrive at the main glacier terrace (Triftjiplateau) at the foot of the summit slopes (2 h.). Slant R (W), cross a bergschrund at c. 3800m. and climb a very steep snow/ice slope to reach the backbone rock crest coming down due N from the summit. This crest is the third outcrop to the R of a large sérac barrier overlooking the Triftji-plateau. Climb the rocks with good incut holds, followed by a fine snow crest up to another group of rocks. Either climb these rocks direct, difficult in icy conditions, or traverse L, delicate, to another rock rib which is climbed more easily. Above this line of rocks, a steep snow slope leads to an abrupt finish, rarely corniced, at the summit ($2\frac{1}{2}$ h., $6\frac{1}{2}$ h. from Gandegg inn).

North Face, Central Summit. A serious ice climb with delicate and normally verglassed rocks on the terminal wall, also exposed to falling ice. The line more or less goes up the R side of the Breithorn glacier headslope, under the barrier supporting the Triftji spur and finishes up the summit wall somewhat R of a direct line. The foot of the face is easily reached across the

Triftjisattel (Routes 170, 171) in $2\frac{1}{2}$-3 h. TD, 750m. First ascent: F. C. Serbelloni with E. and O. Frachey, 1953.

<u>Klein Triftji Ridge (Younggrat)</u>. Now Chli Triftji on map. This ridge descends from a point slightly W of the E summit (4139m.). A famous climb and one still with a reputation. One of the great classics of the Pennine Alps, serious and fairly long. The difficulty increases progressively and the problems are essentially those of a steep and narrow snow crest, delicate, with a technical finish on ice and rocks. The difficulty varies considerably according to conditions. In good snow throughout, rare, AD. Normally about, D-. Rock pitches of III. The lower part of the ridge is not usually climbed except when starting from the Monte Rosa hut. From the Gandegg hut the crest is reached at the Klein Triftjisattel (3498m.) by a traverse from the Triftjisattel. Carry ice pegs. First ascent: G. W. Young, C. D. Robertson and R. J. Major with J. Knubel and M. Ruppen, 18 August, 1906. First winter ascent: V. Lazzarino and P. Aredi, 24-28 February, 1963.

171. From the Gandegg hut follow Route 170 to the Triftjisattel (2 h.). On the other side descend an easy couloir (70m.) to the Breithorn glacier and ascend this SE to the Kl. Triftjisattel at a fairly obvious place on the Younggrat (1 h., 3 h. from Gandegg hut).

Starting from the Monte Rosa hut, descend near the L side of the dry Gorner glacier to a point below the ridge, then turn to climb it, first on moraine and by keeping L on snow and rocks to a snow slope. Go up this to a steepening which is normally best taken on the R, after which more snow on the broad ridge leads to the Klein Triftjisattel (4 h. from Monte Rosa hut).

Now follow the narrow and sometimes corniced snow ridge, turning small gendarmes on the L. In good conditions and crampons you can reach the base of the Grand Gendarme (c. 3740m.), about one-third distance up the ridge, without step

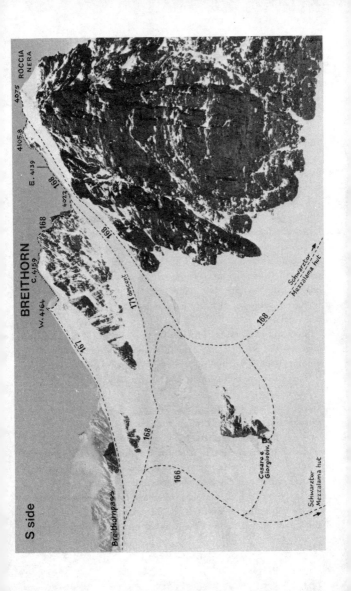

S side

Breithornpass

BREITHORN
W. 4164
C. 4159

ROCCIA
NERA
4075

4105.8

E. 4139

4022

168

169

168

171 descent

161

168

168

166

168

Schwarztor
Mezzalama hut

Cesare e
Giorgio biv.

Schwarztor
Mezzalama hut

cutting. The gendarme is normally turned on the L side by a steep snow/ice slope (30m.) to rejoin the ridge where the crest is very sharp. A direct ascent of the gendarme is IV. The next section of the ridge is steeper, narrower and exposed, with a gap, rocks and snow. Cross pt. 3835m. and descend to a snow gap, after which a traverse L on steep rock enables the crest to be rejoined. Continue up steep rock to where it runs against the summit buttress. About 75m. from these rocks cross a steep ice couloir to the R, 50m., delicate, ice peg belays as necessary. If you cross at this point, where the couloir can be in better condition than higher up, there are a few difficult rocks, usually turned on the R before an open chimney/couloir can be climbed to the summit ridge. However, it is more usual to climb up the snow ridge to the summit rocks where there is a large flake belay, or pegs in place. Cross the couloir at this point, 53°, 35m., generally ice, to the far side and finish up steep snowy rocks or an ice slope near the edge of the couloir to a short rock rib and the summit ridge (6 h. on average, 9 h. from Gandegg hut, 10 h. from Monte Rosa hut).

Descend the frontier ridge easily to a saddle (4022m.). Now descend the S flank and reach the approach line on the Verra glacier leading to the Breithornpass (Route 166) (about $2\frac{1}{2}$ h. to Theodulpass, and another 45 min. to Gandegg hut).

172. North-East Couloir, East Summit. An intimidating route and specialised sort of climb up the great couloir of 55° formed between the Younggrat and NE buttress of the E summit. The enclosed lower section is filled by two thin buttresses, both of which have been climbed (safer on L one) to reach the middle couloir section. The best way starts on rocks at the L foot of the buttress to L of couloir proper and having traversed on to the L-hand constricted buttress climbs this to enter the couloir about half-way up. The climb finishes on the Younggrat shortly before the traverse R across its final couloir. 8-10 h. from bergschrund, 700m., TD with rock pitches of IV, V. First ascent: L. Graf, K. Kubiena and E. Vanis, 21 July, 1954. Climbed several times since.

173. North-East Buttress, East Summit. See preamble above. The climb starts above the foot of the spur, at its L side, reaches the crest near the couloir on the R-hand side of the buttress, and takes the final wall direct. Mixed climbing, TD, pitches of IV, V, rock and ice pegs, 700m. 11 h. from bergschrund. First ascent: E. Cavalieri and P. Villaggio, 31 July, 1961.

174. North-East Spur, Gendarme 4106m. This is the prominent spur L of the one outlined above, marked by pt. 3512m. at its foot. The start can be reached easily across the Schwarztor in 1 h. from the Cesare e Giorgio biv. This is reported to be a route of considerable quality and interest but there appears to be little actual interest in it at present. D, with pitches of V, 600m., mixed climbing. 8 h. from bergschrund. First ascent: A. Mellano and G. Pianfetti, 3-4 July, 1959. Variations made in 1961.

175. North-East Buttress, Gendarme 4106m. This rock buttress lies to the L of the previous spur. Its foot is reached above a defending rock band by climbing a steep snow gangway slanting L to R. Above this, start well R of the foot proper, reach the crest and zigzag up the buttress, finishing with a long movement L to the summit. Mixed climbing, D, 500m., 6 h. from bergschrund. First ascent: A. Molinari with O. Frachey, 23 September, 1951.

BREITHORN E
NE face

Younggrat 171

172

3512
173

Roccia Nera

This most easterly summit of the Breithorn massif is easily reached by Route 168, PD- (1 h. from Cesare e Giorgio biv., $4\frac{1}{2}$ h. from Theodulpass). On all sides except the SW the mtn. is girdled by rockfaces on which various routes have been made of no special interest.

BREITHORNPASS 3824m.

An important crossing point at the frontier on the snowfields at the S foot of the Breithorn. See Route 166.

KLEIN MATTERHORN 3883m.

Chli Matterhorn on map. Any value or attraction that this little imitator of the Matterhorn may have to the climber is likely to disappear with the still pending proposal to complete a branch cableway from Trockener Steg to its summit. Not worth climbing for itself. Reach the summit from the Breithorn plateau, on the way up the Breithorn, Routes 166, 167, by following a broad snow ridge and a few rocks (15 min.).
First ascent: H. B. de Saussure with J. M. Couttet and six other guides, 13 August, 1792.

GOBBA DI ROLLIN 3902m.

A huge glacier dome rising S of the Breithornpass and easily reached by a detour of 20 min. up the snowfields from Routes 166, 167.

PASSO DI VENTINA MERIDIONALE (S) c.3650m.

PASSO DI VENTINA SETTENTRIONALE (N) 3451m.

Large and broad glacier shoulders on the frontier ridge between the Gobba di Rollin and the Testa Grigia cableway terminus. The upper pass is mainly of value as a connection to Routes 166, 167 for parties starting for the Breithorn from S. Giacomo (Fiery) in the Ayas valley. This approach takes the mule path to the Colle Sup. delle Cime Bianche (2982m.), but forks R at the Gran Lago below it to reach the higher col of the Passo del Plateau Rosa (3101m.), from where the Ventina glacier is climbed easily NE to the N pass and adjoining piste slopes of Routes 166, 167. The approach to the S pass for the same purpose is somewhat different and steeper, but quicker (about $5\frac{1}{2}$ h. from Fiery to frontier ridge).

THEODULPASS 3290m.

A very old and easy pass across the frontier from Zermatt to Breuil. CAI hut adjacent to col. See Routes 106, 107.

COLLE SUPERIORE DELLE CIME BIANCHE 2982m.

A broad depression between the base of the Valtournanche-Ventina glaciers and the Gran Sometta (3166m.). An old mule path route from Breuil to S. Giacomo, frequently crossed as such by walking parties, and a cross-roads for various walking circuits. The S. Giacomo side has a jeep road part way up the Cortoz valley, while the Breuil side can be approached from the Cime Bianche station on the Testa Grigia cableway line by a traverse in 1 h. round the E side of the Lago di Cime Bianche. The easiest approach on the Valtournanche side is by the new cableway from Valtournanche village to the Cime Bianche terminus of this line (not marked on any map except KK No. 87), which is found on a terrace due W of the S summit of the Cime Bianche (2973m.), at c. 2820m. This terrace can be traversed N to the Colle Inf. delle Cime Bianche (2896m.), on the S side of the Gran Sometta, in 15 min. Walking all the way from Breuil to S. Giacomo across the main pass, $5\frac{1}{2}$ h., or 7 h. in reverse direction.

MONTE ROISETTA 3334m.

The first of two prominent summits rising on the ridge dividing the Valtournanche and Ayas valleys. It has three summits of which only the highest is indicated on LK. Easily climbed by its SW scree, debris and snow slopes from the Cheneil hotels above Valtournanche village in 4 h. By the Cime Bianche cableway from Valtournanche village you can reach c. 2820m. and from there traverse easily S to the Bocchetta Sud del Colle Inf. delle Cime Bianche (2826m.) in 15 min. This col is reached by a track on the Valtournanche side, at the foot of the S ridge of the mtn. Climb this long ridge to the top, by all accounts

W side

Grand Tournalin

Petit Tournalin

Colletto del Tournalin

Becca Trecare

From Cheneil

rather loose with pitches of II ($2\frac{1}{2}$ h. from col).

First climbed by chamois hunters in the early 19th century.

GRAND TOURNALIN 3379m.

The highest summit on the Valtournanche-Ayas dividing ridge, noted for its exceptionally fine panorama over the Matterhorn-Monte Rosa region and more distant alpine ranges. Frequently climbed from Valtournanche village, but hardly ever from S. Giacomo. The summit is double with a N pt. 9m. higher than the S. The S ridge (normal route) drops to a col, not marked on any map, the Colletto del Tournalin (c. 3075m.), before rising again to the Petit Tournalin (3207m.).

The ordinary route, by which nearly all ascents are made, starts from the Cheneil hamlet (2105m., hotels, etc.) above Valtournanche village, $1\frac{1}{2}$ h. by the main jeep road and mule path. A chairlift can be taken to pastures to the N of Cheneil (c. 1850m.), from where a traverse path leads to the hamlet in 45 min. From Cheneil a large footpath with waymarks goes to Alpe Champsec (2331m.) then contours the valley to the SW base of the mtn. Above this a debris slope and snow are climbed to the Colletto del Tournalin, then a track leads up the S ridge to a ruined hut on the S summit, followed by a rough descent into a gap and a short scramble to the highest pt. (4 h. from Cheneil). F.

First ascent: Edward Whymper with J. A. Carrel, 7 August, 1863.

PART VI

Matterhorn – Dent d'Hérens group

Theodulpass to Col des Bouquetins

FURGGGRAT

Ital: Cresta della Forca. The undulating section of frontier ridge running from the Theodulpass to the base of the Matterhorn. Several named summits are formed on this ridge, a complete traverse of which was once a popular training day. The advent of cableways and snowcat vehicles has diminished the attractiveness for this purpose. At the same time the ridge in part or whole is still frequently traversed by parties using mechanical assistance for moving across or along this part of the frontier to reach or leave climbing routes.

A traverse of the entire ridge is F+, though mostly F, interesting, equally on snow and rock terrain. Superb views of the Matterhorn and of the big sub-ranges on either side of the Zermatt valley. From the Theodulpass end the main summits and crossing points on the ridge are (seperate Italian names ignored): Theodulhorn (3468.6m.); Furggsattel (3349m.), reached by skitow on Swiss (N) side; Furgghorn (3466.6m.); Furgggrat summit (3491m.), reached by cableway on Breuil (S) side; Furggjoch (3271m.); La Madonnina (3348.6m.), nameless on LK; Breuiljoch (3323m.). The latter summits and passes are described in Routes 108, 109, 110, 111 for reaching the Bossi biv. For a traverse of the entire ridge allow $3\frac{1}{2}$-4 h.

MATTERHORN 4477.5m.

Cervin, Cervino. No other mtn. in the world is recognised by sight or name more readily than this great rock pyramid which stands between Zermatt and Breuil. It has a history and literature quite unique in the annals of mountaineering. Certainly the most sought-after mtn. among climbers in the world. It has also been climbed by cats, dogs, monkeys and a bear, and by children (one of seven reached the top in 2 h.). Inevitably this mtn. has attracted showmanship and competitive behaviour. It has been brought to earth at armchair level by television.

By the age of 54 at least one living guide had climbed the mtn. 300 times. The summit has been reached in 63 min. The "top block" has been girdled by traversing from ridge to ridge at or near their most difficult points. All four ridges have been climbed in one day, in $19\frac{1}{2}$ h., 28 August, 1966 by the two Zermatt guides R. Arnold and J. Graven. All four ridges and, exceptionally, the N face also have their own variety of stunts and records. One may conclude this theme with a remark of Guido Rey: "its slopes are still considered unsuitable for skiing".

The summit is a narrow horizontal crest about 80m. long. At the E end is the Italian summit (4476.4m.). The mtn. has four ridges and four faces, all of which are described in more or less detail below. The isolated position of the mtn. makes it particularly prone to bad weather and strong winds.

First ascent: E. Whymper, C. Hudson, D. R. Hadow and Francis Douglas with Michel-Auguste Croz and Peter Taugwalder father and son, 14 July, 1865. First traverse (Italian and Hörnli ridges): John Tyndall with J. J. and J. P. Maquignaz, 1868. First winter ascent: Vittorio Sella with J. A., J. B. and L. Carrel, 17 March, 1882. First solo ascent: W. Paulcke, 1898. Solo in winter: G. Gervasatti, 1936.

<u>North-East (Hörnli) Ridge</u>. The normal Swiss route and the easiest way up the mtn. The ridge is longer than the Italian and Furggen ridges, more regular and on the whole less steep than all the others (average angle, 39°), but has slightly worse rock and is somewhat monotonous, especially in descent. Stonefall is also more serious, but this is often due to human agencies. Fresh snow clears slowly from the rocks; in perfect conditions there is permanent snow only on the shoulder and near the summit. In good conditions the route is easy to follow from the trail of scratches, but there are several false trails. In spite of this the correct route, where the rock is sound, is not at all evident, and there are few good landmarks. With fresh snow, route finding is problematical, more so in poor visability. Accidental variations are loose, steep and always unpleasant. The route keeps more or less to the L (E) side of the ridge, and climbs in a series of curving traverses till the shoulder is reached. Axe and crampons are useful above the shoulder, where there are fixed ropes. It is not wise to start much later

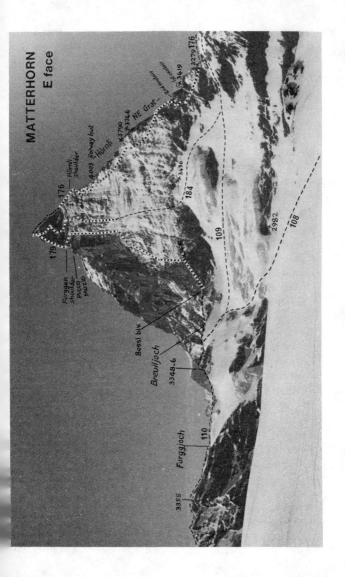

MATTERHORN
E face

179
Furggen shoulder
Pic 010 MUZIO
Bossi biv.
Breuiljoch
3348.6
Furggjoch
110
3355

176
Hörnli shoulder
4003 Solvay hut
×3790
×3714.6
NE Graf-
174
184
3436
3279 176
NE couloir
3419
109
108
2982

than 3 a.m., especially if there are many parties leaving at the same time. In 1974 there was talk of attempting to control the numbers of people climbing the mtn. in one day following reports of long queues just below the summit which can accommodate 40 persons at a time. Including ascents by other routes 200 persons reaching the top on a fine day has become quite common.

PD, numerous short pitches of II. Above the shoulder, pitches of III are avoided by using fixed ropes. First ascensionists. Descended in winter by Sella party (see preamble above). First winter ascent: C. Simon with A. Burgener, A. and J. Pollinger, 27 March, 1894.

176. From the Hörnli hut climb a shaly track behind the hut and go along a hog's back with a slight dip to a rock band on the ridge. Climb this slanting L by a chimney and slab for 15m. (bits of II), then climb straight up for 10m. (slabby, II) to a continuation track in scree and rocks below the crest. Traverse L without losing height to reach the 1st couloir coming down from the crest. Cross this couloir and make a rising traverse on easy rock to a 2nd couloir (stonefall). Climb it for 25m., then move L up a steep open chimney, slanting L, till a third couloir comes into view further L. Now work back R and climb more or less directly and parallel with the 2nd couloir to the crest (1 h.).

Follow a nice rock staircase on the crest for some 15-20 min., then traverse horizontally L for 100m. on to the E face. You are now on a fairly obvious ledge line, so follow it, rising gradually R to where it becomes indistinct, about 25m. below the crest. Traverse L again, curving below steeper rocks, then trend R to a rib (loose) which is climbed to within 50m. of the ridge. Slant L again and reach the foot of a sombre tower, site of old hut, with a plaque (1 h.).

Traverse L below the tower, then climb for a short way towards the crest, before slanting L to reach another rib. Climb it (II) and continue L across a vague hollow, quite large, with a rock band lying across it in the angle-plane of the E face. Climb the band at the correct place (8m., II) and continue the curving traverse till you are directly below the Solvay hut (stonefall). Climb straight up, finally in a near vertical open corner with a peg at the top (Moseley Slab, 8m., II) and reach the hut platform (4003m.) (45 min.).

Traverse L round the hut on to steep rock and climb diagonally L up a narrow slabby gangway with steeper rock above and below: Upper Moseley Slab, 15m., II. Climb R (direct) to the crest as soon as possible (false trail into easy-looking couloir of bad rock on L.) On the crest follow large blocks to a red tower, which is turned on L. Rejoin crest immediately. Continue to broken snowy rocks at the foot of a snow/ice slope: the shoulder (45 min.). Climb this slope (40°) with stanchions at intervals, keeping L of the crest. Reach the crest at the top where the ridge bends L. Climb the pleasant crest at an easy angle on rocks and snow with short turning movements L. Impressive view across N face to R. A slabby rib, usually snowy, leads to the buttressed ridge/step which precedes the summit "roof". The first wall can be climbed L of the fixed rope (8m., good holds, III), the next as you please, L or R of the ropes (II+). A short section without ropes leads to more slabby walls with good ledges between them, usually snow covered, and all draped with ropes. At the top of this section is a vertical pitch (groove on L, III) (45 min.). Reach the upper roof section, a steep rock and snow slope which is climbed direct to the summit. A track is visible when the roof is clear of snow (30 min., 5 h. from hut. 3½ h. in descent but half the parties doing this ridge take as long to go down as up).

South-West (Italian) Ridge. A superb rock ridge, the shortest on the mtn., now draped with many fixed ropes, but a far superior climb compared with the Hörnli. Without the ropes the ridge would be harder than the Zmutt. In fact the average angle is only 36°, but difficulties are fairly continuous. AD, pitches of III. With these ropes it is much less tiring to descend the ridge. The climb is well marked throughout, but is confusing to follow in descent because the fixed ropes are not necessarily placed where the rock appears easiest. There is virtually no stonefall danger. The best time for an ascent is towards the end of the season, when the ridge should be clear of snow. The rock is quite good. First ascent (indirect): Jean-Antoine Carrel and Jean-Baptiste Bich, 17 July, 1865. Route as climbed today: J. J. and J. P. Maquignaz, 13 September, 1867. First winter ascent: Sella party, see introduction to mtn.

177. From the Savoia/Carrel hut (3835m.) climb a steep rock staircase with fixed ropes on the R of the crest to the Grande Tour, which is turned on the R. Pass through an opening between two rocks and climb obliquely up the R side of the ridge, then cross a tiny hollow and move up a step, often verglassed, with a fixed rope. A ledge leads a few m. R, then rises R over slabs, walls and cracks to reach the ridge above the Grande Tour. Go R along a small ledge under the next section of ridge, the Crête du Coq, then pass a small gap in the ridge and some slabs and by a short descent reach the Mauvais Pas in the line of continuation ledges, where a horizontal fixed rope is pinned above a toe ledge. So reach a square-shaped snow/ice patch, called the Linceul. Climb its L edge to a 30m. fixed rope, Corde Tyndall. Climb this strenuously up steep rock with good footholds to the crest where you soon reach a large sloping terrace (snow) on the R, called the Cravate, which stretches far to the R. Cross this in a few steps and go back to the crest. Further on, turn obstacles on the L with a patch of bad rock in crossing a couloir and reach Pic Tyndall (4241m.) (2½ h.).

Continue along a large shoulder, nearly horizontal, which

becomes very narrow and leads in 45 min. to the Enjambée (4244m.), a deep narrow gap which separates the shoulder from the summit mass. Some climbers have jumped the gap, otherwise you descend and pull up awkwardly. The ridge now becomes wider and you climb a scree/snow couloir to Col Felicité, merely a small platform at the foot of a step (30 min.). Turn this step on the L and reach the foot proper of the summit tower; the ridge is not very steep.

Work up L of the crest for several m., then take a narrow ledge leading R and going round to the R-hand side of the ridge, to a fixed rope. Pull up this on a 12m. wall, then make a rising traverse R to a stone covered platform. Above is a fixed rope leading in 15m. to the Echelle Jordan, a ladder hanging in space. Use this to climb an overhang. Above is another rope leading up a slabby wall to a good ledge. Cross this L to the crest and climb the last rope, where you move up a narrow gangway pitch to easy rocks leading to the Italian summit. Go along the airy snow/ice and rock crest, horizontal, to the Swiss summit ($1\frac{1}{2}$ h., 5-$5\frac{1}{2}$ h. from hut. About $4\frac{1}{2}$ h. in descent).

In descent: From the Italian summit follow the ridge to the first rope, swing down it, and cross a ledge L to reach the second rope. Below this Jordan's Ladder and the third rope follow upon each other. Traverse a large terrace R to reach the fourth rope. At its foot, work R along a ledge to the other (R) flank of the ridge, and zigzag down trending R to the Enjambée. Go along the shoulder, turning all obstacles on the R (Swiss) side, but moving L to cross the Cravate. Below the Corde Tyndall, slant R to reach the Linceul, a snow patch situated at the same level as a much larger one further L. Climb down its R edge to the lowest point, then climb R, up to a ledge going behind a buttress, where the horizontal rope of the Mauvais Pas is found. This traverse movement is started before the rope can be seen. Reach a gap in the ridge, step up 2m. to another ledge and follow this till you can descend L, so turning the Grande Tour. The hut is just below (rope).

See approaches to the Bossi biv. (Routes 108, 109, 110, 111) for the most direct way on foot from Zermatt for reaching or returning from the Italian ridge. A reasonably fast party starting from the Hörnli hut can traverse the mtn. and return across the Breuiljoch or Furggjoch to Zermatt in a long day.

North-West (Zmutt) Ridge. The classic route up the mtn., its longest ridge, also the most disjointed. The lower part of the ridge is not climbed. The middle snow section, followed by a few teeth, meets the upper part at the edge of the W face. The direct continuation is the Zmutt Nose, and the route keeps R of this, returning to the ridge proper above the Nose. Needless to say this is one of the most interesting climbs in the Pennine Alps. It is distinctly delicate because the long slab section on the edge of the W face is devoid of good belays. This section is prone to verglas, but when clear of snow there is no rock climbing above grade II. For average conditions crampons are essential for speed and safety. The crossing of Carrel's Gallery and the upper part of the ridge tend to be snowy, and these are bad places to be caught in a storm. In this event it is often easier to traverse off to the R and reach the Italian ridge above the Enjambée. AD, serious. There are two starts, as described below. First ascent: A. F. Mummery with Alexander Burgener, J. Petrus and A. Gentinetta, 3 September, 1879. First solo ascent: Hans Pfann, 1906. First winter ascent: H. Masson and E. Petrig, 25 March, 1948.

178. From the Schönbiel hut follow Route 115 to the snowfields of the Tiefmatten glacier at c. 3000m. beyond Sattelti. On your L hand is an irregular snow bay lying directly below pt. 3424m. on the ridge. Its R-hand side is marked by pt. 3042m. The L-hand side is marked by a rock rib; climb snow immediately

MATTERHORN S face

Pic Tyndall
Furggen shoulder
—Picco Muzio

179

177

179
Bossi biv.

185 Benedetti

Cravate

Corde Tyndall
Mauvais Pas
TESTA DEL
LEONE
Grande Tour
Colle del
Leone
Carrel
hut

Lincon

3558

3243x

111

186

113

Abruzzi
Oriondé hut

3449x

113

113

3976x

R of this rib, up a tongue which near the top is enclosed on the R side by a secondary rib. At the top of the snow tongue move R up a slanting ledge line across the top of the secondary R-hand rib, then cross a watercourse, after which you should climb straight up by scree and rock steps, trending R at one point, to a narrow waterworn gully. Go up this to a scree terrace, then bear L over slabs to reach the watercourse again. Climb its L side to scree and snow leading to the lower end of the Zmutt snow ridge. If there is a lot of fresh snow, reach the precise lower end of the snow ridge by climbing L, away from the watercourse ($4\frac{1}{2}$ h.).

Climb the moderately steep snow ridge to the rock teeth at the top (30 min.).

Starting from the Hörnli hut reach the hog's back of scree behind the hut and follow it to a slight dip. Now descend obliquely R and set foot on the lower terrace of the Matterhorn glacier. Cross this in a few min. to a rock band supporting the upper terrace. This band is surmounted by ice cliffs. To climb it go right under the side of the Hörnli ridge. There is serious stonefall danger at this point, and the sooner it is reached the better. Beside the bergschrund under the ridge flank, climb a break in the rock band where it meets the flank, loose rocks and a snow/ice slope, and so avoid the ice cliffs further R. So reach the upper terrace. All this should be done in 30 min. Now cross the upper glacier terrace WNW and reach the foot of the NE flank of the Zmutt snow ridge, at c. 3400m. Climb steep snow trending first R, then L to a vague rock rib rising S towards the crest. Climb the steep rib to the ridge (3627m.). When icy this ascent to the ridge can be very delicate. Continue up the crest to the rock teeth ($3\frac{1}{2}$ h. on average). The ascent of the rib can be avoided by traversing further R on the glacier, some crevasse complications, then climbing up further R.

Traverse the first tooth on the crest and turn the second on the R, to reach a gap with a jammed block. Now either follow the shattered crest, or keep slightly on the R side, to the gap at the end of the teeth section (30 min.). Climb straight up a series of steep steps on the crest above (II) to a small shoulder, horizontal for a few m. Move a few m. L into an open gully, often icy, and climb it to the crest again at the foot of the Zmutt Nose (1 h.). Now trend R on to the W face for about 50m., following a vague ledge line usually snow covered. At the top of this rising traverse climb straight up an easy rock rib, then in a broad couloir of slabs (verglas) to Carrel's Gallery. This is a large sloping (40°) terrace lying between the Italian ridge (R) and Zmutt (L), and is cut by the aforementioned couloir. When the snow is good move L out of the couloir and cross the terrace to the ridge. Otherwise, after moving L for a few m., climb up the terrace to the wall above it; a steep snow tongue slants L to a knoll of red rocks, from where you continue up an obvious red rock couloir, followed by several red rock steps, to finish trending L to reach the ridge. From the Gallery level, the crest is climbed by pleasant snowy rocks to the Italian summit (up to 3 h. from foot of Zmutt Nose, say 10 h. from Schönbiel hut, 8 h. from Hörnli hut).

<u>South-East (Furggen) Ridge.</u> The hardest of the ridges, entirely on rock with an average angle of 44°. The ridge rises with progressive steepness in three obvious tower/steps. From the main shoulder below the summit, the vertical and overhanging upper one has been climbed or turned in three ways. Some of the rock is poor but it improves higher up. There are sharp gendarmes in the lower part of the ridge which are avoided on the R; most of the approach to the upper shoulder keeps to the E flank, and the rocks are often snow covered. The ridge still has an awesome reputation but is not too difficult in good conditions by the indirect finish. According to conditions, stonefall both in the lower and upper parts of the

ridge can be quite serious. Piacenza climbed further L than Benedetti in getting round the upper step, but the indirect route is still named after the former climber (a ritual with the Breuil guides).

Piacenza (Benedetti) original indirect finish: D-, sustained, with pitches of IV. Direct finish: TD with pitches of V/V+ allowing for plenty of peg moves, and therefore harder if climbed mainly free, fairly sustained. Vertical interval from foot of ridge, 1100m. The final step is 230m. with the difficulties concentrated in the first 150m. First ascent: M. Piacenza with J. J. Carrel and J. Gaspard, 9 September, 1911. Improved finish, described below: E. Benedetti with L. Carrel and M. Bich, 2 September, 1930. Direct finish: A. Perino with L. Carrel and G. Chiara, using 43 pegs, 23 September, 1942. Both routes have now had many ascents. First winter ascent (direct finish): W. Bonatti and R. Bignami, 20-21 March, 1953. First British ascent of Direct Route: C. J. Mortlock and C. W. F. Noyce, 8 August, 1959.

179. From the Bossi biv. just above the Breuiljoch climb rocks and snow patches to the foot of the ridge proper (3478m.) in a few min. Cross several easy rock steps, then traverse L of the crest to a deep chimney, broad at the base. Climb it (30m., III), then some slabs to rejoin the ridge. Move R of the crest to the E side. Easy rocks lead straight up under the crest for 300m. to a shoulder (3087m. IGM) on the crest to the L, which merges into the E face. This is above the top of the first tower. Trend R up a snow/ice tongue, then work L along ledges to a couloir. Cross this (II+, dangerous stonefall) and reach the continuation crest above the second tower. Climb again to the R on moderately difficult rocks below the main Furggen shoulder, then make a rising traverse R up a slabby/snowy gully, and exit L below its top to reach the Furggen shoulder (c. 4240m.) above the third tower, called Picco Muzio (4191m. IGM). On the R are delicate snowy ledges named after Mummery leading to the Hörnli ridge shoulder (4 h.).

Indirect finish: Cross the level shoulder and continue by a delicate and exposed ledge line and cracks to the L (30m., III), then climb a wall/corner (4m.) to a narrow ledge again leading L (peg). Follow this horizontally under an overhanging chimney for about 20m., with a slight descent (III), to reach a projection of rotten yellowish rocks. About 10m. R of this, climb a partly overhanging wall and groove with stiff pull-ups over tiny jutting stances on laminated rock (IV) to a good stance. Continue by traversing L across and up a wet black wall, vertical (IV) and reach a tiny stance (peg belay). Traverse L again for another 30m., then climb direct by easier rocks and a snow/ice slope, skirting a final overhanging balcony. Reach a niche beside snow patches which extend L along the foot of the summit cliff on the S face. Climb R by fairly easy rock, with a crack slanting R (III) to a ledge at the foot of the upper wall. Follow this R, to the base of the last couloir/chimney. Climb it, chockstone (IV), or take the rib between it and the true crest further R (IV+). So reach the terminal crest which is followed without further difficulty to the summit (3 h., about 7 h. from Bossi biv.).

Direct finish: There is more than one way to reach the overhanging crux and this description is taken from that of the third ascensionists. Cross the shoulder as indicated above and climb a large open chimney, easy, which slants R to a slope of scree and loose rock at the edge of the E face. Climb this edge on delicate snowy rocks to where the wall steepens. Traverse R along the top of a snow patch to a chimney/crack. Climb it on the L and R, and up the centre on bad rock (IV) nearly to the top (40m.). Exit L and climb diagonally to a small balcony on the crest. From the L end of the platform climb a chimney (10m., IV) to a large snowy terrace on the R side of the ridge. Trend L up the wall above, to below the overhangs (10m., (IV+). From a peg runner move L using a finger crack and reach the edge of the ridge (V). Climb the overhang above on doubtful rock, with two pegs for protection, mantelshelves on blocks about 1m. wide (V/V+) and reach a stance. Climb the next chimney by jamming (V, icy), then exit L up a cracked wall and pull round the L end of a roof overhanging the S face (V/V+). A loose wall, sometimes verglassed (V), leads to a niche and, a little higher, a large comfortable ledge. Continue up the moderately difficult ridge, soon easing, to the summit (4 h., about 8 h. from Bossi biv.).

North Face (Schmid Route). One of the six famous North Walls of the Alps. Like the others it is no longer considered an extreme undertaking, and this one has justly won the status of becoming in mountaineering parlance a classic route. The face is mainly composed of unstable rock covered with varying amounts of snow, according to the time of year and season. Long sections are usually verglassed and stonefall is frequent. Optimum conditions are a lot of snow on the face, as during the early part of the season, or in a bad year, and after two or three fine days with very cold nights. Then the loose rock will be frozen and the icy rock covered with hard snow. In these conditions crampons can be worn for the entire expedition. There have been fairly frequent winter ascents when similar conditions prevail. Contrary to early reports there are good resting places and even bivouac sites, and pegs can be used for protection all the way. The climbing is more or less very delicate but not sustained. TD-/TD with technical rock pitches of IV, 1000m. from bergschrund. The line slants progressively R, starting up the centre of an obvious ice slope/ bay below the middle part of the Hörnli ridge. The lower L edge of this inlet is marked by pt. 3353m.

First ascent: Franz and Toni Schmid, 31 July - 1 August, 1931. Second ascent: L. Leiss and J. Schmidbauer, 16-18 July, 1935. First solo ascent: Dieter Marchart, 22 July,

MATTERHORN from NW

Pic Tyndall
SW grat
Carrel hut
Testa del Leone
Colle del Leone
Tiefmatten glacier
Sattelti
177
178
3624'
778
3627'
778
3577
shoulder
Solvay hut
176
182
3499'
181
180
178
178
3353'
Hörnli NE grat
Hörnli hut

1959 (in 5 h.). First British (18th) ascent: T. Carruthers and B. Nally, 30-31 August, 1961. First winter ascent: P. Etter and H. von Allmen, 3-4 February, 1962. British winter ascents (3rd): G. Huber and B. Nally, 18-20 February, 1962. M. Burke and D. Haston (5th), 10-12 February, 1967. Climbed during the Matterhorn centenary year, 1965, by a party including a woman, Yvette Vaucher. British solo ascent: Eric Jones, August, 1973 in $9\frac{1}{2}$ h. Climbed about 95 times to end of 1973.

180. From the Hörnli hut reach the foot of the face by Route 178. Cross the bergschrund at c. 3380m. and climb the snow/ice slope (50°) to near its highest point on the R. Next climb steep but straightforward broken rocks and snow up to the R in three or four rope lengths, to below a steep wall, then traverse R towards the bottom of an obvious shallow couloir, the main feature of the face. Descend 15m. and climb a chimney (30m., IV) to the bed of the couloir. It may well be safer to climb the L side of the couloir, where an easy line is protected from above by overhangs. The R side, more towards the Zmutt ridge, is the safest position on the face, but the rocks here are quite difficult. Reach the deep head of the couloir, where it disappears. Traverse R to a band of slabs, then go straight up a steep and very loose wall (IV/IV+) to a ledge. Now an easy traverse R leads to a pulpit and good bivouac site. Follow grooves (III) trending R, which lead to a good ledge on the Zmutt ridge. Avoid this and climb the steep face with a short pitch of IV to the notch between the two summits, near the Italian one on the R (about 12 h. from hut on average, climbed by several parties from foot of face in 6-7 h.).

181. Bonatti North Face Route. Recorded as North Face Direct in some foreign publications. This bold and audacious line, characteristic of its inventor, starts well to the R of the Schmid route and directly below the summit. After an initial section

256

up an ice slope, mixed ground and bad rocks it crosses the vertical and overhanging rock band curving down from the Zmutt Nose further R by a sensational and very difficult "Traverse of the Angels", L-wards to reach the main part of the N face still well to the R of the Schmid Route. This is climbed up a series of very steep walls, slabs, steps and towers with continuous difficulties and artificial climbing till the Zmutt Ridge is joined about 20m. from the Italian summit. Mostly poor rock with difficult pegging, precarious and delicate climbing. ED with pitches of VI and A2/3. 1100m.

First ascent: Walter Bonatti, solo, 18-22 February, 1965. Climbed twice in 1966. Second winter ascent: J. Durana, S. Lednar, M. Kalab and J. Psotka, 15-21 March, 1967. Fifth ascent: V. Kangar and M. Vacik, 21-23 July, 1967.

182. Zmutt Nose Route (North Face). First ascent: A. Gogna and L. Cerruti, 14-17 July, 1969. Second and first winter ascent: E. Oberson and T. Gross, 25-28 January, 1974. Generally considered the "last great problem" of the Matterhorn, but in fact one that is not completely solved because the crest of the Nose remains untouched. On the credit side, the Nose itself would give a relatively short climb if it were done from the Zmutt Ridge before the latter route moves on to the edge of the W face, leaving the Gogna-Cerruti route as a reasonably satisfactory solution. The route starts a little R of the Bonatti and pursues an extremely difficult line up the great curving rock band which at this point lies almost in a perpendicular plane, resembling a pillar below the apex of the Nose. The climbing is extreme with frequent pitches of VI and artificial techniques. Gogna has published a pitch by pitch and for some sections almost step by step description of the route, in 37 stages, which appears in the CAI/TCI Alpi Pennine Vol II guide (1970). There is a verbatim translation into French in the CAS guide of 1970. ED+, VI and A3.

183. West Face. This huge rock wall is contained between the Zmutt and Italian ridges and is 1200m. at its highest point. It is raked by frequent stonefall and is at the best of times dangerous. Early attempts on the face started up the L side, further L than the great couloir named after Penhall and leading to the Zmutt ridge below its Nose. The couloir was reached and crossed about half-way up by the original party who continued on rocks straight up to join the Zmutt ridge route below Carrel's Gallery. W. Penhall with F. Imseng and L. Zurbrücken, 3 September, 1879. A solo ascent of this dangerous, uninspiring but not particularly difficult climb was made by F. Herrmann, 18 July, 1929. From below the avalanche cone entrance to the Penhall couloir a line going almost straight up to the Enjambée on the Italian ridge was made by C. Taddei with L. Carrel, 20-22 August, 1947. TD, difficult and delicate with pitches of IV and V, many pegs used, serious objective danger. Finally, the face between the Penhall couloir and the Carrel-Taddei line was climbed direct to finish at the summit by R. Daguin and G. Ottin, 13 August, 1962, in 10 h. with ideal conditions. TD, pitches of V/V+.

184. East Face. A long, monotonous slope of rotten rocks, generally snowy, inclined at 45-50° up to the horizontal Mummery ledges running from the Hörnli shoulder to the Furggen shoulder. AD, 850m. Bad stonefall. Above the ledges, the summit wall is climbed direct by a big zigzag R then L. Another 200m., TD. First complete ascent: E. Benedetti and G. Mazzotti with L. and L. Carrel, M. Bich and A. Gaspard, 18-19 September, 1932. Second ascent: S. Biel and J. Nostowski, 25-26 April, 1959.

185. South Face. An enormous concave wall bounded on the L (SW) by a twisting ridge coming down from Pic Tyndall on the Italian ridge, and called the Cresta De Amicis, and on the R limited by the Furggen ridge, although a large pillar/spur coming down from the third tower on this ridge just below the Furggen shoulder (called Picco Muzio, 4191m. IGM, see Route 179) really confines the R side of the face.

The middle of the face is marked by a large depression, narrowing to a stoneswept ravine in the lower part. Its immediate L side is contained by a broad buttress, narrowing to a rib near the top which finishes just L of the Enjambée on the Italian ridge. The R side of the depression is marked by one edge of the aforementioned pillar descending from Picco Muzio.

All these features of the face have been climbed by routes exposed to falling stones, and on mainly poor rock and difficult mixed terrain. Only the Cresta De Amicis at the extreme L side is safe and recommendable. To the R of this comes the broad buttress on the L side of the ravine. This buttress is called the Crestone Deffeyes-Carrel (A. Deffeyes with L. Carrel, 11 September, 1942). The route follows its L edge all the way on generally poor rock at grade IV/V with some artificial climbing. Not repeated. Next is the central depression of the wall which forms the S face proper. It was first climbed by E. Benedetti with L. Carrel and M. Bich, 15 October, 1931. It follows an obvious rib on the R of the great ravine, and uses its L flank to pass below the Picco Muzio pillar to reach the centre of the depression below the summit wall. After a fairly direct ascent, a traverse L up a ramp leads to the steep snowbands under the summit wall. This is climbed at its L side, quite close to the finish of the ordinary Italian ridge route, by a steep and very difficult couloir. The rock throughout is generally poor and stonefall is serious except in perfect conditions for this sort of face. The probability of such conditions is more remote than similar ones needed for the N face. Verglas and large snow/ice plaques at a high angle are normal. 1200m., D+, pitches of III/IV, sustained, with one pitch of V in the terminal couloir. Only 5 pegs were used on the first ascent, with a time of 12 h. from the foot of the face. This route is reckoned by Alessandro Gogna as "brilliant, logical and direct ... a magnificent climb which deserves re-valuation despite the fact that it can only be tackled in cold weather if bad stonefall is to be avoided". Repeated in 1942 and 1962, the latter being almost an entirely new line. Fourth and first British ascent: B. Nally and C. Phillips, 9 September, 1966, in 19 h. They declared it more dangerous than the Eiger North Wall. Ascended in winter by a dead heat after seige-like attempts and much preparatory work involving several parties among whom A. and O. Squinobal were prominent, 23 December, 1971.

On the R side of the S face depression is the pillar/spur de-scending from Picco Muzio. The front of this spur forms a large triangular wall. Its L edge (forming the R edge of the depression) is the Cresta Muzio, which is approached as for the Benedetti S face route. The L side of the crest is followed on mainly good rock to the Picco Muzio and Furggen shoulder. Hard, sustained rock climbing in the upper part, pitches of V+ and A1, 60 pegs on first ascent: L. Maquignaz and I. Muzio with L. Carrel, 3-4 September, 1953. Unrepeated. The R edge of the triangular wall (base pt. 3294m.) is taken on its R side by a later and no better wall route of 900m., referred to as the SE face of Picco Muzio. It starts up a prominent couloir for 350m. on the R side of the edge, which is very difficult and exposed to stonefall, before gaining open rock to the L quite a long way up. It finishes up the R side of the terminal crest. ED-, pitches of VI and A2. G. Lafranconi and A. Zucchi, 11-13 August, 1965.

Lastly the buttress/wall front to the L of the previous route, avoiding the dangerous couloir, was climbed as the SE pillar of Picco Muzio by G. Calcagno, L. Cerruti, G. Machetto and C. Di Pietro, 14 July, 1970, reporting a safe, sound climb on reasonable rock. VI and A1.

<u>Cresta De Amicis (South-West Spur of Pic Tyndall)</u>. See first three paragraphs addressed to S face above. This conspicuous spur offers a direct and alternative route to the Italian ridge for reaching the summit from the Breuil side of the mtn. Notwithstanding some stonefall danger in the lower part, while the rest is safe and sure, it is climbed fairly frequently. Having normally to start from the Duca degli Abruzzi hut is a drawback, making the climb a long one, but a bivouac can be made if desired. Some parties have made the ascent to the summit in 8 h. The ridge was first climbed by U. De Amicis and A. Frusta, 11 August, 1906, up to its steep terminal section above the snowy Cravate ledges, where by moving L the Italian ridge can be reached easily. Above the Cravate the last part was finally climbed by A. Crétier and B. Ollietti with A. Gaspard, 7 July, 1933. However this party did not continue to the summit and descended the Italian ridge. The first complete ascent including the last section climbed direct to Pic Tyndall (where previous parties had made a circuit to the L) was achieved by A. Perino with L. and M. Carrel, 19 August, 1940. The "safe" approach to the ridge (described below) was devised by E. Gianotti with G. Bich and L. Carrel, 13 August, 1942. First winter ascent: L. Ratto with G. Ottin, 9 February, 1964.

Topographically the spur falls into three sections/steps. A steep lower buttress, fairly broad, capped by a shoulder where the ridge develops clearly (3558m.). A curving middle section rising to a short shoulder (lower end, 3991m.) forming one end of the snowy Cravate ledges running L to the Italian ridge. A much steeper terminal ridge up to Pic Tyndall (4241m.) where the Italian ridge is joined (Route 177). Up to the Cravate ledges, AD with a few short pitches of III and one of III+/IV on mostly good rock; easier than the comparable section of the Italian ridge if its ropes were removed. The crux pitch is sometimes fully pegged up like a staircase. Above the Cravate, IV+, but easily avoided as is done by most parties by a traverse

L below Pic Tyndall. The original direct start up the front of the spur to pt. 3558m. is difficult and dangerous.

186. From the Duca degli Abruzzi hut follow Route 113 to the small snowfield below the couloir leading up L towards the Testa del Leone. Keep R, along the sloping scree/snow terrace which leads out across a broken rock rib to the Upper Cervino glacier lying below the SW face of Pic Tyndall. Make a rising traverse R (NE) across the glacier, crevasses and mini-bergschrunds in same direction, to its top R-hand side at c. 3420m., now under the side of our ridge where the rocks are yellowish (stonefall). Cross a bergschrund and climb the broken flank of the ridge, trending R up and across shallow couloirs and slabs to reach the crest at the L (N) end of its shoulder marked at the S end by pt. 3558m., ($2\frac{1}{2}$ h.). Now follow the pleasant ridge, turning the first pitch on the L side by a flake ledge. Climb the second step fairly direct by a red dièdre, and turn the next two on the L by traverses across broken walls. Finally reach a steep wall which is normally climbed direct by a zigzag line, L, R, then L again (40m., III+/IV, pegs normally in place). This pitch can be avoided by a wide turning movement to the L on dangerously loose but fairly easy rock, also exposed to stonefall. Above this section easy broken rock and mixed ground lead to the sloping shoulder formed by the R end of the Cravate ($2\frac{1}{2}$ h.).

At this point the difficult terminal section can be avoided by moving L along the snowbands of the Cravate, delicate when icy, to join the Italian ridge above the Corde Tyndall (PD-).

To continue up the ridge. Start L of the crest line below a steep smooth wall. Climb a large black dièdre by a chimney containing several large loose flakes and blocks (IV+, pegs, delicate and strenuous). Exit R to avoid a reddish triangular roof and climb delicately to the crest on the R, about 50m. in all. Follow the loose but fairly easy crest to Pic Tyndall (2 h., 7 h. from Duca degli Abruzzi hut, continued to summit by Route

177 in another 3 h., or save 45 min. to 1 h. by turning the last step along the Cravate).

COLLE DEL LEONE 3580m. 3581m. IGM

Between the Matterhorn and Testa del Leone, a severe pass on the N side, steep, dangerous and quite difficult, attaining notoriety as a result of the description in Mummery's book. AD+. Only of historical interest. The Italian side is reached by the approach to the Savoia/Carrel hut (Route 113). First traversed by A. F. Mummery with A. Burgener, 6 July, 1880.

TESTA DEL LEONE 3715m.

Fr. Tête du Lion. Climbed from Route 113, before moving R along the gallery to the Colle del Leone, by moving L (stone-fall) across snow to the rocky W ridge and climbing this to summit easily. F+ (3 h. from Abruzzi hut). First ascent: A. Gorret with J. A. and J. J. Carrel, 1857.

COLLE TOURNANCHE 3479m. 3484m. IGM

Between the Testa del Leone and Dent d'Hérens, from the Zmutt glacier basin (Schönbiel hut) to Breuil. An important glacier pass amid magnificent scenery, rarely crossed as such, from which the great E ridge of the Dent d'Hérens is climbed. The Benedetti biv. hut is close to the col. See Routes 114, 115. The ridge is crossed further W than the lowest pt., as indicated in these routes. First crossing: F. W. Jacomb and J. A. Hudson with P. Perren and I. Lauber, 25 August, 1864.

DENT D'HÉRENS 4171.4m.

One of the most interesting 4000m. peaks in the Alps, curiously complex, although this is not evident from the Swiss side which is dominated by an elongated N face and a staircase ridge with several imposing steps rising from the Colle Tournanche. Further R (W), and unseen from the Zermatt-Schönbiel foot-path, is the tall narrow WNW face, adjacent to the Tiefmatten-joch. The Italian side is less impressive, more remote and the peak tends to lose its individualism above the immense Grandes Murailles glacier, except in distant views. The mtn. is the most difficult of all major peaks in the Zermatt neighbourhood. The ascent is distinctly more serious than the Dent Blanche and Täschhorn. The main problems are on snow or ice, yet in ideal conditions the climb can be found perfectly easy. Such conditions are not uncommon. In a good season the mtn. is climbed fairly often, probably more often than the Täschhorn but not as frequently as the Dent Blanche. More ascents/descents are made by the W ridge than any other route. Good experience and judgement of steep glacier terrain is essential.

First ascent: W. E. Hall, F. C. Grove, R. S. Macdonald and M. Woodmass with Melchior Anderegg, P. Perren and J. P. Cachat, 12 August, 1863. First winter ascent: M. Piacenza with J. J. Carrel and G. B. Pellisier, 16 January, 1910. First ski ascent: H. Hafers de Magelhaes with A. Schaller and V. Biner, 28 February, 1918.

<u>South-West Flank and West Ridge</u>. The ordinary Italian route and the only straightforward way up this side of the mtn. Comparatively little used, mainly due to the tiresome approach to the Aosta hut. Unfairly condemned in other guidebooks on this account, a criticism that can only relate to better but harder routes on the mtn. and not logically to normal routes on other 4000m. peaks in the region. If this route was transposed to any part of the Mischabel or Zermatt West chains it would be one of the most popular ascents in the region. The route takes the N side of the Grandes Murailles glacier then mixed ground on the SW flank to join the W ridge shortly before the rocks forming a junction with the NW ridge (forepeak). PD-. First ascensionists.

187. From the Aosta hut descend the approach path for c. 50m., then turn L (E) and cross scree to the lateral moraine of the Grandes Murailles glacier. Follow a faint track along the moraine ridge on to the N branch of the glacier, below the Tête de Valpelline. On your R is the Rocher Silvano (pt. 3160m. LK). Ascend E up a wide snow cwm along the S base of the Tête de Valpelline then trend R towards a small icefall at

DENT D'HÉRENS SW side

Tête de Chavannes — Tête Blanche — Col de Valpelline — Tête de Valpelline — Tiefmartenjoch — Col des Grandes Murailles — Pta. Margherita — Jumeaux

Col de la Division — Rocher Silvano — Grandes — Tête des Ro,s,es biv. — Murailles glacier

194 — 196 — 189 — 195 — 187 — 207 — 195

c. 3250m. This is normally best climbed by means of a corridor/ramp rising diagonally R to L, although it may be practical to keep L on the crevassed N edge of the glacier . Either way reach the buttress foot, pt. 3337m.

Continue up the glacier on gentle snow slopes, passing L of most crevassed sections. Above 3600m. the slope steepens . Aim for the foot of the SSW ridge, then bear L (NE) to cross the bergschrund at c. 3800m. After a snow slope start up the SW flank, composed of loose rock and snow patches. A few tiny cairns indicate the approx. line up to the W ridge. Some steep scrambling but otherwise not difficult if the correct line is followed. Deviations from it involve technical pitches. In general slant L and reach the W ridge at c. 4040m.

Climb the W ridge crest or the snow slope to its L (WNW face) without difficulty, up to a broken rock triangle forming a forepeak at the junction of the W and NW ridges. Climb the rocks slanting L up a broken couloir and snow patches to the forepeak. Continue along a fine rock and snow crest to the summit (5 h. from Aosta hut in good conditions, $2\frac{1}{2}$ h. in descent). Parties using this route for descent should take care to leave the W ridge for the SW flank at the correct point.

West-North-West Face. A miniature glacier and icefall, this face is tall and narrow, bounded on the L by the NW ridge and on the R by the W ridge, which meet at the tapered top of the face. At the bottom, the W ridge stands high above the foot of the face, and its lowest point is the Tiefmattenjoch. The face is marginally the most relaible way up and down the mtn. on the Swiss side; it is sometimes impossible. Getting down from the Tiefmattenjoch (W ridge) is not an attractive proposition, so you must on most occasions take pot luck on the face, or choose to escape by the Italian route and thereby fail to return to your starting point. The lower half of the face is at an average angle of 48° and is cut by long crevasses and several ice cliffs. The upper part is a plain snow slope of 35°, crowned by rocks. AD-/AD. 700m. An interesting and variable snow/ice climb with route finding problems. Study the face well before starting up it. Descended by V. J. E. Ryan with J. and F. Lochmatter, 30 July, 1906. Climbed by M. Heywood and G. W. Young with J. Knubel, 18 August, 1910.

188. From the Schönbiel hut take the lower approach line of Route 14 to the sheepfold (site of old hut), near where the route to the Col d'Hérens climbs R (N) to the top of the Stockji. Continue the traverse line and descend from the rognon SSW over rubble to the Tiefmatten glacier. Climb this close to the R side, hugging a buttress to avoid large crevasses which spread from the first icefall at c. 2900m. Continue towards the second icefall, then cross the glacier diagonally L towards the Dent d'Hérens, and climb the icefall near its L side, not too close because of avalanches, at c. 3100m. The icefall can be climbed more awkwardly near the R side. Either way is quite short. Now cross the flat upper glacier plateau towards the foot of the Tiefmattenjoch and reach the foot of the face on your L ($2\frac{3}{4}$ h.).

During the early part of the season, or in a snowy year, an easy route can be found through the ice walls on the face. It has been cramponed in 30 min. Normally three large crevasses cut the slope and progress is further confused by ice walls; these are in two sections above the crevasses. Turn the crevasses on the R, dangerous concealed lips, and seek a way through the ice walls in the centre of the face, to reach the straightforward upper slope. Climb this direct, then slant R towards the W ridge, which is reached without difficulty not far from the rocks forming a junction with the NW ridge. Climb these rocks, slanting L up a broken couloir and snow patches to the apex (forepeak). Continue along a fine snow and rock crest to the summit ($3\frac{1}{2}$ h. on average, $6\frac{1}{4}$ h. from Schönbiel hut). In good conditions the face is a quick descent route.

<u>West Ridge (from Tiefmattenjoch).</u> See introductory remarks
to WNW face. According to fancy, this is either a better or
worse route to the summit when tackled from the Swiss side,
but it is normally a little harder. It has advantages in ascent.
It is fairly sure, but avalanche conditions on the Tiefmatten
slope after midday make it risky for descent. So you should
descend by the WNW face. As the Tiefmattenjoch can be reached
more easily from the Aosta hut (Italian) side, see Route note
193, this is a good option for parties based in the upper Valpelline, i.e. instead of the normal Italian route, or for making
a traverse by descending the latter. Varied and interesting
climbing on a steep snow/ice slope on the Swiss side, and a
narrow snow/rock ridge. AD-, with pitches of II and one of
III+. Not sustained. First ascent: A. G. Puller with E.,
J.J. and P. Maquignaz and L. Carrel, 18 July, 1873.

189. Start as for Route 188 and reach the foot of the Tiefmattenjoch $2\frac{3}{4}$ h.). This col (3565m.) has two crescent-shaped
saddles, separated by rocks and a gendarme. Cross a large
bergschrund and climb a snow/ice slope (51°) directly towards
the R-hand (W) saddle. Half-way up, trend a little R, then L,
where the slope eases (1-$1\frac{1}{2}$ h.). One correspondent has reported a bare rock rib exposed in this slope for more than half
its height, making the ascent easier.

Go along a snow ridge, climb a rock knoll and turn a gendarme on the R. Descend to a fine snow crest, delicate and
possibly corniced. Cross it by the exposed slope of the second
saddle on the L side to the next group of rocks (3602m.). Continue with interest and short difficulties to a small snow
shoulder. There is a close and instructive view of the WNW
face to your L. Now climb steeper rocks on the crest (III, II)
and reach a gendarme. It is best to climb this direct by the
block crest on good holds (III+), and from the top descend to a
small shoulder, from where you drop to a stony saddle. Continue up the easy ridge till it is possible to step L on to the

DENT D'HÉRENS
WNW face

forepeak

NW grat

exit
point
187

187

188

189

top part of the WNW face, not far from the rock triangle forming a junction with the NW ridge. Reach the summit as for Route 188 (3 h., $6\frac{3}{4}$-$7\frac{1}{4}$ h. from Schönbiel hut).

East Ridge. A magnificent expedition, the most formidable ridge on length in the Zermatt district, and one of the longest (2.2 km.) and finest in the Alps, over several huge tower/ steps with their own names, on bad to fair rock. There are also some fine snow crests. The ridge is climbed more fre-quently by parties starting from Breuil. From Zermatt you should preferably go direct to the Benedetti biv. hut in one day (Route 115). The ridge has been climbed in $4\frac{1}{2}$ h. but nearly twice this time is normally required. In good conditions the technical difficulties are not great (III+), but the climbing is sustained, the situations constantly exposed, and care and steadiness are required throughout. Although the vertical interval is only 700m., the length of the ridge makes it a very serious undertaking and there is no easy way off before you reach the upper snow shoulder (4039m. IGM), about $1\frac{1}{4}$ h. from the summit. Standard: D, numerous pitches of III and some of III+ which are notably harder with fresh snow or verglas. First complete ascent: V. J. E. Ryan with F. and J. Loch-matter, 30 July, 1906. Has been climbed in April which is not strictly a winter ascent.

190. From the Benedetti biv. slant L on to the main snow ridge, turning rock outcrops and cornices on the L then go up a loose but easy rock section towards a knoll called Punta Maria Cristina (3706m.). Its summit can be turned by ledges on the L (1 h.). Regain the crest and descend difficult slabs to a gap at the head of a large couloir. Depending on conditions, either cross the narrow, corniced snow saddle (100m., delicate) or traverse the couloir slope on the L below it. Col Maquignaz (3637m. IGM). On the far side continue as far as possible up a snow
270

tongue L of the crest towards the next tower. Finally take the rocks, steep and loose (stonefall). Trend L to avoid a steep pitch and work straight up to reach the SE ridge of the tower, which is climbed up mixed ground to the summit of the tower: Punta Maquignaz (3801m. TCI) ($1\frac{1}{4}$ h.).

Follow a short and very narrow rock crest to a little col at the foot of the next tower, which has two overhanging pts. Climb the ridge on bad rock to below the main overhang, then traverse delicately R on poor rock to a black chimney in the N face of the tower. Climb it (III+, tricky with fresh snow or verglas) and exit through a window on to the other side of the ridge, above which a few short rock steps lead to the top of the tower: Punta Carrel (3841m.) ($1\frac{1}{4}$ h.).

Broken rocks, a snow ridge then slabs to the L lead down to a gap at the foot of the next tower/step. Go more or less straight up the broad steep ridge by not too difficult rocks to where the crest narrows, becomes vague, steep and difficult. Make a rising traverse L on steep rock for 25m. (III+), rejoin the crest line and follow it, or its L side, to the top of the tower; Punta Bianca (3918m.) ($1\frac{1}{2}$ h.).

There follows a mixed ridge with teeth to the next gap. Avoid the teeth by moving down L over an icy rock slope and a couloir, and rejoin the crest at a small snow saddle. Continue on or near the crest which is partly snowy, normally easier on the R side. Take a gendarme direct, then a steep snow/ice pitch to a rock pitch which is climbed by a crack entered from a delicate traverse. Above this easier rock leads to the Spalla (Shoulder) (4039m.) ($1\frac{1}{2}$ h.). Escape to the L, down a glacier cwm leading on to the Grandes Murailles glacier, is possible from here, now that the main difficulties and length of the ridge are finished.

The ridge beyond is now snow and rock and easier. Follow it to a large hoof rock, the Corne-Gendarme (4075m.), which is turned by ledges on the L, then climb a couloir to rejoin

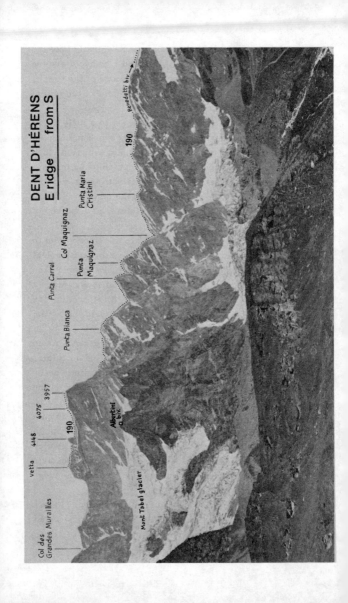

DENT D'HÉRENS   E ridge   from S

Col des Grandes Murailles

vetta   4148   4075   3957   190

Punta Bianca

Punta Carrel

Col Maquignaz

Punta Maquignaz

Punta Maria Cristini

190

Albertini q. biv.

Mont Tabel glacier

benedetti biv.

the crest. The final snow/rock ridge to the summit is easy (about 1 h., 8 h. from Benedetti hut in good conditions, allow at least 10 h.).

North Face Diagonal (Finch Route). About two-thirds way up the N face of the mtn. an outward sloping glacier terrace slants from R to L across the entire face from the NW ridge to the W ridge. The terrace does not connect directly to either ridge and this fact accounts for the main difficulties. Access to it from the R end can be quite awkward and is liable to stonefall. But for the daunting appearance of this entrance, and of the exit, the route would be climbed more frequently. As it is it has been mainly done to date by guided parties, being a speciality of some Zermatt guides. A fine snow/ice route, quite long, with a steep exit on ice to the W ridge. Recommended only in good conditions. AD+. First ascent: G. I. Finch, T. G. B. Forster and R. Peto, 2 August, 1923.

191. From the Schönbiel hut follow Route 188 to the L side of the upper snowfield at 3300m. running to the N foot of the Tiefmattenjoch. Bear L up a snow slope between the NW ridge and the rock buttresses marked at their foot by pt. 3134m. Trend R up this slope to a large bergschrund beside the toe of the NW ridge (3 h.). Cross this, sometimes with great difficulty, and reach the steep loose rocks of the ridge. Alternatively work L along the bergschrund and find an easier crossing point, above which make a steep diagonal traverse back to the R. Climb the ridge for c. 200m. on steep unpleasant rocks, then traverse L across an icy couloir and steep rocks to reach the lower end of the great diagonal glacier terrace above its contorted entrance. This traverse can be very delicate and it may be easier to continue higher up the ridge before moving L. The latter can involve descending across an upper bergschrund to set foot on the terrace proper. In some conditions steep snow/ice can be climbed below the L side of the NW ridge, up to the

192

Weisenbach Route

192

DENT D'HÉRENS
N Face Diagonal
Finch Route 191

terrace, depending on the state of the séracs ($2\frac{1}{2}$ h.).

Climb the terrace which is cut by one or two large crevasses in the upper part, after crossing the line of the Welzenbach route. Near the top it steepens progressively and merges into the N wall below the bergschrund under the Spalla (4039m.) of the E ridge. Cross the bergschrund near the L end and climb the steep snow/ice slope to the small snow saddle gap at the immediate foot of the Spalla. Alternatively cross the bergschrund directly below the Spalla and climb a similar but longer slope of 55° to reach the E ridge below the final pitch leading to the Spalla. This latter line is more usual but a second smaller bergschrund on the steep slope has normally to be crossed or turned on the L before the ridge is reached (2 h.). On the ridge, follow Route 190 to the summit ($1\frac{1}{2}$ h., about 9 h. from Schönbiel hut).

North Face (Welzenbach Route). A superb ice climb, one of the finest of its genre in the Alps. In the same class as the Eiger Lauper Route, safer than the Liskamm NE face modern routes and the Dent Blanche NNE face. Recent major variations, including one completely independent Polish route line of 1971 to the L, have been rightly and severely criticised as pointless and artless. The Welzenbach route is now generally accepted as representing as a standard for good conditions the middle level of the TD grade. In good conditions it is only slightly exposed to objective dangers, and with hard snow throughout (rare) the climbing can be straightforward. Normally the main difficulty is concentrated in an ice wall of two tiers, and in climbing the very steep upper ice slope. The ice cliffs are sometimes impassible; they vary considerably from year to year. The climb is usually done in a day from the Schönbiel hut, but parties often have to bivouac on the descent. TD, 1200m. from bergschrund. Has been climbed in 7 h.

DENT D'HÉRENS
N face

First ascent: W. Welzenbach and E. Allwein, 10 August, 1925. Climbed 9 times up to 1945. First solo ascent: K. Lugmayer, 29 July, 1952. First British (27th) ascent: C. J. Mortlock, C. W. F. Noyce and J. R. Sadler, 5 August, 1959. Climbed previously by the Americans P. R. Burgess and J. R. Sadler, 4 August, 1957. First winter ascent: a combination of Polish, Czeck and Swiss parties, 14-17 March, 1964, with a massive rescue operation during the descent, involving 7 of the climbers and helicopter evacuation. A notable incident for the Zermatt rescue services. Climbed over 120 times to date.

192. From the Schönbiel hut start as for Route 14 on the lower approach to the Stockji. From below pt. 2624m. cross the badly crevassed and mainly dry or stone covered glacier SW, below rognon 2721m. and towards pt. 2861m. at the foot of the face ($1\frac{1}{2}$ h.). This is the L-hand foot of a large triangular rock buttress which is often plastered with snow. Between the buttress and a permanent avalanche cone to the L cross an easy bergschrund and climb an ice slope of 150m. At the top move R up a couloir of ice and rubble and reach the L-hand (on your R) rib of the buttress. Climb this easily on loose spiky rocks to its apex (300m.). Continue up a snow ridge to an ice slope below the first ice cliffs (60m.). These are climbed according to conditions found, usually by a delicate traverse L for 80m. under the prow of the overhanging wall to a couloir which leads back R, finishing with an ice wall on the R (80m.). Above, an ice slope leads to a terrace below the second ice wall. Alternatively, an ice chimney in the lower wall, somewhat R of centre, can be found, and this is often easier. The second overhanging wall is perhaps only 10m. high at its lowest point but it is often the most serious obstacle on the climb. A comparatively easy chimney/gully has been found in it, but normally you traverse R for two rope lengths to its lowest point and climb a very difficult pitch with pegs. On some occasions it has proved possible to turn this wall completely on the R. Finish on the large diagonal snow terrace of the Finch route which slants from R to L across the face.

Above the terrace is the final slope of 400m. This is usually snow at first at 57°, then it eases to 45° but on ice. The last 200m. directly to the summit is on slabby rock at 50-55° which can be very difficult when iced; use snow tongues as far as possible and layers of hard snow on the rocks. It is almost impossible to insert pegs and there are no good resting places. Finish at the summit (12-15 h. in reasonable conditions).

TIEFMATTENJOCH 3565m.

193. Two saddles, W (lower) and E, between the Dent d'Hérens and Tête de Valpelline, a fairly difficult pass from the Schönbiel hut to Aosta hut, rarely used as a regular crossing point. Swiss (N) side, AD-, see Route 189. The Italian (S) side adjoins Route 187 and is easier, either up a rock rib to the col or a simple snow couloir to the R, leading to the E saddle of the col, beside the foot of the W ridge of the Dent d'Hérens. The latter is used by parties starting from the Aosta hut and climbing the W ridge (see Route 189). PD-, 2½ h. to E col. First traverse of pass: A. W. Moore and G. E. Foster with J. Anderegg and H. Baumann, 15 July, 1871.

TÊTE DE VALPELLINE 3802m.

A large snow cap above the Col de Valpelline (3568m.), adjacent to the Col d'Hérens. Climbed from time to time from the Aosta hut and by parties crossing the Col de Valpelline. Occasionally traversed from the Tiefmattenjoch by parties seeking an alternative to descending by Route 189 to the Schönbiel hut, by the rotten rocks of the SE ridge. First ascent: E. Whymper with F. Biener, 3 August, 1866. First winter and ski ascent: R. Helbling and F. Reichert with guides, 13 February, 1903.

<u>North Side (from Col de Valpelline)</u>. Easy snowfields, F. First ascensionists.

194. From the Col de Valpelline, reached from the end of the
278

approach from the Schönbiel hut to the Col d'Hérens and its higher alternative, the Col de la Tête Blanche, by Route 14, where at the head of the Stockji glacier a final snowfield is crossed to the broad saddle ($4\frac{1}{2}$ h. from Schönbiel hut), continue up snowfields to the S and reach the small dome of the snowy summit in another 45 min.

195. From the Aosta hut follow a small track N in zigzags up grass and scree then rocks and snow patches in a cwm below the large rock barrier marking the S side of the Tsa de Tsan Haut glacier. Continue by the track to the foot of this barrier which is climbed slanting L up a prominent snow/rubble couloir to the Col de la Division (3314m.). On the other side descend a little to the snowfields of the aforementioned glacier and cross them NE below a broad crevassed slope to the far side, then go up a snow cwm on this N side to the Col de Valpelline where the previous route is joined ($2\frac{1}{4}$ h. to col, 3 h. to summit). However, a much more direct line can be taken from the Col de la Division to the summit, crevasses permitting, by keeping to the R (S) side of the glacier all the way to the summit.

South-East Ridge. The prominent shattered crest running from the Tiefmattenjoch. It has tempted many parties as an alternative to descending the Swiss slope of the pass. One correspondent lured on to it describes the scramble as "reasonable and scenically splendid". The rock is bad by any standards; while the technical difficulties are low, a relatively high grade is put on the ridge which demands extreme care to avoid dislodging loose rock. PD+, mainly grade I with one section of II+. First ascent: J. Taylor with A. Supersaxo, July, 1880.

196. From the W saddle of the Tiefmattenjoch climb an initial steepness in the ridge on the crest. From a large platform continue by loose rock steps just on the L side to a ridge shoulder. Follow this till it steepens. An obvious ledge line on the L should be ignored. Make a descending traverse R on bad rock down the side of the ridge to a steep snow couloir. Cross this to a steep rock slope/rib, which is climbed direct (II) for 20m. to a short but very steep pitch up to the crest again. Pull up this in two short movements on better rock and good holds (II+ for 15m.) and in a further pitch reach the upper rock knoll (3798.2m.). Cross a small gap to the snowcap summit ($1\frac{3}{4}$ h. from col).

COL DE VALPELLINE 3568m.

An easy but often badly crevassed glacier pass between the Tête de Valpelline and Tête Blanche. The ascent on the Swiss (Schönbiel hut) side corresponds with Routes 14 and 194 ($4\frac{1}{2}$ h. from Schönbiel hut to pass), PD-. The Italian (Aosta hut) side corresponds with Route 195 ($2\frac{1}{2}$ h. to pass), F. First recorded traverse: F.W. Jacomb with J. Kronig, 13 August, 1860.

TÊTE BLANCHE 3724m.

Situated above the Col d'Hérens and adjoining the Col de Valpelline, often climbed for the superb view as a detour by parties crossing these passes. Easy snow slopes. See Routes 14 and 15. First ascent: G. Studer, M. Ulrich and G. Lauterburg with J. Madutz, N. Inderbinnen, A. and J. Binner, 15 August, 1849. In winter and on ski: Dr. Payot and party, January, 1903.

COL D'HÉRENS 3462m.

One of the oldest and most frequented glacier passes in the Pennine Alps. See Routes 14 and 15.

COL DES BOUQUETINS 3357m.

A frontier glacier pass between the Tête Blanche (Tête de Chavannes spur, 3670.6m.) and the Bouquetins ridge, for direct access between the Bertol and Aosta huts. Coming from Arolla and taking two days, this is the most pleasant way of reaching the Aosta hut. Swiss (N) side, F. Italian (S) side, PD-. First traverse: W. E. Hall and K. E. Digby with F. Biner, August, 1862. First winter and ski crossing: Marcel Kurz with M. Crettaz, 27 January, 1920.

197. Swiss side. From the Bertol hut descend a track in rocks to snow below and cross snow slopes W to round the rock base pt. 3229m. Continue over large snowfields SW then S with a few crevasses to the broad saddle of the col ($1\frac{1}{2}$ h.). Note: The Bertol hut is due to be rebuilt in 1975, on another site.

198. Italian side: From the Aosta hut follow Route 195 to the Col de la Division (3314m.). Now traverse the central plateau of the Tsa de Tsan Haut glacier to the opposite side and bear L to the rubble/rock barrier below the col. Climb this generally near its R side by a snow tongue or broken rocks and reach snowy scree at the top. Continue almost due N and R of a snow bowl to the pass (2 h.). Bertol hut to Aosta hut, $2\frac{3}{4}$ h.

VALTOURNANCHE - VALPELLINE SOUTH CHAIN

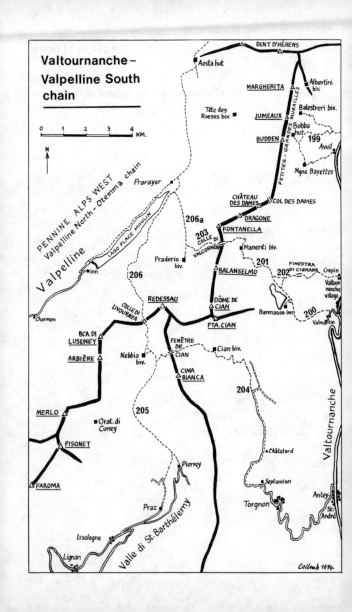

Valtournanche – Valpelline South chain

0 1 2 3 4 KM.

N

PENNINE ALPS WEST
Valpelline North – Otemma chain

Valpelline

DENT D'HÉRENS

Aosta hut

MARGHERITA

Albertini biv.
Balestreri biv.

Tête des Roeses biv.

JUMEAUX

Bobba hut

BUDDEN

199

Avuil

Mgne. Bayettes

Prarayer

Lago Place Moulin

inn

Charmen

CHÂTEAU DES DAMES

COL DES DAMES

206a

DRAGONE

203

FONTANELLA

COLLE DI VALCORNERA

Manenti biv.

Praderio biv.

201

FINESTRA DI CIGNANA

Crepin

206

BALANSELMO

202

Valtournanche village

Lago di Cignana

REDESSAU

COLLE DI LIVOURNEA

DÔME DE CIAN

Barmasse inn

200

Valmartin

PTA. CIAN

BCA. DI LUSENEY

FENÊTRE DE CIAN

Cian biv.

ARBIÈRE

Nebbia biv.

CIMA BIANCA

204

MERLO

205

Orat. di Cuney

PISONET

Châtelard

FAROMA

Pierrey

Septumian

Torgnon

Antey St-André

Praz

Valtournanche

Valle di St-Barthélemy

Issologne

Lignan

Collomb 1974

This is the most prominent and most interesting but least known of all the major Italian branches of the Pennine Alps. It has been re-examined on the ground in some detail by three parties working for guidebook purposes in August and September, 1974. The chain runs S and SW from the Col des Grandes Murailles (3827m.), where it is joined to the main frontier range at the Shoulder (4039m. IGM) on the E ridge of the Dents d'Hérens, down to the Aosta valley between Châtillon and Aosta town. It is enclosed like a great wedge by the long flanking valleys of the Valtournanche and Valpelline. These are two of the most contrasting valleys in the entire Pennine Alps. The first is one of the most highly developed in amenities and facilities for tourists, the second has nothing except a few unspoiled hamlets and a good road for most of its distance to a barrage in the upper part.

At first the chain is simple, consisting of a high rock ridge, the Grandes and Petites Murailles. When this ridge reaches a relatively low point at the Col des Dames (3321m. IGM) it turns SW and immediately changes character. It broadens progressively, forming branch ridges of importance, lateral valleys and cwms, altogether increasing the complexity of the region except for confining the meandering main ridge to the NW side of the wedge, that is to say much closer to the Valpelline than the Valtournanche. Nonetheless the chief summits of the main ridge are at present more conveniently approached from the Valtournanche. The lower (SW) half of this second section of the chain produces rock summits without snow of barely 3000m. or lower. These include the Becca d'Invergnaou (2967m. LK, but highest pt. at least 3000m.), Becca dell'Aquelou (3130m.), Monte Pisonet (3205m.) and Monte Faroma (3073m.). None of these is included in the guide. Descriptions and notes end at the Becca del Merlo (3234m.) just NE of these summits.

This more complex second section of the chain contains peaks with an average height of 3300m., rising to 3500m. in the Becca di Luseney which is the main objective of most unversed parties coming into the district. Some of the other mtns. are much more interesting. To date the area is hardly ever visited by British climbers, a situation which the present guide aims to rectify. During exploration of the region in 1974 no trace of British parties could be found in any hut log books for the 1960s and 70s. (other than those persons associated with researching this project).

The higher and more attractive Grandes Murailles chain is less frequented than the continuation chain which follows the Col des Dames, outlined above, and the reasons for this are elaborated in the climbing section of the guide.

Huts and other mountain bases

Tête des Roéses Bivouac c. 3120m.

Bivacco Tête des Roéses. CAAI property, a tiny refuge near
the top of the Tête des Roéses promontory (3216m.) which
supports the middle part of the Grandes Murailles glacier above
the E side of the desolate upper Valpelline. No record of a
visit by any correspondent. The route to the biv. starts by
the old waymarked track to the Aosta hut (see Route 116), from
which there are two possible levels of approach, involving
climbing short rock barriers at grade I and II, and rough tiring
slopes, $5\frac{1}{2}$ h. from Place Moulin carpark. The biv. serves
as a possible base for the Dent d'Hérens, but primarily for
serious routes, rarely climbed, on the long icy W wall of the
Grandes and Petites Murailles, which form the backcloth to
the entire breadth of the Grandes Murailles glacier. There
are no descriptions of routes on this wall in the guide.

Balestreri (Cors) Bivouac 3142m.

Bivacco Umberto Balestreri. CAAI property, situated on the
E ridge of the Cors group of the Grandes Murailles, directly
overlooking Breuil. There is a good waymarked and numbered
path from Breuil until the ridge proper is reached, after which
the route line is complicated but on easy rock if the correct
way is taken, $3\frac{3}{4}$ h. from Breuil. This biv. hut is rarely used
by anyone because the rock on this part of the Grandes Murailles is rotten and very dangerous. No routes are described
in the guide.

Bobba (Jumeaux) Hut 2770m.

Rifugio Giovanni Bobba. Situated near the top of a rocky spur extending SE from below the S end of the SE wall of the Grandes Murailles, almost directly above Breuil. No warden, places for 16 with blankets, cooking utensils, etc. complete, but only an ancient wood-burning stove. Recommended you take your own stove. Door locked, keys at Breuil and Valtournanche guides' bureaux. The only water available is 5-6 min. away, from snow found on the approach track to all routes from the hut, commencing up the L side of the spur. Water/snow carriers in hut. From Breuil, waymarked, route indicators no. 30. The path line on LK is inaccurate except in the middle section.

199. From Breuil go up the main street to the last turning on L before large carpark at the top. Go down this turning, a smaller carpark and shopping precinct, and continue straight past golf course on your L and through the primitive campsite to a small bridge over a stream on R. On the other side climb straight up an old grass covered moraine fan due W, which enters narrows at the top below waterfalls. Just below the entrance to the narrows the path forks, route markers. Go L, cross a stream and follow path on to bush covered spur to your L, which has the Maberge chalet at its top. The bushy path climbs the spur to open ground and passes directly over the roof of this buried chalet (2299m.). Continue bearing L on pleasant grassy ground under the R side of a low ridge which higher up is crossed L (take care not to continue up ridge on smaller track) into a broad shallow cwm. Follow the path through a small boulder field and make a rising traverse to scree in the bed of the cwm where the main stream is crossed L on rocks. Follow the vague track in a rising traverse L, still with frequent waymarks, working S across the cwm to an obvious saddle on the far side. An improving track rises to this at pt. 2596m. The spur on which the hut is located rises steeply above. Follow an excellent path up its rocks and grass trods on or near the crest directly to the hut which is found under a short rock wall ($2\frac{1}{2}$ h. from Breuil).

<u>Barmasse Inn</u> 2169m.

Rifugio Barmasse. Marked but not named on LK, and detail on LK is not up to latest developments in access. A new private establishment, open to all, situated adjoining the Cignana dam wall directly above Valtournanche village, on the W side of the valley. A large comfortable building with restaurant, lounge, television, hotel service/facilities. Numerous rooms with beds or bunk-beds in twos, fours or dormitory. An important climbing base, unfortunately expensive compared with huts. Impecunious climbers can continue to the Manenti biv., $2\frac{1}{4}$ h. further into the mtns.

200. On the main road just below Valtournanche village a new access road slants back R to cross the river by a bridge. The road then rises briefly on the other side of the valley to Valmartin hamlet. It continues a little further and ends at the tiny Fontaine hamlet. Just before entering Valmartin another new access road forks sharp R and in 300m. reaches the Barmasse hamlet (shown but not named on LK). There is car-parking at Valmartin beside the outer wall enclosing the hamlet, and visitors are not advised to use the tiny parking space at Barmasse. To Barmasse on foot from Valtournanche village, 20 min.

From Valmartin go along the road to Barmasse and just past a water trough on L, before entering the hamlet, turn L up a steep cobble path behind the chalets. Follow this to a fork. Illogically, keep R. The path comes up to the foot of the imposing cliff overlooking Barmasse, where it now turns L and is followed without possible error up through the woods quite steeply, coming into a junction with another path from below, and finally reaching the Cignana intermediate pumping station at c. 1800m. Go up R behind the station (water trough) and cross a gallery/bridge L over the pumping works. The path continues at an easier angle to emerge from the forest and cross a pasture to the chalets at 1912m. IGM. Continue between the chalets and along the fine path on the R side of the valley into the grassy cwm below the Cignana dam wall. The path rises tothe base of the wall about its centre, at a level where tramway lines cross the base of the wall. Follow the tramway L, cross a large wooden bridge over the upper gorge, then turn L and zigzag up a short grass and rock step to the pasture above, now level with the top of the dam wall at its S end. A few min. further S reach the inn (2 h. from Valmartin).

Manenti Bivouac 2789m. CAI

Bivacco Duccio Manenti. Not marked on any official map. Shown on KK No. 87 positioned one km. further S than actual location, a serious error considering the rugged character of the terrain. On the current LK 50m. map, No. 293, a "Biv. Sari" is shown standing on the E side of the location lake, in a position near the approach path not far from the correct spot. This must be some confusion with the Sari section of the CAI, which owns the hut. Precisely situated above the N tip of the Lago di Balanselmo which lies almost directly below the main ridge pass of the Colle di Valcornera, by whose approach path the biv. is most easily reached. Probably the most important climbing base in the Valpelline South-Valtournanche chain. A tiny refuge with places for 2, or 3 using the floor. 3 mattresses and appropriate blankets only. Take your own cooker, utensils, etc. Water from lake infall. Door open. Like all biv. huts in this region, the approach is an easy walk on a mainly good path, but this is the longest.

201. Approach from Valtournanche, route waymarks no. 11 above the Cignana dam. Start as for the previous route to the Barmasse inn, and go up to the foot of the dam wall at the tramway level (1¾ h. from Valmartin). Instead of turning L, go R along the tramway to its N end and climb two or three zigzags to reach a level atop the dam wall. From here follow the excellent path along the NE shore of the Cignana lake. On coming abreast the fine little chapel (2178m.) a short distance L of the path, the route forks. Keep to the upper level rising to Alpe di Cignana (2298m.) which is the lower of two path lines on LK. The path does not go to these chalets but passes below them before passing just above the old ruined chalets shown on map. After this it crosses a stream and reaches a level section along the rim of a cwm. Continue the rising traverse NW into the head of the valley. Near the top the path contours steep slopes and traverses between rockbands round a corner to enter a higher and quite small grassy cwm. The path traverses NW again above the cwm bed into another cwm more like a large shelf with a small tarn (unseen) well to the L of the path. Immediately bear L (another track rises R), cross a small plain and descend to cross the main stream. Track now poor. Continue E up a stony slope with nettles (waymarks) to the rock barrier above this second cwm shelf. Just below a cave at the foot of the barrier the track develops well again. Follow it up R, under the barrier, working N in comfortable zigzags on grass slopes to a break in the barrier further R. Emerge through a small rocky gap on a saddle where the path bears slightly L (NW). Directly above and slightly R is the hut, 5 min. from saddle, with the Balanselmo lake down to your L ($2\frac{1}{4}$ h. from foot of Cignana dam wall, 4 h. from carpark at Valmartin, about $4\frac{1}{2}$ h. walking all the way from Valtournanche village).

202. In fact the shortest route from the Valtournanche is to start from Crépin hamlet (1577m.) above Valtournanche village, which is reached from the main road by a new access road leading to the W side of the river. Carparking. From Crépin a well marked path goes up to the Finestra di Cignana (2441m.), marked but not named on LK, on the other side of which you descend pasture for c. 120m. before traversing R (NW) to join the previous route beside the stream which is crossed soon after passing above the ruined cowsheds ($3\frac{1}{2}$ h. from Crépin to to biv. hut).

203. Access routes from the Valpelline. These are easy but steep and rough, over one or the other of two passes which

291

are rarely crossed in any case, but they are undoubtedly more frequented than any other pass across the main chain with the possible exception of the Colle di Livournea (see Nebbia biv. below). Briefly, from the Place Moulin carpark go to Prarayer at the far end of the lake in 1 h. See Route 116.

By <u>Colle di Valcornera</u> (3066m.). Valcournera on LK. A hard stony ascent, steep at the top, normally only with a little snow slope to finish, $3\frac{1}{2}$ h. from Prarayer. On the other side descend by a two-tier cwm to the Balanselmo lake and biv. hut, in 1 h. This is essential map reading country. The path line on LK is reasonably but not totally accurate, round and over slabby rock barriers.

By <u>Colle di Bellatsa</u> (3047m.). Bella Tza on LK. A glacier pass on the Prarayer side, only half the size indicated on LK due to recession and normally without crevasses except after mid to end August. Easier in terms of effort than the Valcornera pass, $3\frac{1}{2}$ h. from Prarayer. No path line shown on map after reaching from the valley path, Alpe Bellatsa (c. 2475m.). From here a traverse path runs S to large moraines below the Glacier des Dames. Continue this traverse with no path to the next moraine cwm opening under the narrow Bellatsa glacier, which is climbed (stonefall possible) to the pass at the top. On the other side descend a short, loose but easy rock wall. Below this a rough slope due S soon leads via two water pools to the top of a rock barrier, the correct descent of which is not easy to find (i.e. from above). It starts somewhat R of the due S line and is shown with remarkable accuracy on LK. Continue below the barrier round the E side of the Gran Lago (2845m.), ignore the map track line leaving this and working S, and instead continue round S side of lake. Reach a small track going L. This works roughly SW along a grass and rock spur then trending R crosses it and zigzags down to the Manenti biv. hut (about $1\frac{1}{4}$ h. from col in descent to biv. hut). Both these routes on Manenti hut side are fully described under the Dragone and

Fontanella peaks.

Note: The Manenti biv. can be reached from the Nebbia biv. by a fine and not particularly long high level route using three adjoining passes: Colle di Praterier, Col Chavacour, Colle di Cian. F+, 3½ h. in this direction (R. G. Collomb and P. Charles, August, 1974).

Lago Cian (Tzan) Bivouac 2482m. CAI

Bivacco Lago Cian. A new biv. hut owned by the Torgnon Ski Club, open to all (door open), not marked on any map, situated on a hillock above the S shore of the Lago di Cian, a small lake right at the top (N end) and in a cwm to the W of the Torgnon valley. The hillock higher up becomes a spur rising to the Cima Bianca (3009m.). The ground surrounding the lake, which is some distance from hut, is a boulder maze and quite unpleasant. Bunks for 9, blankets, etc., cooking utensils, wood burning stove. No wood in store and best to take your own stove. Water from plastic source pipe located 15m. distance from hut in 1974. This biv. is really a small hut and quite spacious.

204. Bus to Torgnon (1489m.) from the Valtournanche (Antey St. André). All the way on foot from Torgnon, about 4¾ h. Continuing above Torgnon, a new road, tarmac to the large summer campsite (a superb place) at Septumian (1673m.), and beyond this point unmade but quite wide and suitable for all types of cars, etc., is motorable for the greater part of the distance to the biv. hut. None of this detail is shown on LK, and a short road extension above Torgnon on LK is not the new access road into the middle part of the Torgnon valley, which we are concerned with. If the biv. hut is approached all the way on foot it is preferable to take a shorter direct path, fairly accurately indicated on LK, leading from a point not far below Chatrian hamlet (1620m.) to Alpe Châtelard (1891m.), where the new road well above the Septumian camping grounds is joined. This new road is officially private but appears to be used by all-comers, and there are new skitows alongside the first section.

By car follow the main road out of Torgnon and in general keep L at all junctions, up to Chatrian then to the idyllic Septumian camping grounds in glades to the R where the road becomes unsurfaced. Continue in a few easy turns to a great meadow (skitows) where the road bears R at the top to a building at the edge of the forest (1953m.). The path on LK now contouring through the forest, generally N, into the middle valley corresponds almost exactly to the new road. Follow it, passing Châtelard down to your R, for several km., descending at the end to a parking space exactly where the road turns R across the river. This place can be easily identified on LK, at c. 1920m. at the entrance to a marshy plain with a fine cliff (2107m.) at the back of it. Car drivers are advised to stop here.

With small cars the intrepid can continue over the river and follow the road, now narrower but at a reasonable gradient, forking L higher up, into the head of the valley, to the map pt. Alpe Chavacour (2135m.). From here on foot by a short connecting path across valley to rejoin the route described below, shown on map, reducing the walk to biv. hut by 45 min. ($1\frac{1}{4}$ h. from Alpe Chavacour to hut).

From the carpark beside bridge over river, 2 h. to biv. hut, good track with red waymarks, sometimes infrequent and confusing. The path starts at the back of the carpark and the start has been erased by bulldozers. Find it in 20m. and follow it in a rising traverse through forest above the marshy plain. It reaches a small grassy hollow (chalet) just below pt. 2107m. then a small saddle/col behind this pt. From here take the main, slightly descending traverse path on the other side (ignore slightly higher tracks), pass the Château chalet (2084m.) and soon reach a fork (signpost). Take the L branch across a field, keep L and cross a plank bridge to a small plain under the Grotte de Loup chalet. Climb a little L up to this chalet (2161m. IGM), and pass the R side of the building. From the signpost

294

to this point you must ignore all tracks bearing R. Behind the chalet follow a good track in the forest, up rocks and over a small plain to a general rising movement R (N). A little higher the path returns L, having gained open slopes above the last rock barriers, then climbs almost due W towards the cwm directly below Cima Bianca, in which there is a prominent chalet marked pt. 2522m. Well below this reach a tall marker pole, below a large broken crag at the R-side entrance to the cwm. Leave the path and make a rising traverse R to a terrace line of grass and rocks running below the crag. Follow this terrace line R(N), up and down but ostensibly horizontal to reach the biv. hut on its hillock slightly above you, from where the Lago di Cian is seen for the first time further N (2 h. from carpark.

Nebbia Bivouac c. 2590m.

Bivacco Franco Nebbia. Marked accurately on LK, situated below the SE side of the Becca di Luseney, above the E shore of Lago Luseney in the grassy cwm at the head of the St. Barthélemy valley. Standard pattern CAI biv. hut, 4 bunks, blankets, etc. and water carriers. Two more could sleep in discomfort under lower bunks. Take your own cooker, etc. Door unlocked. Approached by a good path and an easy walk from the roadhead for those with own transport. An hour should be added for the road walk by those using public transport to the bus stop at junction of Issologne and Praz roads. In this case follow the new road on L side of valley to Praz and continue along it to a cowshed a few m. before the big bend L, going away from the direction up the valley. None of this detail is shown on LK. Leave the road and cross a wet field for an obvious path coming in from below and follow this to the farm at 1900m. From there by an upper or lower path (nothing in it) over a slight elevation through the woods to the Champlaisant chalets (1900m.) and over a big field beyond in a bend in the river to join the route described below at a bridge over the river.
  Apart from the obvious Becca di Luseney it may not be immediately realised that this biv. is also a good starting point, closer than most, for climbing the Dôme and Punta di Cian.

Grandes Murailles

P. Budden　Becca di Guin　P. Sella　P. Giordano

3760　211　209

212

CONCA DEL BREUIL N-NW segment

205. St. Barthélemy valley approach. Beyond the junction before Issologne leading as the new access road to Praz hamlet (c. 1740m.), not marked on LK, another new road branches R soon after the junction and some distance before Praz. It descends and crosses the river. It continues up the R side of the valley in two or three zigzags to a big, prominent bend at the Pierrey chalets (1910m.). Plenty of carparking space. Those without cars should follow the Praz access road on the other (L) side of the valley, as indicated in the preamble above.

From Pierrey take a waymarked narrow tractor road NNW through woods and out again to pleasant pasture near the river. The grassy road descends gradually to the river (path line on map incorrect) and follows the bank round a bend to the L. You have now passed the conspicuous Champlaisant chapel (1900m.) on the opposite bank. Where a bridge crosses the river just round the bend, join a path coming from the chapel over the bridge. Now the tractor road goes up a short riser above the river and reaches the level bed of the middle valley. Follow this past a chalet to the Ollière cowsheds (2007m.). Continue by a nice easy path past the Praterier chalet on the other (L) side of the stream. In a couple of min. it is easier to walk on the other side of the stream for one km., as the path on the R side is rocky, but you must remember to return to the R side. Ignore map line track on L side of river in upper valley. After the short rocky section on R side the valley bed gradually steepens. Higher up the path crosses a large white scree fan then goes up in short zigzags near the stream with frequent red waymarks to the low terraced walls forming a cow shelter at 2389m., with a slightly higher isolated chalet on other side of the stream. Just below this pt. is the junction, large marker, with a track going E over the Fenêtre de Cian. Continue up the main valley trending L to its headwall with a broad grassy saddle at the top. A series of zigzags through rock outcrops leads to the saddle. Continue on a little grassy plain for 100m.

only, then bear L, cross a stream and climb a large mound of grass and rocks SW, crossing the lake outfall before reaching the conspicuous biv. on the skyline ($2\frac{3}{4}$ h. from Pierrey carpark).

206. Approach from the Valpelline. Normally this would not be entertained if the purpose was to climb the Becca di Luseney, because this mtn. can be climbed directly from the Valpelline. The Colle di Luseney (3162m., marked but not named on LK) is the most direct pass from the Valpelline, starting anywhere below the Place Moulin dam wall, to the Nebbia biv. This pass is fully described under the Becca di Luseney, but is rarely if ever crossed for this purpose. Parties doing a high level tour of the chain account for nearly all ascents from the Valpelline to the Nebbia biv. They invariably use the Colle di Livournea (2858m.) which lies directly N of the Nebbia biv., between the Becca di Luseney massif and Monte Redessau. This is one of the more frequented passes over the main ridge of the chain. The Place Moulin barrage has removed direct access to the valley below the pass on the Valpelline side. You must go up to Prarayer and return along a rising traverse path above the SE side of the lake to enter the valley. On making this entrance, a traverse path just above the tarn at pt. 2374m. is not shown on LK, before the original path is joined just below old chalets at 2410m. A good mtn. walking route, which in the reverse direction is a good plan for climbing the Becca di Luseney before continuing over the pass to Prarayer and up into the Valpelline North area, say to the Collon hut then over the Col Collon to Arolla, or over the Col de l'Évêque to the Vignettes hut (Marcel Kurz, H.E.L. Porter and Mrs. Porter, 1959). The upper part of the pass is easy on both sides, with a small track nearly everywhere. Correct crossing pt. is confusing in poor visability. Prarayer to col, $3\frac{1}{4}$ h. Descent to Nebbia biv., 30 min. (45 min. in ascent).

Note: There is an easy connection between the Nebbia biv. and Cian biv. across the <u>Fenêtre de Cian</u> (2734m.), small path all the way, except for skirting W side of Lago di Cian on approaching Cian biv. Keep high on this side, away from lake shore, to avoid tiresome rocks and boulders. LK path line for this connection is correct ($2\frac{1}{2}$ h. from Nebbia to Cian biv.)

Praderio Bivouac 2450m. CAI

Bivacco F. Praderio. This is the only base found on the Valpelline side of the S section of the Valpelline South chain, situated in the Valcornera valley directly above Prarayer, at the S foot of the rockface capped by pt. 2699m. and adjoining the moraines at the bottom of the N face of the Dôme de Cian. Built in 1972, places for 9, equipped with gas stove, blankets, etc. Door open. The hut is primarily designed to encourage ascents of the Dôme and Punta di Cian from the Valpelline, and should attract more parties to the N face of the Dôme. Not visited by any British party (Frischer-Roberts diaries, Alpinismus 5/1973).

206[a] From Place Moulin carpark follow the path along the lake to Prarayer (2005m.) (1 h.). A little further take a R fork in the valley path and cross the river by a new bridge. Turn R(SW) and follow the good path above the L side of the river, through open forest. In a few min. there is a vague fork L climbing through trees SE into the Valcornera valley. This fork can be missed and is approx. 150m. distance before the main path crosses the Valcornera stream. Climb the intermittent track to grassy slopes on the Alpe Valcornera (2166m.). Continue up the L side of the stream (a variety of tracks), keeping above the stream but never far from it, to stony sections where the track tends to become erased. Near the top pass a R fork, over the stream where another track rises to the Chardonney chalet (2364m.). Ignore this, and continue for a few min. near the stream as before, until the track turns E and rises towards the Colle di Valcornera. Now work due S, leaving the track on your L, and make a line S up debris between two moraine crests, then bear R to the moraine crest on this side where the biv. stands a short distance in front of the rocks directly below pt. 2699m. (2 h., 3 h. from Place Moulin carpark).

PART VII

Valtournanche –Valpelline South chain

Grandes Murailles – des Dames – Cian – Luseney chain
South of the Col des Grandes Murailles

GRANDES MURAILLES

The collective name for the singular and impressive initial rock ridge running from the Col des Grandes Murailles (3827m.) to Col Budden (3582m.), the last being indicated but not named on LK. It is found immediately N of Punta Budden. The latter marks the first summit of the Petites Murailles.

This is the most formidable collection of rock peaks in the whole of the Pennine Alps, comparable in some respects with the lower Morion sub-chain in Pennine Alps West, but with consistent characteristics coupled with great altitude which put the summits in a class of their own. Firstly the rock is intrinsically good but the huge inclined faces are littered with loose material which is constantly falling due to snow/ice melt, wind and rain. Nearly all routes are subject to bad stonefall until the main ridge crest is reached, and key pitches sometimes run up veins of poor rock. The Breuil (E) wall has such a notorious reputation for stonefall and loose rock (the last is mostly unjustified) that most of the Valtournanche guides are reluctant to take people on the climbs. For example, seven recorded ascents appear in the Bobba hut book for the Jumeaux summits in 1973, and this ascent/traverse is much the safest. Four of these were guided parties, mainly led by Jean Bich, who will always go if conditions are right - fine and very cold with no new snow to speak of. The warnings rightly given about two or more parties moving up or down the same route hardly apply, as this event must still be rare. The culminating point of the Grandes Murailles, Punta Margherita (3903m.), is so awkward or dangerous to reach by any route on the Breuil side that anyone determined to do it can succeed far more easily with no objective danger from the Aosta hut.

COL DES GRANDES MURAILLES 3827m. 3831m. IGM

Between the Dent d'Hérens and Pta. Margherita, from the Aosta hut to Breuil. A broad snow saddle on the Aosta hut side and a big rock wall on the Breuil side, with route finding problems, some technical difficulty, bad rock and stonefall. Rarely crossed as a pass, serious and complicated approach on Breuil side. See also remarks under Albertini Biv., following Route 115. The Aosta hut side is described under Pta. Margherita below. Traverse: AD/AD+. J.B. Bich and J.A. Carrel, 8 July, 1868.

PUNTA MARGHERITA 3903m. 3905m. IGM

See introductory remarks above. The culminating point of the Grandes Murailles, seldom climbed and a connoisseur's summit. The best route is from the Aosta hut, but this is hardly simple. From N to S the mtn. forms tops as follows: N Forepeak (c. 3880m.), N. Peak and summit (3903m.), then a ridge section of 120m. to a deep gap, above which rises the S Peak (3894m. LK). Several towers and smaller gaps along the ridge confuse the detail. First ascent: E. Mackenzie with A. and D. Maquignaz, 22 August, 1892.

<u>North Ridge (from Col des Grandes Murailles)</u>. The most direct route from the Aosta hut. The ridge is not technically difficult, pitches of II, but the rock is bad and turning movements round steep pitches are delicate, making the climbing slow and security hard to ensure. Altogether. PD+/AD. First ascensionists, in descent.

207. From the Aosta hut follow Route 187 on the Grandes Murailles glacier to below the SW face of the Dent d'Hérens, then make a rising movement under pt. 3772m. and work up crevassed snowfields SSE to the broad saddle of the Col des Grandes Murailles (3827m.) (3½ h.).

Follow the main snow crest S, keeping to the R side, then a loose rock ridge into a gap (3790m., old LK ref.). Start up the ridge proper, climbing an initial step on the crest, followed by a second larger one where steep bits are turned delicately on the R side. Continue along a knife-edge section cut by teeth and gaps, broken and awkward, up to the N. Forepeak (c.3880m.). A final narrow crest leads to the main summit (2½ h., 6 h. from Aosta hut).

PUNTA DEI CORS (PUNTA GASTALDI) 3852m. 3849m. IGM

A large tower, one of the most formidable summits of the Grandes Murailles. Friable and rotten rock, a serious undertaking. Sometimes several years elapse between ascents. First ascent: (by W flank): E. Mackenzie with J. B. Bich and D. Maquignaz, 14 August, 1891.

COL DES CORS 3721m.

Between the Pta. dei Cors and Pta. Ester (Lioy). The E (Breuil) side is exceedingly dangerous, the W side, a steep snow couloir above the Grandes Murailles glacier, has sometimes been climbed to reach the ridge for approaching the flanking summits. AD. Traversed by E. Mackenzie with A. Maquignaz, 2 September, 1892.

PUNTA ESTER c.3790m.

A secondary pt. on the main ridge between the Col des Cors and Pta. Lioy. The main ridge at this pt. is III.

PUNTA LIOY 3816m.

A fine sugar loaf summit, the ascent of which involves climbing loose rocks of considerable technical difficulty. The approaches are seriously exposed to stonefall. First ascent: C. Broglio and I. Clivio with F., J.B., & L. Bich, 19 July, 1890.

BRÈCHE LIOY c. 3740m.

Not marked on any map. A deep, narrow gap separating Pta. Lioy from Les Jumeaux. Crossing this gap along the main ridge to reach or leave the adjoining summits involves abseiling and rock pitches of III/IV.

LES JUMEAUX

The collective name for Pta. Giordano and Pta. Sella.

PUNTA GIORDANO 3872m.

The lower of the twins, separated from its brother, Pta. Sella, by the prominent gap of the Brèche des Jumeaux. The only route worth considering, undertaken from time to time, is to prolong the ascent of Pta. Sella by continuing along the main ridge to Pta. Giordano. First ascent: Lord Wentworth with J.B. Bich and E. Rey, 6 September, 1877.

<u>South-West (Main) Ridge (from Punta Sella)</u>. By Grandes Murailles standards, a recommended climb as an extension to the ascent of Pta. Sella. Return by the same route. Rock quite good, III. First ascensionists.

208. From Pta. Sella (see below) follow the main ridge for 15m. to a series of short rock steps. Go down these on or near the crest with fine exposed climbing which becomes difficult and delicate with snow on the rocks. (In these conditions you can descend the flank under the ridge, abseiling if necessary, and traverse back to the crest delicately below the steps). Continue down a few steep rocks into the Brèche des Jumeaux (c. 3840m.) (30 min.). From this gap climb the continuation crest to a short wall pitch (III), which can be avoided on the L. Above, loose but easier rocks lead to the summit (30 min., 1 h. from Punta Sella).

PUNTA SELLA 3878m. CAI

Not marked on LK, situated a short distance SW along the main ridge from Pta. Giordano, completing the Jumeaux twins. The most frequented summit of the Grandes Murailles, a worthy climb on mainly good rock, unfortunately marred by stonefall danger. Invariably climbed by one or the other of two routes from the Bobba hut on the Breuil (E) side. First ascent: G. Corona with J. A. Carrel and J. J. Maquignaz, 10 June, 1875.

<u>South-East Side and South-West Ridge</u>. The normal route, the most direct but not the safest way. As many ascents and descents are made from the Becca di Guin along the main ridge (see below). Stonefall occurs along the traverse sections below the Grandes Murailles, and to the same extent on the SE face up to the ridge. PD+ with short pitches of III. First ascent: G. Corona with J. B. Aymond and C. Carrel, 12 August, 1877.

209. From the back of the Bobba hut take a small horizontal track on L side of the hut spur to a hollow and go up this keeping L on to a hogsback leading to the top of the spur. Path gone. Just before this move L up scree and snow to the foot of the grass and rock barriers under the Grandes Murailles E face (15 min.). Climb the first barrier diagonally R, then rise in same direction over grass terraces for 15 min. till a line of barriers is seen above stretching L. Return L over more terraces and short rockbands, gradually approaching the rock barrier, finally working up L below it. Scree slopes lead out steeply to the lowest snow tongues below Punta Budden (45 min.). Traverse R (N) over scree, rocks and snow patches just below the general level of the large snowband under the Grandes Murailles, with increasing stonefall danger, most serious at the far end. A broad flattish rockband interrupts this traverse. The best line across this is high up but stonefall is probably bad there. Most parties traverse low down, rising all the while to just below pt. 3303m. Now traverse the continuation snowband R to its far end where a ridge comes down from the Becca di Guin. This ridge flanks a couloir further R(N)(1¼ h.). Climb the nice ridge briefly to a cairn, then traverse R across the couloir (stonefall). Continue on steep slabby rocks on the R side of the couloir to a large snow patch. From the upper R edge of this climb an easy rockface trending R to the foot of a red wall section. Stonefall still evident. Turn this upper wall by a ledge line up L, short pitches with ledges and snow between, and so reach the main ridge (1½ h.). Follow the pleasant ridge in a fine position on rocks and snow over a forepeak to the summit (30 min., about 4½ h. from Bobba hut). Parties are strongly advised to descend by the route described below.

Main Ridge from Becca di Guin. The nearest thing to a classic route on the Grandes Murailles. By climbing the Becca di Guin first, this way constitutes the safest approach to Pta. Sella, and is obligatory in the interests of safety for descending the mtn. The ascent to the Becca is described after the Main Ridge, below. A fine, airy, mixed ridge of considerable quality and interest, not difficult in good conditions. PD. First ascensionists.

210. From the Becca di Guin descend along the L side of the ridge down a rock and snow/ice slope and return R to the ridge below a step at a snowy section, narrow and corniced on R, running along to a saddle forming the lowest pt. 3742m. between the two summits. Climb the snow and rock ridge above and soon reach the point where the normal route comes in from below, then as for Route 209 to summit (1¾ h. from Becca di Guin to Pta. Sella, 1½ h. in reverse direction.

BECCA DI GUIN 3805m. CAI

Incorrectly recorded on LK as 3742m., which is the correctly measured saddle between Pta. Sella and the Becca di Guin (see route above). A fine rock mtn. often climbed in association with Pta. Sella, sometimes for itself if conditions do not permit continuing to Pta. Sella. The ascent is less exposed to stonefall than Pta. Sella. First ascent: M. Baretti, A. E. Martelli and L. Vaccarone with C. Gorret, J. J. and P. Maquignaz and S. Meynet, 16 September, 1874.

<u>South-East Side</u>. The recommended route, an easy rock climb on sound gneiss but somewhat exposed to stonefall on the long approach. PD, pitches of I/II.

211. From the Bobba hut follow Route 209 to the furthest snowband N, directly under the mtn., and under a sort of E ridge coming down from it which is taken for a short distance by Route 209 (2½ h.). Climb this nice ridge direct, over easy steps and ledges to a large break with scree and snow, above which a steep wall rises to the summit. Work L up a terrace line, narrowing into an open couloir which is followed till an exit R can be made up snow and slabs to the main ridge. Continue up the easy rock ridge to summit (1½ h., 4 h. from Bobba hut).

COL BUDDEN 3582m.

Between the Becca di Guin and Punta Budden, a broad rock saddle used occasionally to reach or leave the main ridge of the Grandes Murailles on the E side. This side is a rock climb with a pitch of III (descended by first ascensionists of Becca di Guin). The W side is a snow/ice couloir above a bay at the S end of the Grandes Murailles glacier. First traverse: E. Mazzucchi with E. Rey and C. Savoie, 15 August, 1918.

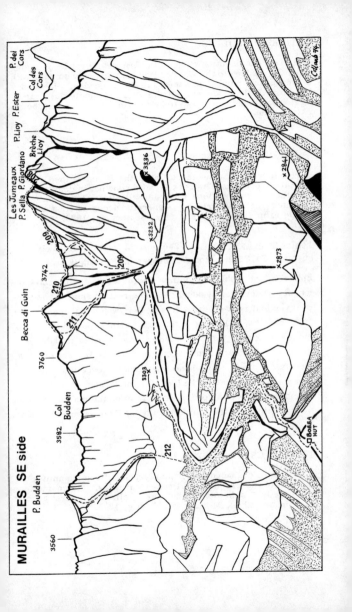

MURAILLES SE side

PETITES MURAILLES

The lower continuation ridge of the Grandes Murailles, running from Col Budden to the Col des Dames. The only summit with a measurable number of ascents is Punta Budden. However a traverse of the main ridge from Pta. Budden to the Tour du Créton and beyond is known to be fine and on good rock, though rarely done.

PUNTA BUDDEN 3630m.

A rock pyramid, conspicuous near the S end of the Grandes Murailles profile. The rock is quite good but in common with all other summits along this wall stonefall can be bad before reaching the main ridge. Generally accepted first ascent: F. De Filippi with A. Maquignaz, September, 1898.

<u>East-North-East Flank</u>. The normal route, relatively frequented. F+. Some stonefall danger in the couloir.

212. From the Bobba hut follow Route 209 to the lowest snow tongues under Pta. Budden. Climb direct up snow to the narrow vertical rock entrance to a couloir which higher up slants L across the ENE flank of the mtn. Climb snow in the bed of the lower couloir, narrow, and reach the broader middle section rising L like a ramp (Couloir Dumontel). Follow this, stonefall from R, to its head where snowy ledge lines slanting L in rocks lead round to the foot of a small facet of sound rock. Climb this direct on good holds to snow on the main ridge L of the summit and a few min. from the top ($3\frac{1}{2}$ h. from Bobba hut).

TOUR DU CRÉTON 3579m.

A fine square-shaped tower, the last significant summit along the wall of the Grandes and Petites Murailles. The main ridge traverse is best known (III+). Rarely climbed. First ascent: G. Corona with P. Maquignaz, 27 July, 1875.

COL DU CRÉTON 3311m.

Marked but not named on LK, between the Tour du Créton and Mont Blanc du Créton. An unimportant and somewhat dangerous pass, much less frequented than the neighbouring Col des Dames. First recorded traverse: Ellis Carr, M.W. Conway and F.M. Davies with U. Kauffmann and J.M. Lochmatter, 20 August, 1890.

MONT BLANC DU CRÉTON 3406m.

A little snowy summit overlooking the Col des Dames, easily climbed by its SW ridge as a detour of 25 min. from the normal route on the Château des Dames. First recorded ascent: C.E. Biressi, G. and O. Dumontel, 14 July, 1904.

COL DES DAMES 3321m. IGM

Neither marked nor named on LK, between Mt. Blanc du Créton and the Château des Dames. An important glacier pass in relation to access routes for climbing the Château des Dames, but infrequently used as a pass from the Valpelline (Prarayer) to Valtournanche (Breuil). Routes to the pass are described under the Château des Dames, below. Traversed by first ascensionists of Château des Dames.

CHÂTEAU DES DAMES 3488m.

A panoramic summit, the second highest mtn. in the secondary section of this chain after the Becca di Luseney. It has three main ridges, one with an important branch, and three rocky faces. All the rock is poor or bad except for short bits on the normal routes. One of the most frequented summits of this area. The mtn. can be climbed directly from Breuil, or with much less effort from the Manenti biv. The Prarayer approach is rarely followed. None of the routes has any notable mountaineering interest. Climbed at least 100 times a year at present.

First ascent: F.W. Jacomb with J. Kronig, 11 August, 1860. First winter ascent: G.M. Spurgazzi with J.J. and J.B. Maquignaz, 3 February, 1890. First ski ascent: A. Alberti and E. Bonomini with J. Pellissier, 4 November, 1932.

approaches to Château des Dames
NE (Breuil) side

Castelletto Whymper

3195

Mont Rous

Colle di Vofrède

3140 IGM

213-4

214 (i)

213

Vofrède glacier

214 (ii)

<u>East-South-East and North-East Ridge (from Col des Dames).</u>
See note on Col des Dames above. This is the short disjointed
main ridge rising from the col. At the bend it is joined by a
prominent SSE branch which attracts today as many ascents.
This branch is described after the next two routes. All approaches from the Valtournanche (E) side of the mtn. reach the
ridge above the Col des Dames, because this side of the pass,
directly below the saddle, consists of a crescent-shaped snow/
ice wall which is not climbed direct. Access to the pass from
the Valpelline-Prarayer (NW) side up the Glacier des Dames
is direct but the ridge can be reached above the saddle to save
a few min. Owing to the remote starting point at Prarayer
this NW approach is rarely practised. On the Valtournanche
side the route has two main approaches, from Breuil and the
Manenti biv., and these are the same approaches for the SSE
ridge variation branch ridge noted above. Both approaches
join on the upper slopes of the Vofrède glacier, from where
the route is mainly on snow and a few rocks to the ridge above
the Col des Dames. F. Suitable for alpinists only.

213. Approach from Manenti biv. hut. The shortest route to
the summit, via the <u>Colle di Vofrède</u> (3130m.). This col is
marked but not named on LK and lies between the Château des
Dames and Mont Rous. Compared with the Breuil approach
in which an overnight stop at a hut is avoided, starting from
the Manenti will appeal to many because of the resulting shorter
approach and the wide variety of ascents which can be made
from the same biv. hut.

From the Manenti biv. move a few m. L to rejoin the approach track. This is now poor but perfectly visible. Follow
it up the L side of the rocky grass spur behind the hut, then
up its broad crest till in 10 min. it slants R along a broad
grassy terrace on the R side of the spur. The track continues
rising a little, keeping near the R side of the terrace, then it
descends, passes a small hut and reaches the small dam wall

on the S side of the Gran Lago (2845m.). The track ends here.
Cross low rock outcrops near the S shore to the R side of a
short steep moraine wall round the E edge of the lake. Now
ascend diagonally L over rocks and debris on the slope below
the Colle di Vofrède, then work up to a line of white rocks
leading to a vague debris rib near the L side of the slope.
Traces of a path on this rib lead up the narrowing slope to a
snow tongue reaching the pass. Climb steep loose scree L of
the tongue, then snow to the narrow saddle level with the
Vofrède glacier on the other (NE) side ($1\frac{1}{4}$ h.).

Alternatively, stepping on to the snow tongue can be avoided
by climbing L up very steep debris to a little saddle below the
main ridge crest which overlooks the Vofrède glacier, so
avoiding the traverse mentioned below, but this variant is
preferable in descent.

From the pass make a slightly descending traverse on snow
under the first part of the SSE ridge of the Château des Dames,
to a rock and debris band stretching R which divides the glacier. Traverse this band horizontally R, away from the SSE
ridge, and after a few min. climb it to the next glacier terrace. (To your R is the top of the long rock promontory dividing
the glacier on the Breuil side of the mtn.). Go up to the foot
of the final glacier slope under the prominent split rock turret
called Castelletto Whymper on the SSE ridge. Now traverse
horizontally R over gentle snow slopes towards the ice wall of
the Col des Dames, pass round the toe of a grey rock buttress,
then climb snow and debris up the R side of this buttress.
Trend a little R, then L up continuous snow bands, fairly steep
and with a few rocks, until steep rocks rise above. Now traverse R onto the NE ridge at a point some 50m. above the
saddle of the Col des Dames. Continue up the broad snow/
rock ridge to a small shoulder marking the junction with the
SSE ridge and where our ridge becomes the ESE section. Climb
on the crest or a little R of it, snow and rock, over a hump

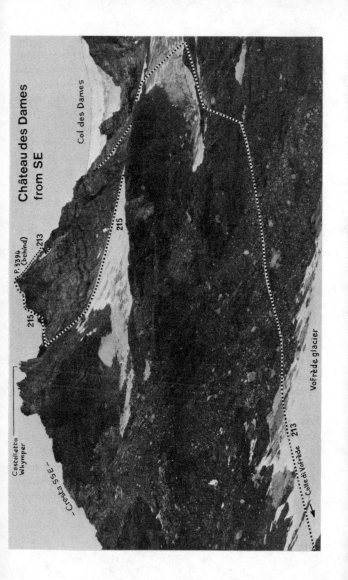

Château des Dames
from SE

Col des Dames

P. 3394 (behind)

213

215

215

215

Castelletto Whymper

— Cresta SSE —

213

Colle di Vofrède

Vofrède glacier

(3394m. IGM) to the foot of two short rock steps below the summit. Climb the first direct on good rock with large flake holds. The second is steeper and can be climbed just R of the crest up a shattered chimney line (15m., II), or turned easily on the L by a slightly descending traverse followed by climbing back R up a slab and short gully pitch, finishing a few m. from the summit cross ($1\frac{1}{2}$ h., $2\frac{3}{4}$ h. from Manenti biv.).

214. Approach from Breuil. A longer route with a choice of at least two ways in the middle section before joining the Manenti route on the traverse below Castelletto Whymper.

From Breuil go down the main road to Avuil (1957m.), access road on R over river. Albergo Carrel, large carpark and construction works. From the rear of the old chalets behind the hotel take a good diagonal track R, soon turning L and rising SW through pleasant forest to emerge among a confusion of cow trails on pasture. Go up to the Montagne Bayettes chalet and continue due N to the upper cowsheds (2288m.), fierce dogs ! (1 h.). From here make an horizontal traverse due W and in three min. find a water supply channel contouring steep slopes in this direction. Follow the narrow grass overgrown channel (delicate, water deep !) which runs to the Vofrède cwm in 7 min. Cross the rock and grass cwm, losing a little height, to the far side, under cliffs of the Tour du Créton (stonefall). Having rounded the lowest rock spur, traces of a path climb steep debris SW into the narrow cwm under the Vofrède glacier. On your L is a moraine ridge rising into a conspicuous rock promontory which divides the glacier, but in view is only the big glacier tongue to its L. Ascend to this ridge and go up it to below the first rocks of the promontory ($1\frac{1}{2}$ h.). One of two ways are now recommended. A third, up the big couloir on the R side of the promontory, snow and debris to a headslope/wall, is considered exposed to stonefall.

(i) Best if the glacier is not icy. Descend L from the mor-

CHÂTEAU DES DAMES
NE side

215
213
3394
213

△ vetta

Col des Dames

Prarayer →

aine ridge and scramble over rough ground to the snow strips in the gutter draining the glacier tip. Climb the glacier keeping L, turning a large rock island in its middle-upper part on the L by a fairly steep snow slope. Return R above the rock island over snow slopes which lead due W to the short traverse just below the Colle di Vofrède, where Route 213 is joined as you approach the rock and debris band dividing the upper glacier ($1\frac{1}{4}$ h.). Continue as for Route 213 to summit ($1\frac{1}{2}$ h., $5\frac{1}{4}$ h. from Avuil).

(ii) Best if the glacier is icy. From the moraine ridge continue directly up the rock promontory. This is a bit tedious, but very direct, and the rock is quite good. Turn the initial rock step on the R, returning L up a scree gangway/gully. Continue up the promontory with traces of a track in places, turning steep bits on the L, and emerging on debris and snow at the top (cairn, 3140m. IGM). From here continue up snow, bearing a little R to join the traverse movement R which is made below Castelletto Whymper as described in Route 213 ($1\frac{1}{4}$ h.). Continue as for Route 213 ($1\frac{1}{4}$ h., 5 h. from Avuil).

<u>South-South-East Ridge</u>. This ridge runs from the Colle di Vofrède (see Route 213) to a junction with the ESE-NNE ridge above the Col des Dames. About half-way along the ridge is a prominent turret, split into several finger-like pinnacles, called Castelletto Whymper, a traverse of which is IV on bad rock. Currently in vogue is the upper part of the ridge, which is a more direct way to the summit than Route 213. However the rock is very loose. PD-.

215. From the Manenti biv. or Breuil (Avuil) follow Routes 213 or 214 to the last snow slope directly below Castelletto Whymper, where these routes traverse R towards the Col des Dames ($1\frac{3}{4}$ h. or 4 h.). Climb the short snow slope, steepening, to a snow/rock couloir coming down from the saddle/gap in the ridge to the R of Castelletto Whymper. Normally it is best to

CHÂTEAU DES DAMES S side

Colle di Bellatsa →

216

213·5

3394·1GM

215

Castelletto Whymper

Cresta SW (3012)

213

Colle di Vofrède

Mont Rous →

climb rocks just L of the couloir, short steps, ledges and debris with 4m. of II. Move R near the top, about 50m. in all to the ridge. Now follow the shattered crest to a steep rock finger-tottering section which is turned on the R by a loose traverse into a couloir, returning L to the crest. In a few min. reach the junction with the ESE-NNE ridge and from there follow Route 213 to the summit (45 min.) ($2\frac{1}{2}$ h. from Manenti biv., $4\frac{3}{4}$ h. from Avuil/Breuil).

South-West Ridge (from Colle di Bellatsa). The most direct way up the mtn. from the Manenti biv., but only climbed occasionally because of loose debris and poor rock. The approach to the Colle di Bellatsa is described under Monte Dragone below. This ridge is not really recommended. The middle section is steep and is turned by a rising traverse across a snow couloir, steep snow patches, steps and debris (pitches of II) leading up to a chimney pitch of III (1 h. to col, $1\frac{1}{2}$ h. for ridge to summit). First ascent: A. Lucat with P. Maquignaz, 4 September, 1874.

MONT ROUS 3224m.

A secondary summit with fine regional view, situated directly above the Colle di Vofrède (Route 213). Reached from this col in 20 min. by traversing up the snow slope adjoining col and returning R to NNE ridge above its steep lower broken section. Frequently "bagged" by parties returning from the Château des Dames.

MONTE PANCHEROT 2614m.

The S rockface of this mtn. dominates the Cignana dam wall and Barmasse inn. Excellent rock climbing not requiring a start before 8.00am. The SE ridge, forming the R-hand profile of the face, is a popular route with pitches up to III+ and a final step which goes at IV-. Two routes on the face are III and IV. Route lines are indicated on diagram.

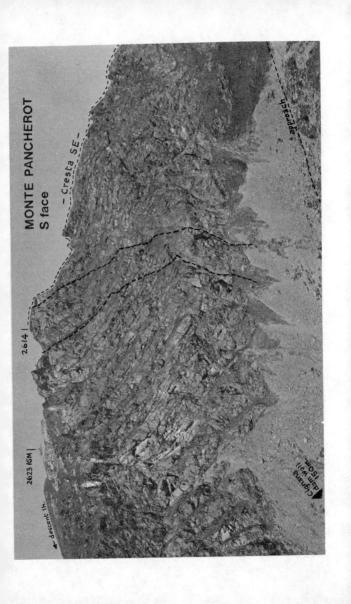

MONTE PANCHEROT
S face

— Cresta SE —

approach

2614

2623 IGM

descent 1h.

Cignana
dam wall
150m.

MONTE DRAGONE 3354m.

This mtn. is coupled structurally with the Fontanella. The pair form an impressive raised ridge on the main crest of the chain, cut about the middle by a gap above which is a 40m. near-vertical step on the Dragone side. The complete traverse of this long ridge is a classic expedition with the Manenti biv. in an ideal position for it. Climbed on its own however, Dragone is worthwhile and recommended. Rock fairly good. First ascent: A.G. Topham with J. Maître and P. Maurys, 24 July, 1894.

East Ridge (from Colle di Bellatsa). Col Bella Tza on LK. The usual route, a rock climb with no snow. F+. Descended by first ascensionists.

216. From the Manenti biv. follow Route 213 to the low moraine wall above the E end of the Gran Lago. Cross large rocks on top of this moraine and commence a gradually rising traverse across debris slopes above the NE side of the lake. Aim to reach the R end of a low but steep rockband which is situated at a slightly higher level than another larger one further L, dropping into the lake. Above both of them is the longer rockband shown on map. Traverse L and slightly downwards on debris between the low rockband and the main one above, for 100m., to where a grassy inlet rises L up the main rockband. Follow this then red slabby rocks, trending L, to the top of the band. Emerge at a water pool and continue directly towards the col, passing in a few min. another pool before reaching the boulder slope below the pass. Go up this direct to a broken rock wall which is easily climbed trending L to the rock saddle level with the Bellatsa glacier on the other side (3047m.) (1 h.).

Start straight up the fine broken ridge, fairly narrow, making slight turning movements of a few m. as desired with pitches of I, up to a secondary top (3228m. IGM). An almost level section runs from here to a gap (1 h.). Climb out of the gap keeping a little R on short steep steps and return to the crest

Fontanella   E face   Dragone

Colle di Valcornera 217   S 218   NE   Passo del Dragone   40m step 218   216   3328 Colle di Bellaza

as soon as possible. Follow it to the summit (30 min., $2\frac{1}{2}$ h. from Manenti biv.).

Note: the Main Ridge traverse is described under the Fontanella below.

PUNTA DI FONTANELLA 3384m.

A fine rock mtn., invariably considered for climbing purposes with its neighbour the Dragone at the opposite end of the high ridge linking them. See preamble to the Dragone above. Recommended as a rock climb on its own account but noted for its main ridge traverse to the Dragone. This ridge has a secondary (NE) summit, not shown on LK, of equal height to the main (S) one, while a third (W) is recognised just off the main ridge and forming the head of the NW ridge. Rock fairly good, excellent in places. First ascent: A. Baltzer and C. Schröder with S. Bessard, July, 1867.

South-East Ridge (from Colle di Valcornera). Col de Valcournera (3066m.) on LK. The normal route, a short climb from the Manenti biv. Between the col and the start proper of the ridge are two incongruous towers. It is possible to turn these but it is more usual to avoid them by not going right up to the col, and instead taking a couloir to the gap between the second tower and the ridge foot. A pleasant entertaining scramble, II. Probable but not definite route of first ascensionists. First recorded ascent: O.G. Jones, G.C. and W.D. Monro with A. Bovier and P. Gaspoz, 22 August, 1892.

217. From the Manenti biv. follow Route 213 for 15 min. only, to where the track reaches the highest pt. on the terrace running across the R side of the spur above the hut. The track line hereabouts on LK is fictitious. Now leave the track and work R under a low reddish rockband and emerge at the top of the spur somewhat R of its highest pt. Below (N) is the Lago del Dragone (2878m. IGM). Make a descending traverse L down slabby rocks and cross the lake outfall on its S side.

FONTANELLA– DRAGONE main ridge traverse

ridge access gap

S 3384

NE 3384

Passo del Dragone

4·0m. step

3228

3354

217

218

216

E FACE

From here traces of a track continue WSW up debris directly
to the Colle di Valcornera above. Go in this direction for about
300m. distance, then move R and climb a debris slope directly
in line with the Fontanella summit. At its top reach a snowfield and climb this near its L edge, with rocks, to the foot of
the obvious couloir descending from the foot of the ridge, with
the second tower along from the Colle di Valcornera on your
L. If there is plenty of snow in the steep couloir climb its
bed, moving R to rocks in the upper half. If it is dry and icy,
climb rocks on the L side of the couloir all the way to the gap
($1\frac{1}{4}$ h.).

Climb the ridge crest direct over an initial gendarme step
with a narrow gap behind it to a final steepening below the S
(main) summit. Traverse L to a couloir in the S flank and go
up this pleasantly to the summit. Alternatively, the final ridge
can be taken direct up a wall (III) (1 h., $2\frac{1}{4}$ h. from Manenti
biv.).

Fontanella-Dragone Main Ridge Traverse. A classic expedition, only grade II except for the step of 40m. about halfway
along the ridge. Done in the direction Fontanella-Dragone
(SW-NE) this step must be climbed (IV). It has been turned
on both sides but the rock is loose and still difficult (III+). In
the opposite direction you make one long abseil needing two
ropes of 40m., or half this length by two abseils, the second
from a peg usually in place. First traverse SW-NE: G. Dumontel
with S. Ottin, 10 August, 1909.

218.From the Manenti biv. reach the S summit of Fontanella
by Route 217 ($2\frac{1}{4}$ h.). Continue along the main ridge, easy,
keeping slightly L and crossing the gap adjoining the head of
the NW ridge before rising a little to the NE summit. From
here descend on the crest more steeply to the gap marking the
lowest pt. between the Fontanella and Dragone: Passo del
Dragone (c. 3280m.) (45 min.). Above this gap is the big step.

326

CIAN GROUP from NE

Col de Fort · Pta. di Cian · Dôme de Cian · Cima di Balanselmo · Colle di Valcornera · Becca di Luseney · Punta di Fontanella S

229 · 219 · 220 · 217 · 203 · 213 · 201

Lago di 2740 Balanselmo · Lago del Dragone 2678 · Manenti hw

À little L, climb a steep grey wall (III) and reach the ridge crest. Climb the crest direct on good holds on nearly vertical rock with a few pegs usually in place (IV) to the top. A narrow horizontal ridge follows to a small gap, then easier climbing to the summit of the Dragone ($1\frac{3}{4}$ h.). Descend from Dragone by Route 216 ($2\frac{1}{4}$ h., $6\frac{1}{4}$ h. for round trip from Manenti biv. without halts).

CIMA DI BALANSELMO 3316m.

A notable summit on the long rock ridge running from the Colle di Valcornera to the Dôme de Cian. Easily climbed by a long debris slope on its SE side, from the Manenti biv. or Barmasse inn. Several rock peaks on this ridge give short routes of quality on excellent rock in grades III/IV. First ascent: G. Bobba with C. Thérisod and G. C. Pession, 9 August, 1899.

DÔME DE CIAN 3351m.

The most varied and interesting summit in the entire chain S of the Grandes Murailles, an elongated snowcap, not well drawn on LK, well seen from some viewpoints on the Valpelline (W) side, but this is not evident on the Valtournanche (E) side. The latter side appears as a long wall of gneiss whose highest towers mark the actual summit points. The summit panorama is exceptional over the Pennine Alps and Mont Blanc range. One of the most frequented summits of the district but this might represent only 70-100 ascents per annum. The rocks are mainly good and one route rates as a rare classic rock climb. The snow climbing is interesting and the ascent has the air of an expedition involving nice route finding. The mtn. can be conveniently climbed from four directions, and inevitably by a fifth from the Valpelline with a much bigger vertical interval, rougher ground and greater effort, although much of this is now cancelled out by the new Praderio biv.

The summit area is complex and confusing in poor visibility. It is a vague ridge orientated S-N. A glacier snow/ice dome rises steeply from the E to form a more or less level walkway about 200m. long and parallel some 50-100m. distance away from the vague edge of the rock escarpment forming the elongated ESE wall of the mtn. The snow ground between is deeply scooped by amphitheatre exits from two large couloirs in the ESE wall. Between these two snow bowls three short snow/rock ridges give walk-ways at R-angles to the top of towers along the rim of the wall. The one furthest S is a few m. lower than the middle one, so that the one furthest N forms the highest pt., a pinnacled rock where the main N ridge of the mtn. becomes well defined again and continues down to pt. 3304m. IGM and thence to the Pta. di Cignana (c. 3320m.). These last two pts. are not shown on LK and precede the Cima di Balanselmo (3316m.) (West Col Archives Memoir, No. 1037).

First ascent: G. Battista and G. Origoni with J.B. Carrel and P. Pession, 16 September, 1889. First winter ascent: O. Mezzalama and M. Scalvedi, 1 January, 1927. First ski ascent mentioned by A. Bonacossa, before 1925.

<u>South-West Flank</u>. There are two distinct approaches to this normal way up the mtn. and both have alternatives according to starting point. A third approach is from the Valpelline (Prarayer) but this is rarely used due to its remoteness. The first and most frequented approach is from the W (Barmasse inn) and NW (Manenti biv.). The routes join and reach the Colle di Cian (c. 3200m., not marked on any map), between the Dôme and Punta di Cian, adjoining the SW flank of the mtn. The second is from the S (Cian biv.) and SW (Nebbia biv.). Again, the routes join at the Col Chavacour (2978m., marked but not named on LK) and continue directly to the SW flank. Illogically, the longest approach, from the Barmasse inn, is the most frequented, and this can be explained by the proximity to Valtournanche village and the short walk from there to the Barmasse inn (Route 200). However, car drivers have a better opportunity from the Cian biv. from where the ascent is relatively short.

All approaches are F, but the final couloir to the Colle di Cian on the W and NW approaches is F+. A splendid outing by any approach, more mountaineering interest from the W/NW than S/SW.

219. From Barmasse inn, W approach. Descend the path returning to Valtournanche and follow the tramway lines platform under the Cignana dam wall, past the pt. where the Valtourn-

until the path leaves it to descend R, to the far end. There take two short zigzags to a level atop the dam wall (15 min.) and follow an excellent footpath along the NE side of the lake. Opposite a small chapel (2178m.) to your L the path forks. Keep L and contour the pastures NW, not approaching the chapel and now well below the R fork, for c. 300m. (no path), to reach the stream entering the NE corner of the lake. Follow this upstream on its R side and soon reach a plank bridge. Cross it. The stream can normally be crossed anywhere. Now make a gradually curving movement L(W) up pleasant pasture to an isolated white cowshed (not marked on map, c. 2240m.) at the top of these grass slopes which are covered in the last part by many large cairns. From the cowshed ascend R for a couple of min., then a path appears which zigzags back L and winds up a rough grassy spur to the W. The path is good, with red waymarks up to an almost level depression. Cross a sort of shoulder at the far end and descend a short grass slope into a narrow stony valley. Cross a stream and climb in the bed of the valley, remote and enclosed, crossing and recrossing small streams, which gradually bends L(SW) and steepens towards a big moraine headwall. No path in this section but intermittent red waymarks. Round the corner move R to the R side of the valley and climb a rocky path in grass to the foot of the headwall. Cross the main stream L and go up a steep loose track, mostly bad, which more or less climbs the moraine directly, halfway up between two prominent rocks, to a large cairn at the top, at the entrance to the upper moraine cwm running up to the conspicuous Punta di Cian at the top (2 h.). Go up the cwm near its bed, keeping somewhat R (fewer cairns and waymarks which soon disappear) and reach snow patches in the bed higher up. Follow these towards the small Roisetta glacier at the top. Keep R below the glacier and climb moderately steep snow and moraine, approaching the fine ESE rock wall of the Dôme de Cian. When close to this wall bear L and

CIAN GROUP from W

PUNTA

COL

220

DÔME

219

Monte
Redessau

221

Col
Chavag coul.

222

traverse diagonally L above the lower steepness in the small glacier and so reach the foot of the snow couloir rising to the <u>Colle di Cian</u> (c. 3200m.). Climb this narrow snow gully of c. 120m. at 35-40° to the narrow gap adjoining broad slopes on the other side (1½ h.). The small Rosietta glacier and the col are not named on map.

From the col make a slightly descending traverse NW on snow and round the base of rocks coming down from the mtn. hidden above (5 min.). Now traverse the snow slope due N for a few min. till the steep snow/ice dome of the summit area rises on your R. Do not continue to a saddle ahead. Turn back R and make a rising traverse on steepening snow towards the fringe of rocks which were turned lower down. Within a few m. of these climb the snow slope direct, this being the easiest and shortest way of reaching the top of the snow/ice dome. After 100m. the slope eases, with small rock outcrops. Bear L and reach the broad horizontal snow walk-way along the top of the "dome". Follow this in a few min. to the N end where a short snow then rock ridge on the R leads to the most northerly and highest pt. (45 min., 4¾ h. from Barmasse inn).

220. From the Manenti biv., NW approach. This joins the previous route in the upper moraine cwm below the Roisetta glacier. Short and pleasant. From the biv. descend across the approach track and traverse two rounded hillocks above the Lago di Balanselmo (2740m.). In this way you pass round the E side of the lake to its S end. Make a rising traverse R on scree and grass up a short slope (traces of path) to a little saddle above the lake. Now traverse grass and stones SSW, passing under hillock pt. 2828m., after which go round the toe of a small rock escarpment. From here traverse upwards a little and pass round the L side of a small lake. Continue the traverse at c. 2800m. and enter the moraine cwm above the headwall climbed by the previous route which is now joined

($1\frac{1}{4}$ h.). From there by Route 219 to summit (3-$3\frac{1}{4}$ h. from Manenti biv.).

221. From the Cian biv., S approach. An easy pleasant route. From the biv. make a traverse over rocks and grass NW, with traces of a path, keeping a respectable distance from the Lago di Cian (2440m.) as you approach it. Continue this line till you reach the good track coming down from the Fenêtre de Cian above. Follow this to where the track crosses the stream coming down from the R (N). Leave the track and climb near the R side of this stream on grass and stones (sort of spur) to narrows enclosed by a rock knoll (L) and barrier (R). Continue directly up the opening taken by the stream into an upper debris cwm. Work up this keeping L (W), small tarn on R (2782m. IGM, not shown on LK), and climb in the bed up a headslope bearing R towards the broad saddle of the <u>Col Chavacour</u> (2978m.). Reach this col by turning a steep snow bank under it on the L (2 h.).

An easy glacier/snow slope lies on the other side of the pass. Traverse diagonally L (ESE) across it, where the snow passes between rock ribs above and below, and continue to rocks. Move R up snow on to mixed ground just below the main ridge crest hereabouts. Work across this flank, keeping to snow where possible, till a moraine of large stones is reached on your L. Follow this, keeping a little L, to reach the foot of the snow slope under the snow/ice dome of the summit. This is a position about 7 min. from the Colle di Cian which lies horizontally to the R, and where on Route 219 you climb diagonally R towards the last steep snow slope just below the summit cap ($1\frac{1}{4}$ h., $3\frac{1}{4}$ h. from Cian biv.).

222. From the Nebbia biv., SW approach, rough, steep and loose at the <u>Colle di Praterier</u>, and trackless. This is not a col in the accepted sense, but a traverse round a ridge slope.

From the biv. descend large blocks N, crossing two streams, to the Alpe Luseney cowsheds (2585m.). From there follow the track N which goes to the Colle di Livournea. When this turns directly N to the col, leave it and keep R (NE), climbing grass, stones, rocky slabs and snow patches in the cwm bed leading to the SW face of Monte Redessau. Go right up to a normally large snow slope/patch under the face of the mtn. above. Climb the slope then bear R (SE) and by rocks and stones reach the broad saddle/crest on this side, below the SW ridge of the SE summit of the Redessau. Cross this saddle L, passing a water pool (3034m. IGM) and get on to the above-mentioned SW ridge. Go up it keeping a little L for c. 100m. till a ledge line is seen running R across the SE facet between two steep rockbands. Follow this discontinuous ledge, steeply sloping, very loose and delicate, to the far end where it opens on to a debris slope not far above the Col Chavacour, which is crossed by a descending traverse L over a knoll, followed by a straight descent to the col ($1\frac{3}{4}$ h.). Then as for Route 221 to the summit ($1\frac{1}{4}$ h., 3 h. from Nebbia biv.).

223. Valpelline approach, from Praderio biv. From the hut traverse R (W) on moraine, down then up below the rock barrier till the main stream coming down from the Chavacour glacier is reached. Indicated as Cian glacier on LK. Cross the stream and traverse up a moraine flank to its crest. Follow this fairly steep crest, with a track, till a traverse L from its head leads to the stream bed again at the foot of a large rocky couloir/ravine carrying the glacier outfall. Cross the stream L and climb a short stiff chimney pitch with a chockstone (2m., II). Continue up steep stones and blocks beside the stream; some sections are best turned by recrossing the stream. The upper part of the couloir is straightforward and reaches the snow/ice tongue of the glacier. Climb this generally on snow at an easy angle due S to the Col Chavacour ($1\frac{3}{4}$ h.) where Route 221 is joined (to summit $1\frac{1}{4}$ h., 3 h. from Praderio biv.).

<u>North Face</u>. A classic snow/ice climb, probably the only one of its kind in the district. Rarely done to the present time due to the remote approach, but this situation should change with the appearance of the Praderio biv. This is a glacier face, formed by the NW section of the characteristic summit dome, whereas the normal route deals with the W section by turning it on the R. Below the dome section is a large bergschrund, while the less steep middle and lower parts of the narrow twisting face are cut by sometimes large and awkward crevasses. Due to recession the glacier tip can be extremely awkward or impossible on account of smooth slabs across its base. 650m. In good conditions, AD+, possibly easier and often harder. First ascent: A. Bonacossa, C. Prochownick and A. Sarfatti, 1923. First winter ascent: G. Ambrosi and G. Machetto, 10 January, 1967.

224. From the Praderio biv. cross moraine L to snow leading SE to a slope rising more steeply to a rockband slanting across the base of the narrow glacier face (falling ice from R). Climb the rockband on the extreme L, depending on conditions delicate and sometimes very awkward. Some parties have found it easier to climb the L enclosing rock rib for a short way. Above, keep in general to the L side of the face, sometimes in the centre. Climb with increasing steepness (40°) the crevassed slopes to the bergschrund under the dome section. Cross this at the L side, normally quite difficult, and climb a snow/ice slope of 50-55°. Keep L under a rockband extending from this direction and finish up icy narrows between the rockband and an iceband further R. So reach the concave slope of the dome and the summit walk-way ridge (4-5 h. from biv. hut). The slope above the bergschrund has been climbed up its centre, finishing over the iceband direct, by an Italian party of four in 1962, using artificial techniques.

225. East-South-East Face. An impressive rock wall of excellent gneiss, but with lichen on the top pitches, long but only
200m. high, which adjoins the NE side of the Colle di Cian,
Routes 219-223. It has a prominent central buttress section
bounded on either side by large deep couloirs of snow and
rock. This section culminates in the S and Central summits
of the mtn. A large terrace slants L to R across the lower
third of the buttress, close to the foot of the final couloir leading to the Colle di Cian. Just after the start of this terrace a
secondary but pronounced couloir splits the buttress at its L
side. The top of this L-hand narrower section is the S summit.
It is climbed more or less up its front by the Via Bazzi (1955),
probably the best rock climb in the district, already classic
and done frequently. III in general with key pitches of IV and
IV+. On the main part of the buttress to the R, rising to the
Central summit, are two separate lines which join rather more
than halfway up. To the L, Via Pellissier (1955), III+. To
the R, Via Carrel (1942). III.

PUNTA DI CIAN 3320m.

The finest looking rock peak in the district, recognisable from
afar by its turreted ridges, one of which provides the most
sought-after classic rock scramble in the whole of the Valpelline South-Valtournanche crest zone. However the southern
aspect of the mtn. is less impressive. The rock is essentially
only moderately good but the routes have been climbed often
enough to produce sound rock almost everywhere. The mtn.
can be easily climbed with the Dôme de Cian in the same day
by several combinations. First ascent: A. Lucat with V. Maquignaz, 26 September, 1874. First winter ascent: A. Falcroz
and L. Rosset, 14 March, 1936.

North-North-West Ridge (from Colle di Cian). The normal
route, climbed frequently for this district, a short rock climb,

interesting. The steep bits are sound but there is quite a lot of loose material on ledges, etc. The rocks and holds are scratched and whereas it is hardly possible to go wrong, parties over the years have blazed little trails up steeper, more direct and difficult bits. Highly recommended. PD-, pitches of II. First ascensionists.

226. You can reach the Colle di Cian (c. 3200m.) from the following starting points. See general comments about this col under Route 219.

(a) Barmasse inn, by Route 219 (4 h.).

(b) Manenti biv., by Route 220 (2½ h.).

(c) Cian biv., by Route 221 (2¾ h.).

(d) Nebbia biv., by Route 222 (2½ h.).

(e) Praderio biv., by Route 223 (2½ h.).

Above the Colle di Cian there is an initial ridge with three or four small steps/towers on it. Turn this section completely on fairly steep broken rock often with snow patches by making an almost horizontal traverse of the slope below it on the R (W) side. There is a track in places. Rise a little after rounding a steep rock head and reach a small snow saddle on the crest. Cross this and a rock knoll on the crest in a few paces to a snow/rock nick at the foot of the large summit tower (c. 3210m.) (20 min.).

Climb broken rock direct for a few m. then trend L up a nail-scratched staircase to a slab. At the R side of this go up a crack (10m., II) to the crest line again. Almost immediately trend L and climb easy rock for 30m. distance to a snowy platform below the steep terminal wall. At the R side of the wall climb a large shallow chimney/dièdre slanting L to R at a high angle with fine climbing on good holds (40m., II), and exit over a short wall by a pull up (II) on to a small terrace R of the summit. Step up a few m. to the top (35 min., 45 min.-1 h. from Colle di Cian).

PUNTA DI CIAN N face

Cresta Rey (E) –

3180

230

– Cresta NNW –

226

Colle di Cian

219

Roisetta glacier

229

219

Col de Fort

227. South-West Ridge (Cresta Dentini). The fine looking ridge of towers seen in profile from the Colle di Cian, which is not a practical starting point. The ridge is less interesting than it looks. It is often used in descent for reaching the Cian biv. and Torgnon valley. Most of the towers are avoided by turning them on the S side. Pitches of II and one of III+. First recorded ascent of complete ridge: F. Cavazzani and L. Carrel, 9 September, 1947.

228. South Face. Though rarely climbed this route gives the most direct line to the top from the Cian biv. About 2 h. from this hut the route starts up the edge of a couloir directly below the summit. After slanting R, rocks are climbed in the same direction till a line of weakness leads L, up a chimney, slabs and a small couloir to just below the SW ridge near the foot of the summit tower. By moving R along a ledge the summit tower is climbed by a long chockstone chimney in the S side. 200m., II (2½ h. for face). First ascent: L. and M. Sinigaglia with L. Carrel and C. and A. Gorret, 7 October, 1895.

East Ridge (Cresta Rey). From Col de Fort (2906m.). The most famous rock climb in the area. There were 20 entries in the Barmasse inn hut book for 1974 up to end July, and many more in other biv. hut books up to end September. The first part of the ridge is straightforward, followed by an horizontal middle section. The difficulty is concentrated in the conspicuous penultimate tower/step just before the lesser summit tower. The first ascensionists avoided the main step by a wide flanking movement L, which is tedious and misses the whole point of the climb. The route is well-scratched and fairly obvious. III+. Rock good. First ascent: Guido Rey with A. Maquignaz, 1896. Main step as climbed today, c. 1910.

229. Routes to the Col de Fort, a broad saddle of snow and rock

PUNTA DI CIAN S side

Cresta Dentini

227

228

Cresta Rey 380

230

Col de Fort

229 var.

229

between the Punta di Cian and Becca di Salé.

From the Barmasse inn follow Route 219 to just below the Roisetta glacier, where you slant R below its lower tongue. Instead, slant L over moraine, rock and an easy snow slope to the wide col (3 h. from Barmasse inn). F.

From the Manenti biv. by Route 220 join the Barmasse inn approach above ($1\frac{1}{2}$ h.). F.

From the Praderio biv. by Route 223 to the Colle di Cian ($2\frac{1}{2}$ h.), then descend the couloir of this pass (Route 219) and traverse below the Roisetta glacier tongue to the pass ($1\frac{1}{4}$ h., $3\frac{3}{4}$ h.). F+.

From the Cian biv. make a traverse over rocks and grass NW with traces of a path, keeping a respectable distance from the Lago di Cian (2440m.) as you approach it, and go up a short grass slope above the NW corner of the lake to the good path coming down from the Fenêtre de Cian. Follow this path to the E. It descends slightly all the way to a point above the Grand Drayère chalet (2350m.). At c. 2400m. continue by a small track for another 250m. to a small L fork. Follow this poor and vague track N up the side of a spur, past a large rock outcrop to a small plateau above pt. 2580m. Continue up steep grass to the R end of a rock barrier. Climb blocks and stones, working L above the barrier on to a rough spur above pt. 2835m. Climb diagonally L across slopes of the spur to reach the stony slope below the pass which is followed to the top (2 h. from Cian biv.). F.

There is a more direct route to the pass, leaving the Fenêtre de Cian path above the NE corner of the Lago di Cian, and following rough slopes directly towards the rocks of pt. 2835m., which are turned on the L side up a steep stony couloir to reach the upper slopes of the pass ($1\frac{1}{2}$ h. from Cian biv.). F+.

230. From the Col de Fort start up the ridge crest on loose rock and reach a steep slab which is climbed by a wide crack

(10m., II). Continue for 30m. to a short step and go up this trending R for 10m., then return L to the crest line. Follow the crest with one bit of II to the top of the first ridge summit (3180m. IGM). There follows an undulating but more or less horizontal and easy ridge with a gendarme towards the end. Turn this by scree and rocks round its base to the L, and return to a rocky saddle/gap at the foot of the big ridge step.

Start at the L side of a wall, climb diagonally L for a short way then trend R to the top and the crest again (15m., III-). There are other ways up this wall pitch. Next, avoid the crest by following a rising ledge line just L of it for 10m., finishing on the R side. Now trend R up a slabby wall and higher up turn a jutting block delicately on the L (III). Continue directly to the crest, above and slightly L. All this section can be climbed at III+ by a more direct line to the L, nearer the crest. From the crest slant L up a narrow slabby ramp for a few m. and get into a steep chimney which is climbed (III) to the crest again. Go directly up the crest with a short overhang (IV-) to the top of the step. The overhang can be turned delicately by a circuit to the R.

From the top of the step follow the sharp exposed crest slightly downwards, across a long-stride gap, and in 80m. reach the foot of the summit tower. Follow a track in loose rock up this to a large chimney which is climbed (10m., II+) to the top (2 h. from Col de Fort).

MONTE REDESSAU NW 3253m. SE 3237m. IGM

231. An important summit topographically but of little mountaineering interest. Its SE summit is evident but not marked on LK. Climbed infrequently but normally from the Nebbia biv. by a traverse starting from Route 222 up the L side of the SSW ridge of pt. 3237m. to the lower summit (2 h.), then along the main ridge, narrow and exposed in places, turning steps/gendarmes quite easily, to the highest pt. (1 h. more). A descent can be made from pt. 3253m. across a large sloping

scree band on the S face, breaking through the lower barrier by going down a couloir slanting L to R (as you look down), so returning to the approach of Route 222.

First recorded ascent: O. G. Jones, C. D. and W. G. Monro with A. Bovier and P. Gaspoz, 23 August, 1892. Party found a cairn on top.

CIMA BIANCA 3009m.

232. The "Gornergrat" of the Torgnon valley but you have to walk up this one. Situated almost directly above the Cian biv. from where it is nowadays usually climbed by day-visitors. (The St. Barthélemy side is seen to advantage from the main approach to the Nebbia biv. - an unattractive lump of grass and bad calcareous rock). From the Cian biv. return along the approach path and go round a terrace into the cwm to its S, with a path up to the Erbion chalet (2522m.). Continue up the grassy cwm then bear L up a steeper grass, scree and rock slope in a shallow side cwm opening to the E shoulder ridge. Follow this broad stony ridge to the main crest (2969m. IGM) and continue along a similar ridge to the highest pt. F. (1¾ h. from Cian biv.). (Frischer-Roberts Diaries).

BECCA DI LUSENEY 3504m.

The highest mtn. in this Italian sub-range of the Pennine Alps and the most sought-after summit in the district. A superb viewpoint with a magnificent panorama perhaps not quite as interesting as that from the Dôme de Cian.

A mtn. of remarkable contradictions. Described by Adams-Reilly as "one of the most graceful snow peaks in the Alps", an observation supported to recent times by several correspondents remarking on the beauty of its profile in views from the Western Pennines (but also asking what the peak was !), but in more informed 'opinions regarded as the most disappointing major mtn. in the region. It rises too far S and outside the main zone of gneiss which makes up many parts of the chain further N. Consequently only a few bits of good gneiss occur and rotten schists and others predominate. The rock is very bad. The danger of two or more parties moving together on the same route cannot be emphasised too strongly in respect of rocks knocked down from above. The snow face on the N side of the mtn. can be used to avoid the bad rock, but this is steep and generally icy after mid August. Even so it is used frequently for descent by Italian parties when conditions permit. It explains the number of entries for this descent in the hut book.

The Nebbia biv. on the S side is the only convenient starting point. But this mtn. is historically and topographically part of the Valpelline, being only 3 km. map distance from the Buthier river in its bed. However there is no intermediate hut on this N side, nor anywhere to sleep directly below the approach valley. The vertical interval from river to summit is 1900m., and you have to get to the river crossing point first from somewhere higher up or lower down the valley. This is not an effort normally expected for a peak of 3500m., with really rotten rock to finish up the last 350m.

All the same its fine snowy profile seen from Valpelline viewpoints tantalises and attracts some ascents from this side. But these must be few compared with those from the Nebbia biv. Apart from those described below, no other routes are worth considering (West Col Archives Memoir, No. 2777).

First ascent: A. Adams-Reilly with J. A. Carrel and H. Charlet, 2 August, 1866. First winter ascent: G. Fillietroz and L. Rosset, 26 December, 1934. On ski: A. Bonacossa and B. Salvi Christiani, 6 May, 1919. The ascent and traverse by R. G. Collomb from the Nebbia biv. in 1974 was the first British recorded in the hut book since the biv. was opened in 1958. Probably about 80 ascents per annum at present.

East-North-East Ridge (from Colle di Luseney). The col is pt. 3162m. on LK, between the Becca di Luseney and Cima di Livournea (3289m., marked but not named on LK). This is the traditional normal route when starting either from the Valpelline (N) or St. Barthélemy valley (S). Nowadays from the latter most parties go up the more satisfactory SE ridge and join the ENE ridge at the junction pt. 3389m. IGM. From the col the easiest route is complicated and not easy to find. It makes a steeply rising trayerse L of the ridge, crossing the SE ridge and joining the main ridge above pt. 3389m. F, to the col on either side, but PD for the ridge on account of very bad rock. First ascensionists from Valpelline side.

233.South side approach. From the Nebbia biv. descend the rock covered grassy hump N and descend to the outfall from the Lago Luseney. It is not necessary to work further R and join the path running beside the Luseney Alp chalet. Continue near a stream coming down from the N, then cross this L at the foot of a long grassy slope covered with stones which narrows progressively and becomes a scree fan emerging through the rock barrier directly in line with the Colle di Luseney above. This opening in the barrier is the first one L of the one carrying the stream coming down from the col. Climb the grass slope direct, no track, into the scree gully entrance with large chimney rocks on either side. Continue up scree and boulders in the gully to a stony plain at the top. Go up this near its bed, gradually steepening into a headwall of moraine. Climb this by a choice of low relief moraine ribs, very loose, to reach the narrow upper cwm leading in a few min. to the small snowfield and steep snow slope under the col. Climb the snow keeping somewhat R and go up the narrows to a steep headwall. Traverse up R, using rocks as necessary, then return L to finish on the broad saddle ($2\frac{1}{2}$ h. from Nebbia biv.).

234 North side approach. From the Valpelline start from La Ferrera chalets (1691m.) which stand just under the road line and can be missed when driving by. Parking room on road for 2 or 3 small cars. A lane descends L without passing the chalets, down fields towards the Buthier river in the bottom. Further along the road a large mule path goes down more steeply to join the lane. Cross the river by a bridge to the Pouillaye chapel and chalets (1616m.) (10 min.). Very comfortable bivouacs in the open or with a tent can be made here. Army summer camp in 1974. The terrain all round has been greatly disturbed by a huge landslide in 1952, which has destroyed the original path, still marked on map. Climb away from the river by a steep path with red waymarks in the rocky forest due S, higher up making wide zigzags, returning under a rock barrier towards the gorge of the Montagnaya valley. The path rounds a spur and immediately after traverses a narrow grassy cwm with a few trees (c. 1880m.). At this pt. leave the path (45 min.) and climb WNW up the cwm with occasional tracks (not indicated on LK) to reach a saddle at the top, marked above and to the N by pt. 2144m. Now make a more or less horizontal traverse, no path, across the Arbière cwm, cross the main stream and continue rising a little on the other side to join the old path line coming up from below. Work N up a grassy knoll, keeping R to avoid rocks, and reach the ruined Pra de Dieu chalet (2277m.) (1¼ h.).

To this pt. the entire approach from the river ignores the well marked direct path line on LK. This has been destroyed by the aforementioned landslide and the ground is a jungle of broken trees, large rocks and shifting earth.

From Pra de Dieu the original path can now be used till it peters out. It zigzags steeply NW in a valley bed, on grass to the L, and reaches scree further up. At c. 2500m. exit R (SW) from the valley by going up a scree fan between two large rock outcrops situated just L of the central part of the narrow rock barrier below the Luseney glacier. Scramble over the top of the barrier on to snow and rocks leading R in a few min. to the lower edge of the glacier at c. 3000m. (2 h.). Climb the L side of the glacier snowfield, no crevasses, and reach the Col di Luseney at the top (30 min., 4¾ h. from La Ferrera).

In practice, parties going to the Becca di Luseney need not reach the col. Before this slant R under a steep step in the glacier and go up a fairly steep slope to the R to join the ridge at a small saddle (see below) where the main steepness starts.

235. From the Colle di Luseney (3162m.) turn the lower section of the ridge by climbing up and round R, keeping low until a small snow/ice saddle can be seen above where the main steepness in the ridge commences. Reach this saddle (15 min.), with a big drop down a couloir on the far side. Several alternatives are now possible.

(a) A direct ascent of the ridge crest to pt. 3389m. is steep and very loose. Grade III pitches, some of them sound but

BECCA DI LUSENEY SE side

Colle di Luseney

233

ENE —

lower ridge gap

3389

235a Cresta

235c

Cresta SE —236

— Cresta S —

236

very unstable rock between. Not recommended.

(b) For good conditions in early part of season. Climb steep snow/ice under the R (N) side of ridge, really at the L edge of N face. The steepness rises to 50° and there is no advantage in using rocks on L. After rounding a projection coming down as the side of the ridge continue climbing until you are below pt. 3389m. Continue still higher till the ridge flank on your L is only 50m. high. Now very loose rocks can be climbed to a convenient, level ridge section. This seems to be the place where most Italian parties descend when snow conditions permit. This is also the place, about 50-80m. distance up the ridge from pt. 3389m., where alternative (c) finally reaches the crest. This snow climb alternative is the route line taken by first ascensionists. Crampons assist greatly.

(c) This is undoubtedly the easiest way up the bad rock on this approach to the summit. Complicated. From the small saddle at the bottom of the steep ridge climb the loose crest on its R side for 30m. then move L to the crest. At a not too obvious place, below a lighter coloured steepness, traverse L off the ridge to a broad sloping scree terrace. Work L along the top of this and trend L into an opening with two couloirs above. The one on the R runs up below the ridge. Climb the L-hand couloir, away from the ridge, by fair grey rocks on its L side to a gap between two small distinctive rocks. Up to the L again the couloir line continues across the mtn. face, ending in a gap between the two most prominent gendarmes on the top part of the SE ridge. A rough, loose scramble leads into this second couloir which is again climbed by grey rocks at the L side, quite sound. Near the top move R and pull up into the gap. From this pt. the SE ridge can be climbed to pt. 3389m. (bits of II). However, only climb 6-7m. on the gendarme above, then descend L for a few m. off the SE ridge into a narrow rock couloir. Immediately climb reasonable rock up its L side. Keep trending L on steep debris, aiming

349

for the summit ridge above and L. The rock deteriorates rapidly. Cross low rockbands and pass above a subsidiary ridge in the face to arrive below the main ridge which is steep-sided for the last 30m. You have now passed the pt. which overhead is in line with pt. 3389m. A zone of red coloured broken slabs about 20m. high offers a way to the crest. Climb its L side, very loose, returning R along the top of the band to reach terraces from which the crest can be grasped at one or more points. This place corresponds with the ridge exit for alternative (b).

While the crest is now at a reasonable angle it continues in almost vertical little steps to the summit. Climb these direct, or turning the last few m. of each on the L or R by foot ledges, where the rock is better. Continue thus to the summit which is soon reached.

Time from Colle di Luseney: $1\frac{3}{4}$ - $2\frac{1}{4}$ h. according to route and conditions. From Nebbia biv., average $4\frac{1}{2}$ h. From Valpelline, average 7 h.

<u>South-East Ridge</u>. This ridge comes down from pt. 3389m. on the ENE ridge. It is entirely rock and avoids climbing to the Colle di Luseney. It is now the normal ascent route from the Nebbia biv., having reached this status over the col route because the rock is slightly better and the line more direct. However by any standards the rock is bad and great care is needed. The approach is tedious. PD with short pitches of II. First ascent: M. Borelli, P. Costantino and S. Noci, 27 November, 1921.

236. From the Nebbia biv. start as for Route 235. After crossing the stream below the long grass slope leading to the lower rock barrier below the Colle di Luseney, turn L (W) and climb grass at an easier angle, aiming for the lower L-hand side of the barrier. Reach a small moraine plateau forming the bed of the big moraine cwm under the Becca d'Arbière. Climb

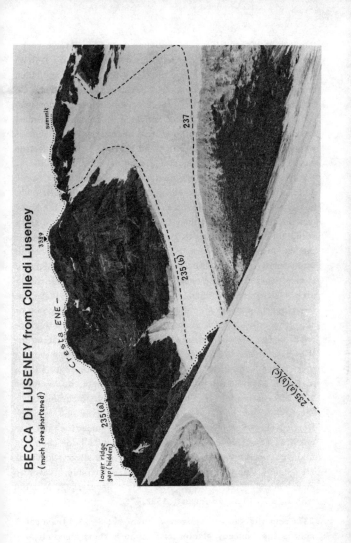

BECCA DI LUSENEY from Colle di Luseney
(much foreshortened)

— Cresta ENE —

3389

summit

237

235(b)

235(a)

235(a)(b)(c)

lower ridge
gap (hidden)

the R side of this till you have turned on the L a lateral rock-band marking the base of the SE ridge overhead. Turn R (NW) and climb steep debris above the top of the lateral band, then traverse R to join the ridge. The crest is vague at first. Go up steep loose rocks L of a black scree couloir and continue up a steeper step to a broken rockface which can be climbed anywhere, but easiest on the L, to a secondary ridge junction where the crest becomes distinct and narrow. All this section can be turned by a laborious, steep loose debris slope on the L.

Follow the crest, climbing or turning minor outcrops on the L to a series of small teeth. These can be climbed quite easily. Turning them involves using terrible rock, but some can be conveniently avoided L. Continue up debris and short steps for some distance to a prominent gendarme. Traverse this on fairly sound rock to a gap which is the place reached by alternative (c) in Route 235. Continue up the next gendarme/ step steeply (II on the crest, easier by moving L) to a rather airy position on the ridge. Having improved in the last 80m. the ridge now breaks down into rubbish again. Climb on or near the crest with a few little steps and minor gaps to ridge junction pt. 3389m. From here there is a short but steep in-itial step up the ENE ridge on reasonable rock, then a narrow crenellated section to the point where alternatives (b) and (c) of Route 235 join the main ridge. From this pt. as for Route 235, alternative (c) ($4-4\frac{1}{2}$ h. from Nebbia biv. to summit).

North-North-West Face. A short, steep snow/ice face with possible objective danger. Average angle 50° for 200m. in main part and a rather unpleasant delicate finish on short rock ribs below summit where conditions are variable. Climbed and descended fairly often. AD. First ascent: F. Mondini with L. d'A. Bich, 16 August, 1892.

237.From the Colle di Luseney (Routes 233, 234) traverse R across the Luseney glacier and climb a short steep slope to

BECCA DI LUSENEY from E

235(b) 237

the W to reach a broad sloping band in the glacier above its central step. This band crosses to the N ridge on far side. From the middle of it, directly below the summit, climb straight up to the top (2 h. from Colle di Luseney).

BECCA D'ARBIÈRE 3319m.

A large rock mtn. joined to the Bca. di Luseney by a long N-S ridge. The summit is well seen from the Nebbia biv. Unfortunately, tedious to climb and rock quite bad. Not recommended. First ascent: E. Canzio and F. Mondini, 30 June, 1894.

BECCA DEL MERLO 3234m.

A fine rock mtn. of some difficulty situated remotely about midway along the main ridge between the Bca. di Luseney and Monte Faroma. No hut base but climbers can stay by arrangement at the Benedictine refuge of the Oratorio/Santuario di Cuney, found in the cwm below E side of mtn., and easily reached from the Ollière chalet on the approach route to the Nebbia biv., in 2½ h. The normal route by which nearly all ascents are made takes rocks up the R side of a large couloir coming down from the NE ridge, up to a pinnacle (3150m. IGM) on the R side of the couloir ridge gap. From here you descend on the R to the gap and climb the NE ridge, fairly easy then steeper (II) to a shoulder section. After crossing this the final ridge steep gives a pitch of III on its R side, to the summit. Fairly good rock (3¾ h. from Santuario).
  First ascent: E. Canzio and F. Mondini, 1 July, 1894. First winter ascent: A. Berthod, V. Marcroz and R. Willien, 3 January, 1938.

ADDENDA

BREITHORN
NW Face. Route 169, page 228. The solo ascent recorded was of the Bethmann-Hollweg line by Helmut Kiene, 18 August, 1973.

DENT D'HÉRENS
WNW Face. Route 188, page 267. Descended on ski by E. Meier and H. Ritter, spring, 1941.

N Face Diagonal (Finch Route). Route 191, page 273. Descended on ski by J. Zimmermann and H. Wäffler, 26 April, 1943.

BECCA DI GUIN
Route 211, page 308. On LK25 a higher but still incorrect spot height of 3757m. is recorded in the approx. position of summit.

INDEX OF ROUTES SHOWN ON DIAGRAMS

Other locations shown on diagrams

GENERAL INDEX

364